Alan Millard

TREASURES FROM BIBLE TIMES

A LION BOOK

Tring · Belleville · Sydney

For my parents,
Ralph and Joyce Millard,
on their golden wedding

Copyright © 1985 Lion Publishing plc

Published by
Lion Publishing plc
Icknield Way, Tring, Herts, England
ISBN 0 85648 587 X
Lion Publishing Corporation
10885 Textile Road, Belleville, Michigan 48111, USA
ISBN 0 85648 587 X
Albatross Books
PO Box 320, Sutherland, NSW 2232, Australia
ISBN 0 86760 568 5

First edition 1985
Reprinted 1985

Bible quotations are from the *Good News Bible*, copyright
1966, 1971 and 1976 American Bible Society, published by
the Bible Societies/Collins

British Library Cataloguing in Publication Data
Millard, Alan
    Treasures from Bible times.
    1. Bible — Evidences, authority, etc.
    2. Bible — Antiquities
    I. Title
    220.9'3   BS621
    ISBN 0-85648-587-X

Library of Congress Cataloging in Publication Data
Millard, A. R. (Alan Ralph)
    Treasures from Bible Times.
    "A Lion book."
    Bibliography: p.
    Includes index.
    1. Bible — Antiquities.   I. Title.
BS621.M55 1985   220.9'3   84-9652
ISBN 0-85648-587-X

Typeset in England by PFB Art & Type Ltd.
Printed and bound in Hong Kong by
Mandarin Offset International (HK) Ltd

Cover: River Nile at Qena, Upper Egypt
Endpapers: Men gather with their flocks
in the cradle of civilization, where the Tigris
and Euphrates rivers join
Title page: gold head from Persia
Preface: bronze lion-weights from Assyria

CONTENTS

PREFACE

For more than a hundred years people have been writing books to show what archaeological discoveries made in the Near East can tell us about the Bible. Some use archaeology to try to prove that the Bible is true; some think it is less important than other ways of studying such ancient records. Opinions change and new discoveries bring fresh information, so there is always a place for another book to describe what has been found and to show its value.

This book looks at particular discoveries, at the sorts of things found, the ways some of them have been interpreted and the ways they can be understood now. There are many more discoveries than are presented here, especially documents naming people or using Hebrew or Greek words found in the Bible, but to try to include them all would have made the book too big, and perhaps too tedious.

Several friends and institutions have generously supplied photographs, and I am grateful to them. For advice on ancient Egypt I thank my friend Dr Kenneth Kitchen, and for unfailing encouragement and help, my wife.

Alan Millard

THE LAND OF ISRAEL

THE LANDS OF THE BIBLE

Black Sea

ARMENIA

Lake Van

Lake Urmia

Caspian Sea

Harran

Gozan

Khorsabad

Nineveh

Calah (Nimrud)

Aleppo

MESOPOTAMIA

ASSYRIA

Ebla (Tell Mardikh)

Ashur

Nuzi

Ecbatana

Tadmor
(Palmyra)

Mari

River Euphrates

Behistun

River Tigris

Babylon

Kish

Nippur

Susa

BABYLONIA

SUMER

ELAM

Tello

Ur

Persepolis

ARABIA

Teima

Persian Gulf

BIBLICAL ARCHAEOLOGY — THE BEGINNINGS

Someone forgot to shut the door, and changed the history of Europe. The Turks were attacking Constantinople in May, 1453. Its walls were strong, its defenders brave. Some had crept out through a little door for a hit-and-run raid, and failed to bar it when they came back. A group of Turks broke through, then a stream. Elsewhere they beat down the defenders, and soon the city was theirs.

Many citizens had already left, fearing a Turkish victory. Others, who could, fled afterwards. They were Greeks and they were Christians. The only places where they could hope to find shelter were in Italy and France. Some of those who settled there were scholars who brought with them their inheritance from classical Greece. Under the influence of ancient Greek philosophy, coupled with other changes, the Renaissance flowered.

As interest in ancient Greece and Rome grew, rich men began to collect statues and coins found in the ruined cities. Scholars began to study and write about them. In a few cases connections could be made with the Bible, especially with the New Testament. People began to see that knowing about the ancient world and the way people lived could help them to understand ancient writings better.

Throughout the seventeenth and eighteenth centuries wealthy, adventurous young men travelled to Italy, Greece and Turkey exploring, describing and collecting from the remains of Greek and Roman cities.

A few went further, to Syria and Palestine. There they found the spectacular ruins of Baalbek, Palmyra and Petra, Roman cities with architecture derived from the Greeks.

Of course, pilgrims had been visiting the holy places for hundreds of years, but few had taken any interest in them as historical sites, or studied the ruins visible.

Ancient Egypt had drawn a few adventurers who brought back accounts of the enormous temples, painted tombs, and the pyramids. Beside straightforward travellers' reports, these journeys also brought ancient Egypt into the scope of fantasy-writers. They thought they could tell the future or learn some other secrets from the design of the pyramids — a false idea that is still current.

But if anything was known about ancient Egypt, it was the subject of mummies, the bodies of Egyptians carefully bandaged and preserved with natural chemicals. Powdered mummy was reckoned a powerful medicine!

With the opening of the nineteenth century, a new era dawned in the study of the ancient world. Exploration began in earnest in the lands where civilizations grew up before the time of classical Greece — in Assyria and Babylonia, and in Egypt. At first those cultures themselves were the objects of study. But when inscriptions were read which named kings known from the Old Testament a new interest was stirred, and the studies attracted a much wider audience.

Soon books were written to apply

Names from the Bible leapt to life with the discovery by archaeologists of palace walls carved with the triumphs of Assyrian kings. This stele shows the Assyrian king, Tiglath-pileser III.

The mystery of the great pyramids of Egypt has long haunted the imagination of travellers and writers of fantasy. Sir Flinders Petrie's accurate surveys put an end to much speculation.

the new discoveries to the Bible. Suddenly names that had been almost meaningless became real. The Assyrian tyrants actually appeared, carved on palace walls, with their armies and their miserable captives. The great kings of Persia spoke through their own writings, and the pharaohs of Egypt could be identified.

All this gave a rich background for biblical history, the setting for the story of ancient Israel.

At the same time, views about the Old Testament were gaining ground which seemed to deny what the Hebrew books themselves said. Stories of Abraham and his family came, it was argued, from the times of the kings of Israel or later. Many of the laws attached to Moses' name grew up over a long period of time, some of them being the ideals of priests in the time of the exile. These, and related views, became very popular. They still are.

Some writers believed archaeological discoveries weighed against them, and began to use archaeology to 'prove' the Bible. But to do that, as some continue to do, is to ask archaeology to do more than it can.

Archaeology can neither prove the Bible nor disprove its major claims, for they are about God. There is no way archaeology could bring evidence to show that God spoke through Moses, for example, or that God sent Nebuchadnezzar to destroy Jerusalem. It is unlikely that anyone will ever find anything to do with, or written by, Moses.

Where archaeology can be helpful is over questions of human history and customs. If the Bible, or any other old book, says that people followed certain patterns of behaviour at a certain time, archaeological discovery may reveal whether or not they did.

If the results of archaeological discovery agree with the reports of ancient writers about an ancient practice, they still cannot prove that a particular instance mentioned in a text did take place. That would require independent written evidence about that occasion. But the fact that what the Bible states often agrees with ancient practices is a good basis for a positive approach to the biblical records (see, for example, *A Golden Temple, From Persian Postbags*).

Placing those records in their ancient setting is a major service of archaeology. It allows modern readers to appreciate them better on historical and cultural levels. Rarer discoveries, relating directly to passages in the Old or New Testaments, can give support to the witness of those passages, and add to them (see, for example, *No Hidden Treasure, 'The Assyrian Came Down...'*).

As all these discoveries increase our knowledge of the world in which the Bible was written, so they enable its distinctive religious message to stand out more boldly.

ENTREPRENEURS IN EGYPT

Napoleon Buonaparte invaded Egypt in 1798 and the team of scientists he took with him virtually founded modern Egyptology (see *The Mystery of Egyptian Hieroglyphs*).

Ancient Egypt became fashionable. The leaders of society bought furniture decorated in Egyptian style, and some imported ancient carvings from Egypt itself. Museum keepers, too, wanted fine objects. So people went to Egypt to bring back whatever they could.

One of the most unusual men involved was an Italian who had worked in a circus in London as a strong man, 'the Italian giant'. This man, Belzoni, had brains as well as brawn and invented a water-wheel much better, according to him, than any used in Egypt. In 1815 he displayed it in Cairo, but no one wanted it. He turned, instead, to transporting stone monuments from Egypt to England.

Belzoni's actions, breaking open tombs and ransacking temples, were deplorable when judged by later standards, yet he made many important discoveries and helped ancient Egypt to gain the hold on public imagination which it has never lost.

A number of other collectors and dealers in antiquities followed Belzoni's example. But there were scholars who worked more methodically. A German

The sun rises over the River Nile at Nag Hammadi, in Egypt.

team directed by Richard Lepsius worked from 1843 to 1845 investigating and making exact records of the tombs and monuments, at the same time collecting exhibits for the museum in Berlin. Lepsius edited twelve volumes of drawings and descriptions, *Denkmäler aus Ägypten*, which remain a basic source of knowledge.

Three Englishmen did a valuable job making copies of paintings and inscriptions which have since been destroyed or damaged. Some of their discoveries produced material for a famous book which one of them, Sir John Wilkinson, wrote: *The Manners and Customs of the Ancient Egyptians* (first published in 1837).

Bringing some order to archaeology in Egypt was the job a young Frenchman took on himself after a few years in the country. He was Auguste Mariette, who initiated the Cairo Museum in 1858, set up a local antiquities service and introduced laws to control the export of antiquities from Egypt. Mariette made a number of careful and important excavations.

Later in the nineteenth century,

excavation in Egypt was put on to a regular scientific basis by the energetic British archaeologist, Sir Flinders Petrie. Petrie was born in 1853 and educated by his parents and his own passion for collecting and arranging things. His father was a civil engineer who taught him the elements of surveying, which he then applied to ancient monuments in Britain.

In 1880 he went to Egypt in order to survey the pyramids, a task which took him the best part of two years. Tradition has it that he worked with only a walking-stick and a visiting-card, yet obtained very accurate results. Certainly he was a spartan, living on the barest necessities.

In 1883 the Egypt Exploration Fund, founded the year before, employed him to excavate in Egypt. Working there for most winters until 1926, he dug at about thirty different sites, making it a habit to publish a report of his work within a year of its completion.

Where earlier diggers had been seeking big buildings and objects for museums, Petrie gave his attention to the precise noting and comparison of small details. He was able to put earlier discoveries into their historical context, to rescue important evidence ignored by others, and make an orderly study of the amazingly varied things found in ancient Egypt.

When Petrie left Egypt, in 1926, there was no longer any room for archaeologists who ignored the humble potsherds or discarded animal bones. Archaeology had become a proper, scientific study.

It was Sir William Flinders Petrie who put excavation in Egypt onto a regular scientific basis, late in the nineteenth century.

CURIOSITIES FROM ASSYRIA

The name of Babylon never left people's minds, even after the place had turned into a wilderness. Babylon stood for luxury and evil living, for the Bible book of *Revelation* used its name for the centre of human wickedness.

What it was really like no one knew. A few Europeans who went to Baghdad saw the dusty mounds of Babil and picked up bricks with strange writing on them to bring home as curiosities.

The first to survey and describe the ruins was a remarkable young man, Claudius James Rich. At twenty he arrived in Bombay to work for the British East India Company, having travelled in Turkey, Egypt and the Near East. As well as speaking French and Italian, he could also speak Turkish, Arabic and Persian, and read Hebrew, Syriac and a little Chinese!

A year later the company appointed Rich to be their Resident in Baghdad, so he went there in 1807 with his eighteen-year-old bride. In 1811 they made an excursion to Babylon. Rich toured the mounds, making sketches and rough plans, and setting men to dig for inscribed bricks, seals and other objects.

His *Memoir on the Ruins of Babylon* was first printed in 1813 in Vienna and reprinted in London in 1815, 1816 and 1818, so much interest did it arouse. He made another visit in 1817 to check his earlier results, and published a *Second Memoir on Babylon* in London in 1818. Two years after that, the Riches made a long tour including Mosul, chief city of northern Iraq.

On the east bank of the Tigris, opposite Mosul, were the ruins of Assyria's former capital, Nineveh. Rich explored and surveyed these, and collected inscribed bricks and clay tablets. He kept notes of his travels but did not live to publish them. In 1821, while in Shiraz on his way to visit the ruins at Persepolis, he fell prey to a cholera epidemic and died, aged thirty-four.

His widow, who had gone ahead of him to Bombay, edited his diaries and they appeared in print in 1836 *(Narrative of a Residence in Koordistan)*. The British Museum bought the seals, inscriptions and manuscripts he had been collecting for £1,000 in 1825.

Rich's books were read widely. In France the government was persuaded to provide money for excavation in the promising mounds of Nineveh. Paul Emile Botta was sent to Mosul and opened his first trenches in the ruins of Nineveh in December 1842. He found very little during six weeks' work, so he was glad when local people told him of a place called Khorsabad, 22 km/14 miles to the north, where carved stones could be seen. Botta started digging there in 1843, continuing until 1845.

Only a little below the ground surface were the walls of a great palace. Lining the brick walls were slabs of stone carved with pictures and with cuneiform writing. At the main doorways stood enormous winged bulls, up to 4.8 metres/16 feet high.

Botta was delighted. He gathered more workmen to load the carvings on to carts, take them to the River Tigris to put them on rafts, and float them down to the port of Basra. Before packing them, Botta arranged for an artist to make drawings, thus recording them before any further damage could happen.

When the stones reached Paris they caused a sensation. Public interest rose higher when it was proved that the palace belonged to Sargon, the king of Assyria named in Isaiah 20:1, whose existence had been doubted because he was otherwise unknown.

In 1839 a twenty-two-year-old Englishman set out with a friend to walk from London to Ceylon, where a relative could find him a job. In 1840 they reached Mosul, then floated by raft down the Tigris to Baghdad. Soon afterwards they parted company.

One went on to finish his journey. The other, Austen Henry Layard, was spell-bound by the region and stayed behind. He spent some months in Persia, living among the tribesmen of the mountains, then returned to Baghdad. From there he was sent to the British ambassador in Istanbul with

political messages. On the way he met Botta in Mosul.

The ambassador at that time was interested in antiquities so, after employing Layard on diplomatic errands, he gave him funds to begin an excavation in Assyria, with the approval of the Turkish sultan.

Late in 1845, Layard dug into the mound called Nimrud, which he had seen to the south of Nineveh. At once his workmen's shovels hit stone slabs lining the walls of rooms. Carvings in relief, cuneiform inscriptions, metal objects, and fragile pieces of carved ivory appeared.

Layard was convinced he had found Nineveh, and went home to London after eighteen months' work to write a best-selling book, *Nineveh and Its Remains* (1849).

Layard returned to Mosul in 1849 and began to dig in earnest in the mounds of Nineveh where he suspected more sculptures could be found, despite Botta's failure. He was right. During the years 1849-1851 he and his local assistant, Hormuzd Rassam, uncovered rooms lined with almost 3 km/2 miles of stone carvings. These belonged to the palace of Sennacherib (king of Assyria, 705-681 BC) and included his famous pictures of the siege of Lachish (see *'The Assyrian Came Down . . .'*).

In one room lay thousands of small

The Illustrated London News *publicized many dramatic finds by early archaeologists such as Austen Henry Layard.*

Decorating the palace of King Sargon of Assyria at Khorsabad was a great winged bull (left). Paul Emile Botta was the first to excavate the mound. When the carvings he found were taken to Paris, they caused a sensation.

Some of the most famous Assyrian carvings are those which show King Ashurbanipal and his courtiers hunting and killing lions.

clay tablets covered with cuneiform writing, part of the library of the palace. Important and exciting as the sculptures are, these documents supply the really vital information about Assyrian history, religion and society. All these treasures were shipped to England, to the British Museum. Layard finished his digging in 1851, becoming a politician, diplomat and art collector.

Assyria and Babylonia now became a hunting-ground for show-pieces to fill museum cases. In the south, only clay tablets, metal-work and other small objects were found, rather to the disappointment of explorers. Assyria continued to yield sculptured friezes to the spades of French excavators at Khorsabad and, supremely, to Rassam at Nineveh. There he found the palace of Ashurbanipal, the last great king of Assyria (669-627 BC). Another large collection of clay tablets came from it, and the magnificent scenes of the king hunting lions and other wild animals which are now so famous.

The pace of discovery slowed down with the Crimean War (1853-56) and other problems. Scholars worked to interpret and publish the discoveries. In 1872 George Smith, an assistant in the British Museum who was studying the clay tablets, identified on one a

Marsh Arabs with a cargo of reeds work their way across the River Euphrates. Their way of life in the southern part of the great kingdom of Babylon has changed little over the millennia.

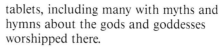

story of a great flood very similar to the story of Noah's flood in Genesis (see *The Babylonian Story of the Flood*). This created a new wave of popular interest, and a leading newspaper, *The Daily Telegraph*, paid for new excavations at Nineveh.

Now more French scholars set to work in Babylonia, uncovering remains of the Sumerian culture from before 2000 BC. At Tello they found fine statues of a prince Gudea who ruled about 2100 BC.

A team from the University of Pennsylvania excavated in the Sumerian religious centre of Nippur from 1887, recovering thousands of cuneiform tablets, including many with myths and hymns about the gods and goddesses worshipped there.

At the very end of the century, a German expedition opened trenches in Babylon. Led by an architect, Robert Koldewey, it set new standards of precision in digging and recording.

Archaeology in Assyria and Babylonia had moved from a treasure hunt to become a scientific exploration of the past.

At Nimrud, close to Nineveh, Layard discovered rooms lined with stone slabs and doorways guarded by stone bulls. Arabs stare amazed at the first one to be unearthed.

IN THE LAND OF THE BIBLE

An American, Edward Robinson, stands at the beginning of archaeology in Palestine, although he never dug into an ancient site, and even thought that the mounds of earth *(tells)* which mask them were natural hills.

In two journeys to Palestine, in 1848 and 1852, Robinson and his friend Eli Smith explored the country and, by careful study of the landscape, identified a hundred places named in the Bible which had not been properly located before. This basic work, together with a description of the country, was published as *Biblical Researches in Palestine* (1841) and *Later Biblical Researches* (1856).

Mapping the land accurately was a major task. Another American, W.F. Lynch, made an essential contribution when he and his men sailed from the Sea of Galilee down the River Jordan in two prefabricated metal boats. The journey took them a week, 10-18 April 1848. He made the first detailed map of the river's twisting course, and found out that the Dead Sea's surface lies 1,300 feet below sea level.

The major work, the geographical survey of western Palestine, was done by the Palestine Exploration Fund, founded in London in 1865. British army officers were sent by the Fund to map Jerusalem and the countryside.

Between 1872 and 1878 C.R. Conder and H.H. Kitchener (later Lord Kitchener of Khartoum) surveyed over 6,000 square miles of country, marking more than 10,000 sites. Their maps, although replaced in recent years, underlie all others.

The Palestine Exploration Fund also made some excavations, especially around the edge of Herod's Temple in Jerusalem (see *Herod, the Great Builder*). Not much productive digging was done, however, until 1890, when Flinders Petrie made a short visit from Egypt.

For six weeks he worked at a mound called Tell el-Hesy. There he saw the importance of relating the pottery, commonly lying on ancient sites, to the different levels of earth in which it was found. From the relative positions of the pieces he was able to work out which types were the oldest and so classify the pottery by age.

Thus he set the pattern for all later work in Palestine. Where there are no inscriptions or coins the pottery offers some clues about the date of the building in which it lies.

In Palestine there are none of the enormous stone temples or brick palaces of Egypt and Assyria. The Palestinian mounds demand much more attention from the archaeologist for fewer spectacular rewards. Observing and recording are vital. After Petrie's new approach, others gradually realized this.

An American expedition began to explore the site of Samaria in 1909 and 1910. King Herod's builders had destroyed much of the Israelite palace when they built a new temple (see *Herod, the Great Builder*), so it was very hard to trace the plan of the palace and its history. Happily G.A. Reisner, the director, was a meticulous and sharp-eyed excavator with

The hill-country of Judea and its small towns form the backcloth to much of the biblical record.

Dame Kathleen Kenyon was one of the most influential archaeologists to work in Palestine. She is most famous for her excavations at Jericho.

Petrie had the pottery found in his excavations at Tell el Hesy drawn on site before the objects were removed to the safety of a museum.

The aerial view (above right) shows the great 'tell' or city-mound of Lachish. The Bible records how the city fell to the invading Assyrians.

experience in Egypt. He noted the layers of soil with care, so that he could unravel the story. Reisner did not dig any more in Palestine and his methods were ignored by other excavators.

W.F. Albright, the leading American archaeologist, began to excavate in 1922 and refined the dating of pottery by comparing pieces from one site with pieces from all the sites, through his own unrivalled knowledge of them.

One of the most influential archaeologists to work in Palestine in the past fifty years was Dame Kathleen Kenyon (1906-1978). When she joined an expedition at Samaria in 1931 she used a technique of excavation she had learnt working in Britain with Sir Mortimer Wheeler. In her own excavations at Jericho (1952-1958) she applied this stratigraphic method of digging and recording with brilliant results, even though they proved disappointing for biblical studies (see *And the Walls Came Tumbling Down*).

The Kenyon excavations at Jericho, and her later series at Jerusalem (1961-1967), trained or influenced many of the archaeologists who have worked in Palestine since, although some Israeli scholars follow slightly different procedures. All are concerned to learn as much as possible from an excavation, aiming first to learn about the whole history of a place, and then looking at its value for interpreting the Bible.

DECIPHERING ANCIENT WRITINGS

The languages of the Bible, Hebrew, Aramaic, and Greek, have always been understood by some people, but the other languages of people who lived in biblical times were mostly forgotten. They are completely lost, of course, if their speakers did not write them down, and write them on stone or other materials that will survive over a long period of time.

These two factors mean that the scales are weighted against the recovery of ancient writings, yet they do survive in large numbers from certain places. From some places and some peoples we have no written documents at all. This is the case for the Philistines, for example. Their language is unknown, apart from one or two words and names preserved in the writings of other peoples (such as the Philistine name 'Goliath', recorded in the Bible).

The ancient written documents we read today survive by accident. Often they are not ones which modern scholars would have chosen if they had had any say. Accounts from Samaria tell us about administration and taxes in ancient Israel. There are no texts about the running of the king's court or dealing with crime, no hymns to Baal or letters from foreign kings.

Even when a wide variety of documents is available, as in Egypt or Babylonia, they are still a selection, and they give incomplete and unbalanced pictures. Often the letters sent to one man exist but his replies are lost, so their contents are a matter of guesswork.

Again, texts recovered in groups or archives tend to belong to the last generation or two of people who lived in, or used, the building. They threw away older documents unless they had a special value — as, for example, legal deeds and other family records.

Reading ancient writings is often difficult because they are damaged or broken. There may be more than one way to fill the gap, each resulting in a quite different sense (for an example see *Jesus and the Dead Sea Scrolls*). If part of the record is missing, its purpose or its date may be unknown, or the end of a story be lost.

To read the forgotten languages of the biblical world demands time and hard study, but all the major ones are now understood. Less than 200 years ago they were mysteries. Deciphering Egyptian hieroglyphs and Babylonian cuneiform was a great achievement of nineteenth-century scholarship, and the stories deserve to be told. There is now no doubt about the interpretation of most ancient texts. New discoveries serve as checks on older views, in language as much as in archaeology.

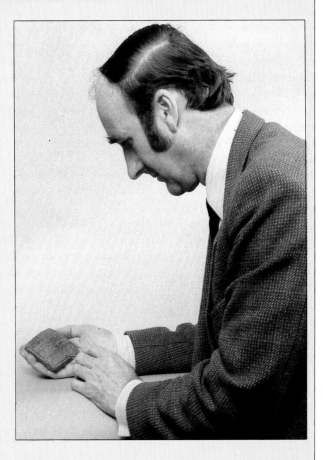

The author holds in his hand a clay tablet from Nuzi dating from about 1400 BC and written in Babylonian cuneiform script.

THE MYSTERY OF EGYPTIAN HIEROGLYPHS

Until the discovery of the Rosetta Stone no one was able to read the ancient hieroglyphic writing which could be seen everywhere on the walls of the tombs and temples of ancient Egypt.

A warship sailed away from the coast of Egypt. On board was Napoleon Buonaparte, with a small party of officers. It was August 1799.

Little more than a year earlier, Napoleon had invaded Egypt with a fleet and a large army. Now he was leaving his army, and the British Admiral Nelson had destroyed his fleet. Napoleon had hoped to make Egypt a French possession, so that he could move on to attack the British in India. His adventure was a failure in every way but one.

With his army had travelled 175 French scientists. They were to map and describe the land. They did their work thoroughly, returning to Paris with notes and drawings that were eventually published in twenty-four volumes as *Déscription de l'Egypte* (1809-1828). Their work was the foundation of modern Egyptology.

Among the large collection of ancient Egyptian carvings which Napoleon's men collected was a stone slab found near Rosetta on the River Nile. The stone itself, with the rest of the collection, was brought to London as a prize of war when the army Napoleon had left behind surrendered to the British. Drawings and plaster casts had already reached Paris. There the Rosetta Stone caused a lot of excitement, for it seemed to be the key to the mysteries of ancient Egyptian writing, the hieroglyphs.

At the top of the stone are fourteen lines of hieroglyphs, then thirty-two lines of a sort of Egyptian handwriting, demotic, and finally fifty-four lines of Greek.

Reading the Greek was not difficult. It was part of a decree issued by King Ptolemy V in 196 BC. But, try as they would, no one could make progress in reading the Egyptian, beyond two or three names.

Napoleon failed to conquer Egypt, but it was a Frenchman who was victorious in the struggle to decipher the writing of ancient Egypt. This man was Jean-François Champollion. Born in 1790, he showed himself a gifted child, studying Latin, Greek and Hebrew at the age of eleven.

Shortly after that, Champollion saw Egyptian inscriptions for the first time.

When he was told that no one could read them, he announced that one day *he* would. That became his passion.

He turned all his energy to learning ancient and obscure languages and to collecting everything he could about Egyptian history. At seventeen he went to Paris to study further, enduring poverty and the political troubles of turbulent France. When he was twenty-three he published a thorough history of Egypt (*L'Egypte sous les Pharaons*, 1814). Although he was chased from his university post, he never halted his study, and made himself a master of Coptic, the language of the church in Egypt.

Suddenly, in the autumn of 1822, Champollion saw the true explanation of the writing. Until then he had thought the hieroglyphs had some sort of symbolic meaning, used as letters only to write foreign names. Now, looking at recently copied texts, he recognized that the signs were used for sounds as well as for words. Within a few days he successfully made sense of many kings' names, and announced his discovery in Paris on 17 September 1822.

Copies of newly-found inscriptions reached him a few weeks later and he was able to apply his system to them, with success. In 1824 he set out a full account of his discovery in a book which gave birth to modern knowledge of ancient Egyptian *(Précis du système hiéroglyphique des anciens égyptiens)*. It was quite clear he had deciphered the hieroglyphs correctly.

Champollion was appointed curator of the king's new Egyptian Museum in Paris in 1826 and led an expedition to Egypt in 1828-29. He made many discoveries and brought more objects home to France. He was highly honoured by his fellow-countrymen, but died of exhaustion in 1832 at the age of forty-one.

The Rosetta Stone was the key which unlocked the mysteries of ancient Egyptian writing. It records a decree of King Ptolemy V in three languages: Greek (bottom), Egyptian demotic script (middle), and hieroglyphs (top).

Ra' - mes - (s) sw

One of the groups of hieroglyphs that gave Champollion the key to deciphering ancient Egyptian was the name of Ramesses. The third sign is strictly unnecessary, simply helping to 'spell' the value of the second.

SECRETS FROM THE ROCK OF BEHISTUN

Travellers on the road going west from Tehran, through Kermanshah in Persia, towards Iraq, pass a great cliff known as the Rock of Behistun (or Bisitun).

Three hundred feet above the ground, men can be seen carved in the stone. A tall figure raises his hand towards ten standing men, and two others stand behind him. No one knew who they were. Guesses ranged from Christ and the twelve apostles to a school-master and his class!

Beside the picture the rock was polished smooth. Some who climbed near it reported that it was covered with arrow-head marks cut into the stone.

The same marks had caught the attention of visitors to parts of Persia from the seventeenth century on. The few Europeans who saw them made drawings of them which intrigued and puzzled the readers of their books. During the eighteenth century more men went to see them, and some began to decipher them.

There was agreement that they were a form of writing, not decoration, as some people had said. Cuneiform, 'wedge-shaped', was a name invented for them for French and English, derived from Latin (in German the name is *Keilschrift*).

First to make headway was the hardy explorer Carsten Niebuhr. Reading books about Persia had excited him. He learnt Arabic and led an expedition from Denmark in 1761.

He travelled through Arabia to India, arriving in Bombay with a doctor, the only other survivor of the party. Undiscouraged, he set off for Persia, where he spent three weeks copying the inscriptions at the ancient ruined capital, Persepolis (see *Persian Splendours*). After studying what he had seen, he published an account of his journeys and of the inscriptions in 1774-1778 *(Reisebeschreibung von Arabien und anderen umliegenden Ländern)*.

Niebuhr added to his copies an attempt to translate the writing. He saw that there were three different kinds, the simplest one being an alphabet. Out of the forty-two letters he recognized, thirty-two turned out to be right when the inscriptions were finally understood.

Neibuhr's work spurred a number of men to try to improve the understanding of this cuneiform alphabet. One correctly argued that it was written by the kings of the Persian Empire, Cyrus, Darius and their successors — but could not read it.

The one who succeeded was Georg Grotefend, a school-master at Göttingen in Germany. His hobby was to solve puzzles, especially puzzles with words. One day, about 1800, a friend who had been drinking with Grotefend made a bet that he could not read the Persian writing. In 1802 Grotefend announced that he had deciphered the writing and identified the names of Darius and Xerxes with words for 'son' and 'king'.

Unhappily, Göttingen University was not interested in Grotefend's work, so its full publication was delayed until 1805. He did not carry his work much further forward, that was done by other scholars.

Behistun and its inscriptions were the means of completing the decipherment of what we now call 'Old Persian' cuneiform. At the same time, they opened the door to deciphering the much more complicated Babylonian cuneiform writing.

An energetic Englishman squeezed the secrets from the Rock of Behistun.

Henry Rawlinson went to work for the East India Company in 1827, at the age of seventeen. He learnt Indian languages and Persian, served with the army in the 1st Bombay Grenadiers, and went to Persia in 1835 as military adviser to the Shah's brother, governor of Kermanshah.

Near the city were two inscriptions on rocks. Examining them, Rawlinson worked out the names of Darius and

Gigantic sculptured figures on the Rock of Behistun stand above the cuneiform inscription cut into the cliff face. Henry Rawlinson, copying the inscription into his notebook, did so at considerable risk. The prize was the deciphering of cuneiform signs for the first time.

Major General Sir Henry Rawlinson (1810-1895) was one of the great pioneers in deciphering Babylonian cuneiform.

Rawlinson's notebooks, preserved in the British Museum, show how he worked to achieve his decipherment. This is a detail from one page.

Xerxes, apparently unaware of what Grotefend and others had done. Then he went to the Rock of Behistun.

In 1835 he began to copy. At the end of the year he was ill and spent some time in Baghdad where he evidently discussed ancient inscriptions with the British Resident. After military exercises, he returned to Kermanshah to find papers sent by the Resident explaining Grotefend's work.

Later in 1836, in 1837, and again in 1844 and 1847, Rawlinson copied the texts at Behistun. It was not easy to reach parts of them.

He described the work on the cliff face: '. . . ladders are indispensable . . . and even with ladders there is considerable risk, for the footledge is so narrow, about 18 inches, or at most 2 feet in breadth, that with a ladder long enough to reach the sculptures sufficient slope cannot be given to enable a person to ascend, and if the ladder be shortened in order to increase the slope, the upper inscriptions can only be copied by standing on the topmost step of the ladder, with no other support than steadying the body against the rock with the left arm, while the left hand holds the note-book and the right hand is employed with the pencil. In this position I copied all the upper inscriptions and the interest of the occupation entirely did away

with any sense of danger.'

In another passage he told how a ladder he was using to bridge a chasm came apart and left him hanging over a precipice to be rescued by his friends. Such was the price of decipherment!

Rawlinson sent a first essay to London, translating and commenting on 200 lines of the inscription in 1837. His major study, *Memoir on the Persian Version of the Behistun Inscriptions*, appeared in 1846 and was completed in 1849. With that, the study of Old Persian was firmly founded.

Rawlinson guessed that the two other sorts of cuneiform writing on the cliff gave translations of the Persian inscriptions. In one of the scripts there were over 100 signs, too many for it to be an alphabet.

Grotefend identified a few signs, and a Danish scholar, Niels Westergaard, several more, using examples of the same writing found elsewhere in Persia.

It was Rawlinson, again, who made the major contribution. He sent his copy of the text to London, with a translation and notes, and it was printed in 1855 after careful editing and improving by Edwin Norris of the Royal Asiatic Society.

The language of this second sort of cuneiform writing was named Susian or Elamite, because it was found mostly at Susa, capital of ancient Elam (see *Persian Splendours*).

With two of the three writings deciphered, Rawlinson turned to the third. This is the most complicated and was the most awkward to reach of the inscriptions at Behistun. In 1847 Rawlinson paid a local Kurdish boy to clamber across the sheer rock face, hanging by a rope, banging wooden wedges into cracks to gain a foothold.

The boy reached the right part of the rock where, dangling in a rope cradle, he took an impression of the engraved signs with large sheets of damp paper. Little more than a year later, Rawlinson felt he could understand the sense of the inscription.

He spoke about his work in London in January 1850.

Other discoveries of cuneiform inscriptions had been made, and other men were trying to read them. In a quiet Irish rectory an Anglican clergyman, Edward Hincks, devoted himself to the mystery. Already, in 1847, he had published lists of signs with their values, and the meanings of some words. Hincks deserves great credit beside Rawlinson as a pioneer in deciphering Babylonian cuneiform. It was he who told Layard the meaning of the inscriptions he unearthed in Assyria (see *The Price of Protection*).

The papers by Hincks and Rawlinson were sent to other scholars who interested themselves in cuneiform, so that all could share in the work. There were many mistaken attempts before everyone accepted that Hincks was right in claiming that the signs stand for syllables (*ba, ad, gu, im,* etc.), although some of them could also be words (*an* is also 'god', *ilu*).

Hincks also observed that the signs were originally invented to write a different language from the Semitic Assyrian and Babylonian. Later, the language was revealed to be the quite unrelated Sumerian.

Were Rawlinson, Hincks and others right, or was their decipherment mistaken?

1 ya - ú - a son of

1 khu - um - ri - i.

One of the first Assyrian inscriptions to be deciphered was on the Black Obelisk which bears a picture of tribute sent by a king named as 'Jehu, son of Omri', one of the kings of Israel (see The Price of Protection).

In 1857 one man interested in the subject, Henry Fox Talbot, a pioneer in photography, proposed a test. A text should be sent to the decipherers for each to translate independently, the results being submitted to an independent judge.

Rawlinson, Hincks, Talbot and a French scholar, Jules Oppert, took part. The translations were so similar as to make it certain the script had been deciphered.

Now the publication and translation of the inscriptions could go ahead. The records of Assyria and Babylonia could speak again, 2500 years after they had fallen silent.

DIGGING UP THE PAST

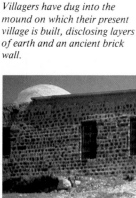

Villagers have dug into the mound on which their present village is built, disclosing layers of earth and an ancient brick wall.

Stories of buried treasure are common all over the world. For as long as people have built houses and lived in towns and villages, they have been finding things their forebears lost or buried.

Usually these things are found by accident, and most of them are so uninteresting, they have simply been thrown away. The only things people have kept are objects of gold and silver, or things which they can admire.

This is still true today. Farmers ploughing fields will keep anything they think is valuable that their ploughs turn up, and throw away the rest. People combing the beach or countryside with metal-detectors hope to find money or valuables. They leave behind the nails and other odds and ends their machines locate.

Archaeologists are scientific

treasure-hunters. When they find gold and silver, or beautiful works of art, they are pleased. But everything people have used is valuable to them.

In certain circumstances a single piece of broken pottery may tell the archaeologist more than a gold ring. If, for example, the pottery was marked as an import from a country overseas, it could be a sign of foreign relations through trade or warfare.

Equally important are the ruined buildings, houses, temples, palaces, fortresses that people have built in the past, and the tombs they dug for their dead.

Digging ancient remains out of the ground can be exciting and rewarding. But simply pulling a jar or a jewel out of the earth, or clearing the rubbish down to the floor of a building, destroys valuable evidence.

Observing exactly where the things lie, the different colours and textures of the soil, and how they are arranged in the ground, can reveal a great deal.

Was this pot underneath the earth floor or on it, or in the rubbish lying on it? If the first, it is older than the floor. If the second or third, it is likely it belonged to the people who used the building. If it was on top of rubble fallen into the house, it could belong to a much later date. Even if it was below the level of the floor, careful inspection might discover that it lay in a pit dug from a higher level long after the building was forgotten.

In the same way, following the layers or strata of earth may show that one wall was built earlier than another, if the layer of soil running up to the first wall was cut through by the foundations of the second.

It is as vital for the archaeologist to observe and record all of these matters

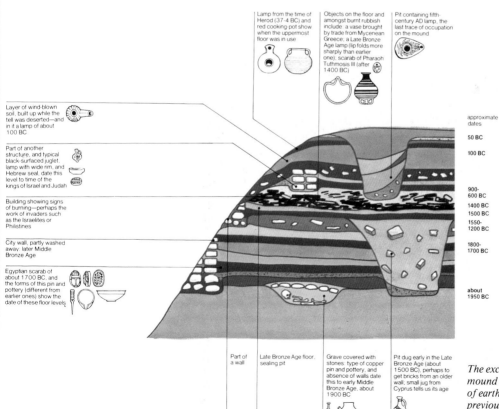

Lamp from the time of Herod (37-4 BC) and red cooking-pot show when the uppermost floor was in use

Objects on the floor and amongst burnt rubbish include: a vase brought by trade from Mycenean Greece; a Late Bronze Age lamp (lip folds more sharply than earlier one); scarab of Pharaoh Tuthmosis III (after 1400 BC)

Pit containing fifth-century AD lamp, the last trace of occupation on the mound

Layer of wind-blown soil, built up while the tell was deserted—and in it a lamp of about 100 BC

Part of another structure, and typical black-surfaced juglet, lamp with wide rim, and Hebrew seal, date this level to time of the kings of Israel and Judah

Building showing signs of burning—perhaps the work of invaders such as the Israelites or Philistines

City wall, partly washed away: later Middle Bronze Age

Egyptian scarab of about 1700 BC, and the forms of this pin and pottery (different from earlier ones) show the date of these floor levels

| approximate dates |
| 50 BC |
| 100 BC |
| 900-600 BC |
| 1400 BC |
| 1500 BC |
| 1550-1200 BC |
| 1800-1700 BC |
| about 1950 BC |

Part of a wall

Late Bronze Age floor, sealing pit

Grave covered with stones: type of copper pin and pottery, and absence of walls date this to early Middle Bronze Age, about 1900 BC

Pit dug early in the Late Bronze Age (about 1500 BC), perhaps to get bricks from an older wall; small jug from Cyprus tells us its age

The excavation of a town mound ('tell') shows the layers of earth and remains of previous buildings, with buried objects which may provide clues to the date.

in notes, photographs and drawings, as it is for him to describe the objects and the building he finds. All excavation is destructive; disturb the soil and it is impossible to replace it as it was before. What the archaeologist's eye misses is lost.

These essential facts have gradually become obvious over the last century and a half. In recent years all sorts of refinements have developed, and a wide range of techniques have entered archaeology from physics and chemistry, all aimed at extracting as much information as possible from what is found. In the end, the observant eye of the archaeologist is still the most vital tool.

In the lands of the Near East, where most of the Bible was written, people have been building their houses of stone and brick for more than 7,000 years. The stones may have fallen from their places, but they often survive. Bricks, however, were made of mud dried in the sun, not baked in a kiln, and so they usually disintegrate quite quickly, unless they are buried in the ground.

The life of a simple mud-brick building, therefore, might span only thirty years or so before the walls started to give way. Where this was the normal building material, repairs and total rebuildings were frequent.

That is the process which built up the great mounds of ruined towns and villages visible all over the Near East, one house rising upon the remains of the earlier one. (The same process can be seen in many other lands; in cities of Europe, for example, streets of the Roman period lie 3–7 metres/10–20 feet below the modern roads. The stumps of walls and the debris of medieval and later times make up the difference.)

The need to observe all the time digging is in progress, and the need to record all that is found, makes excavation a slow and demanding task. Consequently, the excavation of an entire town is very rare. Expeditions may concentrate on the buildings of one period or, more commonly, dig in selected areas.

The archaeologist may choose to dig where a farmer has uncovered a carved stone, or explorers have noted the lines of walls or large quantities of pottery. He may hit a part that has always been important, perhaps as the highest quarter of the town, or the best situated for sun and wind. On the other hand, he may miss the chief buildings, learning much about the houses of the poorer people.

So the restricted areas cleared, as well as the amount of destruction worked on the ruins over the course of

Carved stones from earlier buildings, like the bull (below right) were often reused by later builders on the same or nearby sites.

At Nimrud in Iraq, workmen dig and basket boys carry away unwanted earth.

Excavation is in progress at a Sumerian burial site in northern Iraq.

centuries by mankind and the elements, mean that the complete history of a site is beyond recovery. What is found can never be more than a part, a sample of what once existed.

This is an important condition to keep in mind when reading any study based on archaeological discoveries. Unless the evidence is very soundly established and is evaluated in the light of other knowledge of the time and region, it may be misleading. And what applies to archaeological discoveries also applies to written documents. They, too, are only a sample of all that was written in ancient times. Although thousands of them lie in modern museums, many thousands more have been lost.

Few buildings, few texts, and few objects were made in order that they should last for distant generations to read. The majority survive by accident and are found by accident. Indeed, some things found may not even be typical of their kind. This means that a new discovery can force scholars to change their accepted positions completely, or to revise them.

To take just one example, the recent finding of a palace at Ebla in north Syria with thousands of clay tablets written about 2300 BC is opening new areas of study in history and language (see *Headline News: The Lost City of Ebla*).

As farming and towns spread across parts of the Near East where no one has lived for centuries, ancient sites risk destruction. Excavating these places has priority, but others can be studied at leisure. There is much work yet to be done, and many more discoveries to be made.

A DAY ON A DIG

It is dark when we get out of bed. After a quick wash in a basin of cold water, we walk across the courtyard of the mud-brick house to a long room. This serves as the expedition's meeting-place and dining-room. Cups of tea, pieces of bread, and a tin of apricot jam are on the table, a snack before the day's digging starts. Chattering and clattering in the court-yard tell us that the workmen have come to collect their shovels and pick-axes, and baskets for carrying earth.

Sleepily, we pick up our notebooks, pencils, tape-measures, labels, paper-bags and boxes, and walk out after them across the mound to the trenches. The sun is about to rise. Over the hill to the east shines a rosy glow, then, quickly following, the sun's disk blazes light over the countryside.

After the workmen had left yesterday, we had assessed progress to decide where to dig deeper, and where to stop. Now we show the two pick-men the area for today's work. Part of a brick wall is showing, and we want to follow it down to the floor, then trace its course across the area of our trench. At first the work is heavy, vigorous digging, to clear away mud-bricks that have fallen from the wall and weathered into a mass of hard mud with nothing else in it. The picks swing, the mud-bricks give way and soon there is a pile of loose earth.

The two men stop, and step aside to rest. In their place come the four shovel-men and the basket boys. They scoop up the earth, two or three shovelfuls to a basket. The boys swing the baskets to their shoulders and pad away to tip the earth over the edge of the mound. (Excavating is often done after harvest, when the men have little work to do in the fields and the boys are on holiday from school.)

We watch, checking that the earth is nothing but decayed brick, until the picks strike into different-coloured soil. Under the fallen bricks is a layer of rubbish. Perhaps we are near the floor. The pick-men wait while we test the ground with trowels. The dark, ashy soil is several inches thick and stretches for some distance. All the fallen brick-work has to be cleared away before deeper digging is done.

As the picks hack into it we describe the change in the notebook, give a number to the new layer and prepare a bag, marked with the number of the trench, the layer and the date, ready for any finds. At last the sterile brick-mass is gone. The wall stands clear at one side, patches of fine mud-plaster still sticking to it.

Now the pick-men dig very gently into the ashy level. They are trained to detect any hardness or object in the ground by the feel and sound of the steel point as it touches the

earth. Often, the soil will fall away from a stone or a pot as soon as it is loosened. The paper bag begins to fill as pieces of pottery come out of the ground. Less earth is being shifted, the basket boys need not run so fast!

As we are examining the pottery, one of the pick-men calls. He has hit a black square a few inches long; it is a piece of wood, charred in a fire. Is it only a piece of wood? Is it shaped or carved? It is too delicate to handle. With trowel and knife we cut it from its place in a block of mud and lay it on a cotton-wool bed in a cardboard box to be taken to our make-shift laboratory.

Expert treatment can solidify it before it is studied. Even if it is simply a lump of wood, botanists can identify the tree and atomic physicists can measure its age by the Carbon 14 test. (All living organisms contain a radio-active carbon isotope, C14, in a regular proportion. After death this substance begins to decay at a known rate, so that half of it will have disappeared after

5,730 years. Measuring the proportion of Carbon 14 in the material enables its age to be calculated.) There is a great deal of broken pottery — ancient people were very careless and very untidy. Two bags are full, we need to commandeer a basket to hold all the pieces.

A lot more wood is uncovered, bigger pieces from the beams of a roof or floor, so more samples have to be taken and the position of each one measured and noted on a sketch-plan. Putting their picks aside, the workmen scrape and dig gently with trowels and knives.

As well as pottery and wood, there are green spots in the ground at one place. Very slowly the earth is cut away. Lying there, complete, though badly corroded, is a copper ring with an Egyptian scarab as its stone. Before we lift it, its position is noted, for

A Danish archaeology student sieves earth, looking for coins, at the site of a fifth century AD Jewish village on the Golan Heights.

that may help to tell us why it was lying just where we found it. Everyone is pleased. We have made a good 'find'.

Hardly is the ring packed in a clearly labelled box, when one of the basket-boys comes running back. As he tipped his load away, his sharp eyes saw a flash of bright colour. In the palm of his hand he holds a tiny bead of polished red stone. It goes into an envelope, is duly labelled, and a note is entered in the book. The boy's name is written on the envelope, too — a good mark for him!

We've been busy and three hours have passed. It's time for breakfast. Back at the dig house we eat eggs, boiled or scrambled, bread and more apricot jam, with tea or coffee to drink. There's half an hour to rest, discuss finds and progress, warn the registrar that more finds may be coming. His job is to draw and describe them for the records of the expedition and of the national Department of Antiquities.

In the second half of the morning the pace of work slows as noon approaches. Soon it will be time to end the digging for the day. In the strange way things happen, a few minutes before work finishes the pick-man stands up, nursing something in his hands, and comes to us. He has picked up something he has never seen before.

Everyone gathers round to stare at a small lump of brown mud. One flat side has little marks impressed all over it. It is a Babylonian cuneiform tablet, an outstanding discovery, a written document perhaps bringing names and personalities to the mute walls and potsherds. But as we gingerly take it from him we see that two edges are newly broken. Are the other parts still in the ground, or did we all miss them?

The man's face falls; he goes back to look, the shovel-men and the basket-boys sift the loose soil. Soon they are all happy. One piece was in a basket ready to be carried away to the tip, two more were still in the ground. The positions of the pieces are recorded, then all are solemnly borne to the house, where the news has already spread.

Hurrying from the other side of the mound comes the epigraphist, the expert in writing and languages, who has spent a miserable three weeks without a single inscription to study. With paintbrush and pin he cleans the dirt away from the first two lines, a grain at a time. Everyone is waiting. What does it say? It is a letter addressed to a king, the king of the city everyone has believed the place to be. Now there is no room for doubt.

Dinner is ready, an interruption, but a welcome

An artist makes a careful copy of a relief portrait of Pharaoh Tutankhamun, on site.

one. Discussion goes on around the table. Records from other cities speak of this king and his contemporaries, so we can give him an approximate date. How long after that did the tablet stay on a shelf in the building? Is it the palace we are digging into? Will there be more tablets, more rings?

After dinner most of the expedition takes a siesta for an hour or two, to wash and shave, write letters. Refreshed, we continue to clean and draw the finds, sort and mend the pottery, draw plans, take photographs and pore over the tablet. The sun sets, paraffin lamps are lit. The cook has a special supper ready — frogs' legs from the nearby river — a change from tinned meat bought in the town twenty miles away. Contented, we retire to bed, stumbling

across the rough courtyard in the moonlight, to dream of more tablets, more pots, palaces, rings and archives. The mound has many more treasures waiting to be found!

The 'day on a dig' describes the traditional way of excavating in the Near East. A director with a small team of experts from Europe, or America, or from the near eastern country itself, works with local labour. In recent years, some directors have welcomed students and other volunteers to work on their sites, almost completely dispensing with local workmen.

'OF COURSE, IT'S THE FLOOD!'

Leonard Woolley, the archaeologist in charge at Ur, instructed his workman to dig a small pit, to find the ground surface on which the first settlers had built their reed huts. That would mark the birthplace of the great city Ur of the Chaldees.

The workman dug down to a clean bed of clay, with no broken fragments of pottery. 'That's the bottom sir,' he shouted. But Woolley was not so sure.

The workman was still standing more than 2 metres/6 feet above sea-level and Woolley reckoned that was also the original level. Unwillingly, the man agreed to dig deeper. He dug and dug, through 2.5 metres/8 feet of clean soil, and then more pottery began to appear. At last he hit true virgin soil, 1 metre/3 feet below modern sea level, and about 19 metres/62 feet from the surface of the ruin mound.

What was this thick layer of sterile soil?

Woolley thought he knew, and when two assistants could give no answer, he turned to his wife.

'Well, of course, it's the flood,' she remarked.

When the soil was analysed, it was shown to be silt deposited by water. On the basis of that, and related discoveries, Leonard Woolley claimed he had found physical evidence of the great flood which Sumerian, Babylonian and Hebrew stories recall.

All sorts of writers took up Woolley's discovery. Some seized on it as proof of the biblical story of Noah. Others saw it simply as the remains of one of the many floods that overwhelmed the cities of Babylonia.

News of the flood-level at Ur had hardly broken before another excavator claimed he had found a layer of silt left by the flood. He was working at Kish, 220 km/137 miles north of Ur.

Now the debate began.

The Ur layer, deposited about 4000 BC, was much older than the one at Kish. Did either represent the flood?

Excavations at other places in

Babylonia produced clean levels like those at Kish, and belonging to roughly the same date, about 2800 BC.

None of the levels at other sites belonged to the same time as the level at Ur. Many scholars now argue that some of those later deposits mark the time of the flood.

They argue this because the date fits information preserved in Babylonian traditions. Some of the lists of early kings begin with the gods setting up kingship. After a few reigns the sequence is broken — 'Then came the flood' — and a fresh start follows. Other lists begin with the first king after the flood. Not so very long after that king, and within his line of succession, we meet a ruler whose own inscriptions survive. Since they have an archaeological date of about 2600 BC, the floods can be set a century or two earlier.

There is no doubt the flood was a catastrophic event that stayed in human memory as long as Babylonian civilization lasted. A variety of writings refer to it as a point in time. It was evidently more than a small local flood, the sort of thing most of the low-lying riverside towns of Babylonia could expect. Yet we are still not sure that these deposits of silt and clay are traces of it.

At Ur, Woolley admitted, the silt did not cover the whole site. The great depth of clean soil he dug through appeared to be the result of water running against part of the ruin mound, perhaps over a long period of time. Some of the other deposits, too, seem not to have destroyed or drowned the buildings where they are found. Perhaps Mrs Woolley was wrong, after all, and it was only a flood, not *the* flood.

The snow-capped peak of Mt Ararat, in eastern Turkey, reaches to the sky. The Bible says it was on the mountains of Ararat that Noah's 'ark' came to rest, after the flood.

Another exciting discovery about the flood was made long before the excavations at Ur. In the 1850s Sir Henry Layard dug out of the ruins of Nineveh thousands of pieces of clay tablets. They were once the library of the Assyrian king Ashurbanipal, and were left lying broken and forgotten when his palace was destroyed in 612 BC. Layard brought the tablets to the British Museum in London. Over the years scholars catalogued and identified the pieces, making their work known in books and learned journals.

In 1872 George Smith was busy at this task when he realized the fragments on his desk belonged to a story of the flood. This was no ordinary flood, nor just a story of a flood. It had striking resemblances to the story of Noah in the biblical book of Genesis.

Smith described his discovery to a meeting of the Society for Biblical Archaeology, and it created a sensation.

The Babylonian story and the biblical one clearly shared so much that there could be no doubt there was a strong connection between them. But what was it? Did the Hebrew story derive from the Babylonian, the Babylonian from the Hebrew, or did both have a common source?

Ever since the discovery was announced, the first possibility has won greatest support. The second is held to be unlikely because the Babylonian account dates back to at least 1600 BC, well before the Hebrew one was written.

A small number of scholars have always taken the third position, that the stories have a common origin. Abraham's migration from Ur to Canaan could have carried the story westward; many scholars think the Israelites learnt it from the Canaanites.

What is the Babylonian Flood Story? Chapters 6−9 of Genesis tell of the flood as part of the continuing story of God's relations with mankind. The story George Smith found is also part of a longer tale. It is in the eleventh, and last, tablet of the Epic of Gilgamesh.

This epic tells how the ancient king Gilgamesh tried to win immortality. After many adventures he reached a distant land where lived the only man who had become immortal, a man named Ut-napishtim, the Babylonian Noah. He told Gilgamesh about the flood to explain why the gods gave him his eternal life. After the story was told, he showed Gilgamesh that he could not hope to become immortal, and sent him home.

Several details and oddities suggested that the Babylonian Flood Story did not begin as part of the Gilgamesh Epic. Thanks to the discovery of another poem, known as the Atrakhasis Epic, the story can now be seen in its proper setting.

Like Genesis, the Atrakhasis Epic tells of the creation of man and his history to the time of the flood and the new society which was set up after it. Here the reason for the flood is clear, which it is not in the Gilgamesh Epic. Mankind made so much noise that the chief god on earth could not sleep. The gods, having failed to solve the problem in other ways, therefore sent the flood to destroy these troublesome humans and silence them for ever.

The similarities between the

Records of the excavations at Ur, published in 1956, include this cross-section of the pit which cut through a thick layer of silt. Leonard Woolley claimed this was evidence of the flood.

40

Buildings of reeds, on the banks of the Euphrates, serve as reminders of a low-lying riverside area prone to flooding.

Babylonian and the Hebrew stories are easy to see. But there are notable differences which should not be overlooked. The basic one lies in the monotheism of the Hebrew account contrasted with the many gods acting in the Babylonian story. Equally different is the moral attitude. Details differ, too, about the form and size of the ark (the Babylonian one, a cube, would be unlikely to float on the water), the duration of the flood, and the sending out of the birds.

The similarities in the stories and the recognizably Mesopotamian background imply that they had a common origin. The archaeological evidence for floods in Babylonia, and the strong tradition of one major, disastrous flood, taken with the stories about it, point to a catastrophic event early in history. When it comes to the interpretation of the event the biblical record clearly stands apart from the others, supporting its own claim to be not just a human tale but the revelation of God.

THE BABYLONIAN STORY OF THE FLOOD

The Babylonian Flood Story, as it is told in the Epic of Gilgamesh, occupies almost 200 lines of poetry. The following extracts show how the story runs and give the flavour.

The gods in council decided to send the flood, and Ea, the god responsible for creating man, took an oath with them not to tell mankind about it. Ea, however, wanted to warn his worshipper Ut-napishtim, and so spoke to his house:

'Reed-hut, reed-hut, wall, wall!
Reed-hut listen, wall pay attention!'

He was really addressing Ut-napishtim:

'Pull down the house, build a ship!
Leave riches, seek life!
Spurn possessions in order to stay alive!
Take the seed of all creatures aboard the ship.
The ship you are to build Its measurements shall equal each other
Its width and its length shall be the same.'

There follows a discussion about how Ut-napishtim should explain his work to his fellow citizens, and how he is to know when the flood will come. The solution was to hide the facts from them, and lead them to think the gods would bless them. Then the building of the boat is described. When it was made, Ut-napishtim continued:

'Whatever I had I put aboard it,
Whatever silver I had I put aboard it,
Whatever gold I had I put aboard it,
Whatever living creatures I had I put aboard it.
I made all my family and relatives board the ship.
The domesticated animals and the wild,
All the craftsmen, I made go aboard . . .
The fixed time arrived . . .
I looked at the pattern of the weather,
The weather was terrifying to see.
I boarded the ship and closed the door . . .

This seventh-century BC inscribed clay tablet, the eleventh tablet of the Assyrian version of the Epic of Gilgamesh, contains a Babylonian account of the flood.

With the first glow of dawn,
A black cloud rose up from the horizon.
Inside it the storm-god thunders . . .
The god of the underworld tears out the posts of the dam.
The warrior-god leads the waters on.
The gods raise the torches,
Setting the land on fire with their blaze.
The fearful silence of the storm-god reached the heavens,
And turned everything bright to darkness.
[   ] of the land shattered like a pot.
For one day the tempest [raged]
It blew hard . . .
Like a battle the divine might overtook the people.
No one could see his neighbour.
The people could not be recognized from heaven.
The gods were frightened by the flood.
They went off up to the heaven of the chief god.
The gods cowered like dogs, crouching outside the door.
The goddess Ishtar cried out like a woman in labour . . .
The gods weep with her . . .
For six days and seven nights
The wind, the flood, the storm overwhelmed the land.
When the seventh day arrived, the storm and flood ceased the war
In which they had struggled like a woman in labour.
I looked at the weather: it was still,
And all mankind had turned to clay.
The countryside was flat as a flat roof.
I opened the window, light fell upon my cheek,

Crouching down, I sat and wept . . .
On Mount Nisir the ship grounded . . .
When the seventh day came,
I sent out a dove, releasing it.
The dove went, then came back,
No resting-place appeared for it, so it returned.
Then I sent out a swallow, releasing it.
The swallow went, then came back,
No resting-place appeared for it, so it returned.
Then I sent out a raven, releasing it.
The raven went and saw the waters receding,
It ate, it flew about, to and fro, it did not return.
I brought out sacrifices and offered them to the four winds,
I made a libation on the peak of the mountain,
The gods smelled the savour,
The gods smelled the sweet savour,
The gods clustered like flies around the sacrificer.'
When at last the great goddess (Ishtar) arrived,
She lifted up the big fly (beads) which the chief god had made to amuse her.
"All you gods here, as I shall never forget my lapis lazuli necklace,
I shall remember these days, and never forget them . . .".'

Following a dispute over the survivor and advice to punish individuals for their sins, the gods ordained immortality for Ut-napishtim and his wife.

The biblical story begins in Genesis 6. Its tone and flavour is quite different from the Babylonian.

'God looked at the world and saw that it was evil, for the people were all living evil lives.

God said to Noah, "I have decided to put an end to all mankind. I will destroy them completely, because the world is full of their violent deeds. Build a boat for yourself out of good timber; make rooms in it and cover it with tar inside and out. Make it 133 metres long, 22 metres wide, and 13 metres high. Make a roof for the boat and leave a space of 44 centimetres between the roof and the sides. Build it with three decks and put a door in the side. I am going to send a flood on the earth to destroy every living being. Everything on the earth will die, but I will make a covenant with you. Go into the boat with your wife, your sons, and their wives. Take into the boat with you a male and a female of every kind of animal and of every kind of bird, in order to keep them alive. Take along all kinds of food for you and for them." Noah did everything that God commanded . . .'

'The Lord destroyed all living beings on the earth — human beings, animals, and the birds. The only ones left were Noah and those who were with him in the boat. The water did not start going down for a hundred and fifty days.

God had not forgotten Noah and all the animals with him in the boat; he caused a wind to blow, and the water started going down. The outlets of the water beneath the earth and the floodgates of the sky were closed. The rain stopped, and the water

gradually went down for a hundred and fifty days. On the seventeenth day of the seventh month the boat came to rest on a mountain in the Ararat range. The water kept going down, and on the first day of the tenth month the tops of the mountains appeared.'

ROYAL TREASURES FROM UR

Sir Leonard Woolley had been excavating at Ur for only a few days in 1923 when one of his workmen dug out a small hoard of gold and stone beads. The men were new to the work, untrained, and Woolley was afraid that the sight of the gold might lead to secret digging and smuggling. He knew there was more to be found, but he stopped the digging at that spot for four years, until 1926.

He was uncertain, too, about what the man had found. No one had seen jewellery like this before. One experienced archaeologist reckoned it belonged to the Middle Ages and was 5–600 years old. Woolley himself thought it might be 2,000 years older, from the Persian period or just before.

When Woolley put the men to work in that place again the result was astonishing. They found a cemetery with hundreds of graves dug over a period of several centuries into an older rubbish tip. The majority of the burials were quite simple. Each grave contained a skeleton with a few pots, perhaps a little jewellery, some tools or weapons.

Sixteen burials were very grand. Great pits were sunk some 9 metres/ 30 feet from the surface to make a space up to 11 × 5 metres/32 × 16 feet at the bottom.

To reach the bottom, the tomb-builders cut a sloping shaft leading in at an angle. On the floor they built a small stone- or brick-vaulted chamber for the dead man. But these great shafts were designed to hold more than one body. To the excavator's amazement, dozens of bodies were

The golden head-dress of flowers and leaves once belonged to a queen of Ur.

lying on the floor of each shaft. Near the foot of the ramp were skeletons of oxen, once harnessed to a wagon. The reins had decayed, but some had been threaded through beads which were still on the lines where the reins ran.

Human skeletons beside the oxen Woolley identified as their grooms. Other bodies belonged to guards with spears and helmets stationed at the foot of the ramp. Still more were the court attendants. Musicians had their harps and lyres, the ladies wore bright headdresses of flowers and leaves cut from gold and silver sheets.

All the bodies were so neatly placed, Woolley concluded the people

had walked down the ramp to their positions, lain down, and drunk poison from a small cup. (Some of the cups were beside the bodies.) Undertakers then tidied the scene, killing the oxen, some of which lay on top of their human attendants, and left. With great ceremonies and offerings, the shaft was refilled with earth.

Ancient robbers had tunnelled into the tombs and disturbed the central burials. They took all they could, still leaving plenty for Woolley's men. What was left made it clear these had been the tombs of kings. Royalty had to pass into the grave with all the trappings of state they had enjoyed in life. Their servants had to go with them, too, and it was probably an honour to be chosen.

Processes of decay had destroyed the clothing, basketry, leather and woodwork, yet, with brilliant makeshift techniques, Woolley was often able to preserve traces of rotten wood, or at least record them. If his workmen found a hole in the ground, he poured plaster of Paris down it. When the plaster had set, they would chip away

the soil to see what had been there. In this way the shapes of harps and lyres, spear shafts and many other wooden objects were recovered.

Through Woolley's skill and observation more was learnt about the culture of Ur about 2500 BC than any other Babylonian city of that time.

The Royal Tombs of Ur reflect the wealth of the city. Kings and queens drank from gold and silver beakers. For

Music as well as art was part of the cultural life at Ur. Only the gold bull's head and mosaic decoration of this lyre (below, left) could be recovered, but Woolley's careful records of the decayed woodwork made this reconstruction possible.

One of the finest treasures of Ur is the figure of a goat (below), decorated with gold, silver, lapis and shell.

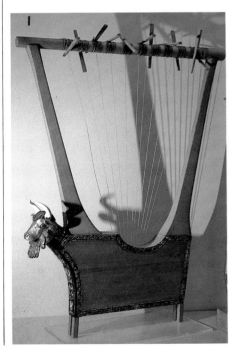

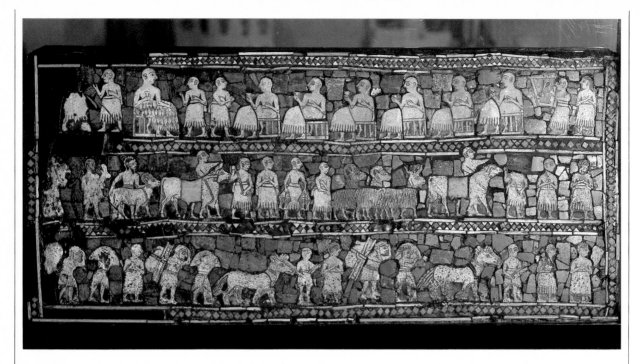

The 'standard' from the Royal Tombs at Ur is a mosaic of shell, red limestone and blue lapis lazuli. One side shows scenes of war, the other (pictured here) shows the victory feast and parade of booty. Several hundred years before the time of Abraham, the craftsmen of Ur were able to produce work of consummate skill.

The gold tools are also from the Royal Tombs at Ur.

show, the kings wore daggers with golden blades, the queens exquisite jewellery of gold and coloured stones. As they feasted they listened to singers accompanied on strings and pipes.

Metals and stone are not found in Babylonia. These had come by trade or conquest from foreign lands, the blue lapis lazuli from distant Afghanistan. In some of the tombs were the owners' seal-stones with their names and titles engraved on them. These allowed the dead people to be

put in their historical setting.

The treasures of Ur have no direct connection with the Bible. Like many less spectacular discoveries they reveal the craftsmen's consummate skill and hint at the beliefs of the time — in this case a form of self-sacrifice abhorrent to both Judaism and Christianity. They date from several centuries before Abraham's time, reminding us that the beginning of Israel's history is set, not in an age of primitives, but in a world of men already highly civilized.

HEADLINE NEWS
The Lost City of Ebla

Week after week the workmen toiled under the hot Syrian sun. Italian archaeologists hired them for two months each year and they dug into the mounds they and their fathers called Tell Mardikh. 1964 saw the first season; 1965, 1966, 1967 came and went.

Obviously, an important city lay hidden here. A high bank all round the site marked the city wall, and a strongly-built gateway led through it at the south-west. A local man turned up a carved stone by the hill in the centre of the enclosure, and the archaeologists found more, large stone basins ornamenting a big temple.

All these buildings belonged to the Middle Bronze Age, 2000 to 1600 BC. Yet no one knew the city's name. In 1968 an answer came. Builders in the Persian era, about 500−400 BC, had found part of an old statue and taken it as a useful stone. Written on it was the name of the king who had had it made over 1,000 years before. He presented the statue to Ishtar, goddess of love and war, the Babylonian Venus. Beside the king's name was his title, 'King of Ebla'.

Ebla was the name of a city the powerful Babylonian kings Sargon and Naram-Sin claimed they conquered about 2300 and 2250 BC. Scholars had been looking for it for years. Usually they looked near the River Euphrates, 160 km/100 miles from Tell Mardikh. Of course, a king could travel a long way from home to set up a statue in another city, so this single stone did not prove that Tell Mardikh was Ebla.

In 1975 the answer was made certain. In a building below the big temple thousands upon thousands of cuneiform tablets were uncovered and they made the identity of the place clear beyond doubt. Ebla was found!

The tablets lay in a pile on the floor of a small room at one side of a courtyard. They were the archives of a palace that had flourished for a few generations, then burnt down. In the heat of the flames the brickwork was baked, and the tablets too, so that both were stronger to stand the wear of time.

Enemy soldiers did not leave visiting-cards but, because we have no reason to doubt the boasts of conquest by Sargon and Naram-Sin, we can assume the army of one of them sacked Ebla's palace. They looted it hastily, leaving behind plenty of things precious to the archaeologist. Pieces of stone statues modelled in Babylonian styles, morsels of gold plating and intricately carved woodwork, charred by the fire, had fallen to the floors to be covered by the crumbling building.

Ebla hit the headlines when a leading Italian expert began to study the tablets. Valuable as the other discoveries are, the written words bring life to the picture. Dates, names and personalities add vividness to the dusty objects and broken walls. The very first news from the tablets was intriguing. In the oldest written documents ever found in north-west Syria the language was closer to Hebrew than to Babylonian.

Then the names of some Eblaites were announced. Among many strange ones were some which had a more

familiar sound: Ishmael, Adam, Daud (David). Some names ended in *el*, the word for 'god', and some in *ya*. Was this a pattern, like the biblical name 'Michael', meaning 'Who is like God?' and 'Micaiah', 'Who is like the Lord' (Jehovah, or Yahweh, shortened to Yah)? Was this *ya* really the name of the God of Israel (see *The Engraver of Seals*)?

The expert asserted it was so, and some scholars agreed with him. He went further. Places Ebla ruled, or had some power in, covered a large area, even to Hazor, Megiddo and Lachish in Canaan, and the cities of the Dead Sea plain, Sodom and Gomorrah.

One king of Ebla had the name Ebrium. Might his name be the same as Abraham's ancestor, Eber, mentioned in Genesis 10:21, or as the word 'Hebrew'?

Journalists seized on this news. Ebla featured in magazines of all sorts and was hailed as 'proof' of the Bible. The tablets themselves had not been made accessible to other scholars. Only reports from the one in charge were circulated. Irresponsible writers then imagined that the modern political prejudices of the Near East were hindering the flow of information, a charge which was untrue.

The Ebla tablets are one of the outstanding archaeological discoveries of the 1970s. Regrettably, its size and its novelty led the Italian scholar to move too fast, to neglect normal precautions in dealing with a strange language. Now, an international team of experts, principally Italian, with representatives from Belgium, Britain, France, Germany, Iraq, Syria and the USA, has the responsibility to edit the entire collection.

They have discarded most of the sensational claims.

Canaanite places do not occur in the tablets. Ebla had no contacts so far south, certainly not with the cities of the Dead Sea plain.

Names ending in *ya* may be short forms like Jimmy, Tommy, or the names may be read another way. There was no god Ya at Ebla, and no connection with Israel's God.

Ebrium did rule Ebla, his name might be the same as Eber, but there is

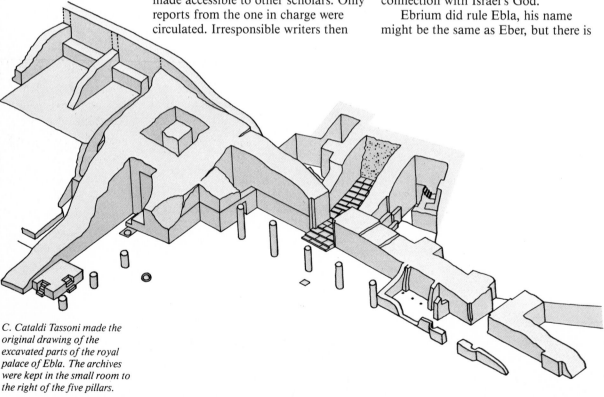

C. Cataldi Tassoni made the original drawing of the excavated parts of the royal palace of Ebla. The archives were kept in the small room to the right of the five pillars.

no reason to connect the two men. An association with the term Hebrew is unlikely.

Even the language of the tablets may prove closer to a Babylonian dialect than to Hebrew, although some citizens of Ebla did speak a language belonging to the same West-Semitic group as Hebrew.

Ten thousand documents written in a place from which none were previously known may well be full of difficulties. Long years of research will be needed for solving them. Meanwhile, the tablets are valued for their evidence that Babylonian writing spread to north Syria before 2300 BC, for their evidence of a readiness to write down every sort of administrative and legal activity, to write letters and literature, even to make dictionaries of different languages, and for their witness to the presence of West Semitic people there at that early date.

The later remains at Ebla illustrate the biblical texts more directly.

In its plan the big temple foreshadows Solomon's, with a porch, inner hall, and holy room. The proportions, however, are different.

Local royalty were buried in tombs hollowed out underneath a palace of the same period, 1800–1650 BC. Robbers had plundered the burials, but some treasures escaped them. Finely-worked gold beads were threaded for necklaces. There were gold bracelets, and a sceptre with a pharaoh's name spelt out in gold hieroglyphs.

A beautiful ring of gold, covered

with minute golden balls, had hung in a lady's nose. One may imagine the ring Eliezer gave to Rebekah at Harran was like it.

Ebla was a flourishing city in the days of the patriarchs.

Great discoveries often create rumours which excite false hopes and mislead people. In due course it is possible to make a balanced judgement and see what is really important. This is the case with Ebla.

When the dust raised by the first reports has died away, Ebla will be seen as a key site in early Syrian history, giving a brilliant insight into the level of culture there before the days of the patriarchs and during their period. The tablets will make knowledge of the early Semitic languages clearer, and so broaden our understanding of Hebrew.

It was the discovery of thousands of clay tablets, the palace archives, which made the identity of the 'lost city' of Ebla certain.

UR: CITY OF THE MOON-GOD

The train trundled through the night, privileged passengers asleep in bunks, others dozing on hard seats. With a jolt it stopped; bleary eyes looked out of the windows. The station's name, 'Ur Junction', had an air of unreality. We climbed down to the ground and spent the last part of the night in a convenient rest-house. Next morning, a mile or two across the flat plain, we reached the ruined city, Ur of the Chaldees.

The place is marked by a massive block of brickwork which can be seen from miles away. This was the temple of Sin, god of the moon, the chief god worshipped by the people of Ur.

Although the temple is even older, the bulk of the building standing today was erected by a king of Ur over 4,000 years ago. He made it as a series of platforms, one on top of another, each smaller than the one below. On the third platform stood the chapel where the people believed the god would live.

The Babylonians called the tower a ziggurat, meaning a mountain peak. A temple like this was a typical feature of a Babylonian city (see *The Glory that was Babylon*), rising above the flat countryside, a landmark to honour the gods and display the wealth of the king. In the city around the temple are ruins of other temples, palaces and

The temple of the moon-god dominates the ruins of Ur. It is more than 4,000 years old and was built as a series of stepped platforms with the house of the god on top. The biblical 'tower of Babel' was probably a temple tower of this kind.

tombs, and the houses of rich families.

When Sir Leonard Woolley, the archaeologist in charge of the excavation at Ur, cleared the dirt and fallen bricks from the houses, he found two areas quite well-preserved. A king of Babylon had destroyed Ur about 1740 BC, setting fire to some of the buildings. The inhabitants ran away, and only some came back to live in the houses again. Woolley was able to draw the plans of many streets, houses, shops and small chapels set among them. From his discoveries he was able to reconstruct their appearance and imagine life in the city.

In a typical town house the street door opened into a small lobby, perhaps provided with a jar of water for those arriving to wash their feet. A doorway at one side gave onto a courtyard. There were other rooms around the sides of the courtyard, among them store-rooms, a lavatory and a kitchen. In the kitchen there might be a well, a brick-built table, an oven, and grinding stones for making flour, as well as the pots and pans the last owners left behind. A long room at the centre of one side could have been the reception room.

Arab houses built in recent times in the towns of Iraq follow almost the same plan. All the rooms may be on the ground floor. Houses in Babylonia 1,000 years later than those at Ur were also single-storey dwellings. In the houses at Ur there is usually a well-constructed staircase at one side of the courtyard. None of the walls stands high enough to prove there was an upper storey, but it seems very likely there were upstairs rooms.

The furnishings did not survive. Carvings, pictures on seal-stones and models made in clay, probably as toys, represent the folding tables and chairs,

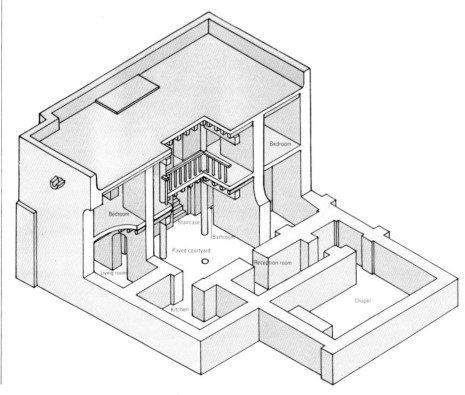

At the time of Abraham some well-to-do citizens of Ur may have lived in two-storey houses built in this style. In the centre was a paved courtyard, with bathroom, kitchen, chapel and other rooms around it.

wickerwork and basketry containers, wooden bedsteads and rugs that made the houses comfortable.

In larger houses one room could be set apart as a shrine. An altar of mud-bricks, carefully plastered, stood in one corner. An installation like a hearth nearby had a flue reaching to the ceiling, possibly for burning incense, and a mud-brick bench served as a table for cups of drink and dishes of food. Nothing reveals the sort of worship carried on in the houses. But probably the owners made offerings, praying to their family gods and commemorating their ancestors. Family feeling is demonstrated in twenty of the sixty-nine houses excavated. Vaulted chambers under the floors were tomb chambers. They might hold the remains of ten or a dozen people, earlier burials being pushed aside to make room for later ones. A proper burial, the Babylonians believed, prevented the dead from haunting the living.

Clay tablets left in the houses, some in small archive rooms, tell what the occupants of those houses were doing. Among them were merchants who traded to the south down the Persian Gulf, east into Persia, and north-west up the River Euphrates to Syria. There were local businessmen, priests and others in the service of the temples.

A beautiful gold dish was among the treasures discovered in the Royal Tombs at Ur.

A great flight of steps led up to the first level of the temple.

Their records deal with the sale and purchase of houses and land, slaves and goods, with adoption, marriage and inheritance, and all the affairs of a busy city.

In a few houses there were scores of tablets of a different sort. On round balls of clay, flattened to a bun shape, pupils had copied the teacher's handwriting in exercises to learn how to form the cuneiform signs. The next stage was to copy out the inscriptions of earlier kings, or hymns and prayers to gods and goddesses, or myths and legends about distant days.

We owe our knowledge of Sumerian and Babylonian literature to the activity of these teachers and their pupils. To help them learn the old Sumerian language they had tables of verbs, and for arithmetic they had tables of square and cube roots and reciprocal numbers. Tablets from other cities of the eighteenth century BC in Babylonia display a correct understanding of 'Pythagoras Theorem' — 1,200 years before Pythagoras formulated it!

Citizens of Ur between about 2100 and 1740 BC were able to enjoy quite a high standard of living in their prosperous city. So it is no surprise to find that they felt superior to the nomads who lived in the semi-desert beyond the areas watered by the River Euphrates. People who had 'no fixed abode', who ate raw meat and did not give their dead a decent burial were hardly human!

The nomadic people were called Amorites and seemed to come from Syria. They came in such large numbers that kings of Ur built a wall across Babylonia to try to keep them back. More and more Amorites came,

overran the wall and brought to an end the rule of Ur over Babylonia in about 2000 BC. Gradually, the newcomers took up city life and lived in places like Ur alongside the original inhabitants. These Amorites spoke a language more like Hebrew than Babylonian, but the scribes still wrote Babylonian, since it was a more respectable language. Hammurabi, the famous king of Babylon (see *King Hammurabi's Law-code*) belonged to an Amorite family.

The names of Abraham and his family are very much like these Amorites' names. The biblical records point to a date about 2000 BC, or a little before or after, for Abraham's career. The book of Genesis, chapter 11, tells us that Ur of the Chaldees was his birthplace. So it is against this background that we should set his early life.

How stark is the contrast with the life he turned to. At the call of God, Abraham left the sophisticated city, with all its security and comfort, to become one of the despised nomads!

The New Testament letter to the Hebrews (chapter 11) puts its finger on the key to this remarkable response:

'It was faith that made Abraham obey when God called him to go out to a country which God had promised to give him. He left his own country without knowing where he was going. By faith he lived as a foreigner in the country that God had promised him. He lived in tents, as did Isaac and Jacob, who received the same promise from God. For Abraham was waiting for the city which God has designed and built, the city with permanent foundations.'

THE PALACE OF THE KINGS OF MARI

Nomads leave very little evidence of their existence for archaeologists. Once they have pulled up their tent-pegs and moved away, a few stones in a circle blackened by fire may be all they leave. So it is only from contacts with settled farmers and town-dwellers that something can be learnt about the nomads, and their opinions may be rather biased. However, there is one discovery which is giving direct information about the nomads in Mesopotamia about 1800 BC.

In 1933 a party of Arabs dug into a hill by the River Euphrates in order to make a grave. They dug out a stone statue. They reported their find and before the end of the year a team of French archaeologists began work. They soon dug out more statues, and read the name of the city of Mari inscribed on one of them in Babylonian. Other records showed that Mari was an important place, but it had not been found until this moment. Excavations have continued in the ruins, with some interruptions, to the present time.

Temples, a palace, statues, inscriptions and a jar of buried treasure, all dating from about 2500 BC, are signs of Mari's importance at the time when the kings of Ur were buried with such magnificence. Long after that flowering, Mari had another short spell of power. About 1850 BC an Amorite chieftain took over the city and made it the centre of a kingdom controlling trade along the River Euphrates between Babylonia and Syria. With the income from taxes on this trade, and from other business and farming, the kings of Mari were able to

build themselves a huge palace. This ranks as one of the major discoveries in the Near East.

The palace of Mari covered more than 2·5 hectares/6 acres of ground and had over 260 rooms, courtyards and passages. Enemies had ransacked the place and set it on fire. Then the desert sands filled the rooms until they were entirely covered. Thus the walls were still standing 5 metres/15 feet or more high when the archaeologists dug into them, and now a roof has been erected over parts of the palace to protect the walls, so that visitors can walk into a most impressive ancient building.

After shifting the tons of sand from each room, the excavators hoped for great rewards. Some rooms were empty, some rooms were stores: rows of great jars stood ready for oil, wine or grain. There were living-quarters — spacious for the king, his wives, and his family, more cramped for officials and servants. We can imagine craftsmen were busy in workshops, secretaries in their offices, pastry-cooks in the kitchens. There were even singing-girls practising to entertain the king's foreign guests.

As always, the most informative discoveries are the written documents. Clay tablets were scattered on the floors of various rooms. One in particular was the archive room where they were stored. Altogether over 20,000 cuneiform texts awaited the archaeologists in the palace of Mari.

The scribes kept their eye on every detail of palace life. Tablets record the amounts of food coming into the palace, grain and vegetables of all sorts, and several hundred list the provisions provided for the king's table each day.

Hundreds of letters carry news to the king from all over his realm. One official reports progress in making musical instruments the king had ordered, another that there is not enough gold to decorate a temple as the king wanted. A small group of letters brings accounts of messages given by the gods to prophets or to ordinary people. Some advise the king to act in a certain way, others assure him of divine protection.

The nomadic tribes and their movements were a serious matter for military officers. They constantly reported about them to the king. Tribesmen moving in hundreds were a threat to small farming towns and even to Mari itself. They stopped traffic on the trade-routes and pinned down the king's forces. In attempts to keep the

The statue of a bearded man found at Mari and dating from the eighteenth century BC is inscribed with the name Ishtup-ilum, king of Mari.

The great palace at Mari was enlarged and rebuilt by King Zimrilim in the eighteenth century BC. The complex includes state reception rooms, apartments for the royal family, rooms for scribes, and an inner sanctuary.

peace, treaties were agreed with some groups who were allowed to settle in parts of the territory of Mari. This is one picture of a situation that has repeated itself throughout the history of Mesopotamia.

The letters name several of the tribes. All fall under the blanket-term 'Amorites'. When scholars first studied these texts they were excited to read one name as 'Benjaminites'. Was this the

Israelite tribe, or an ancestor of it? Later research decided the name was actually 'Yaminites', meaning 'southerners' (like the Yemen in the south of Arabia). Another name means 'northerners', and they both seem to have to do with the origins of the tribes. There is no reason to see a biblical connection here.

In the same way, the initial enthusiasm of discovery led to a claim that the name David was current at Mari

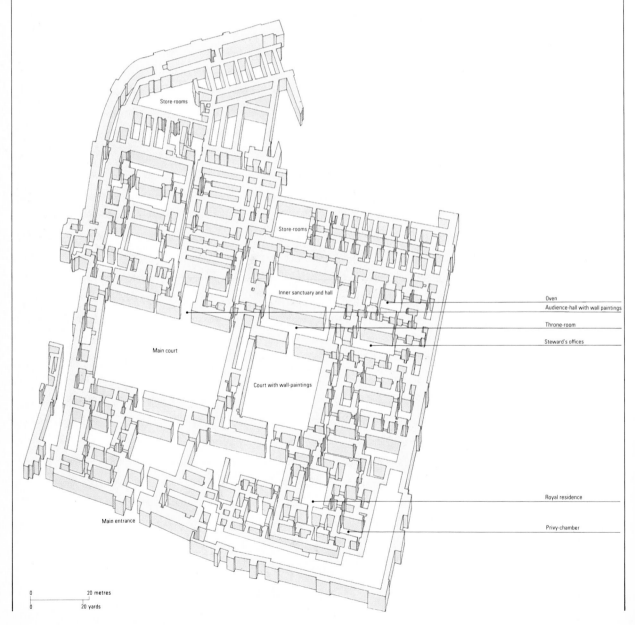

Store-rooms

Store-rooms

Inner sanctuary and hall

Oven

Audience-hall with wall paintings

Throne-room

Steward's offices

Main court

Court with wall-paintings

Royal residence

Main entrance

Privy-chamber

0   20 metres

0   20 yards

as a title 'chieftain'. On that, theories were built about David's name originally being a different one, 'David' only adopted when he became king.

A long-standing problem could be solved by this means. According to 1 Samuel 17, David killed Goliath, whereas Elhanan killed the giant according to 2 Samuel 21:19. If 'David' was a title, David and Elhanan could be the same person. It is now certain the word at Mari is not a title and not related to David (it is a word meaning 'defeat'), so this solution disappears. (Although there are difficulties, the simplest answer may be to suppose the Philistines had more than one champion named Goliath.)

Apart from David, hundreds of Amorite names occur in the Mari tablets. Similarities with Hebrew names abound, notably in names of the patriarchal age. Sometimes the names are identical, as in the case of Ishmael, but this does not mean a reference to the same man (see *Headline News: The Lost City of Ebla*), simply that the name was common, perhaps fashionable at the time.

Mari's great palace displays the organization and the bureaucracy of a small though powerful state. Its archives give a wealth of unexpected knowledge about the life of nomads in the eighteenth century BC. Despite diplomatic alliances with other kings and with the tribes, Mari fell to the forces of Hammurabi of Babylon soon after 1760 BC. Other towns flourished in the area from time to time, the nearest today is Abu Kemal. But none was as great as Mari.

Among discoveries at Mari was a life-sized statue of a goddess. She holds a vase through which water flowed, and her robe is decorated with representations of streams in which fish are swimming. The statue dates from the eighteenth century BC.

THE PATRIARCHS: AN ARGUMENT FROM SILENCE

Abraham and his father Terah lived at Ur in southern Mesopotamia and at Harran in the north. Nowhere, in those two cities or in any other Babylonian city, have their names appeared in ancient texts. Harran is unexcavated; the early levels lie beneath the medieval castle and mosque. Ur, as we have seen, has produced hundreds of written documents.

Once out of Mesopotamia, the patriarchs' story is set in Canaan. There, Genesis 21 records, Abraham had a quarrel with the king of Gerar over water-rights. The quarrel ended with a peace treaty. Abraham's son, Isaac, had the same trouble, and reached the same solution. Today we can read a variety of ancient treaties, is it not surprising that nothing is known about these outside the Bible? Canaanite cities have not given any sign at all of Abraham's presence.

At one stage Abraham went to Egypt. The pharaoh took his wife Sarah from him, then, faced with God's disapproval, gave her back, sending Abraham away with rich gifts (the story is told in Genesis 12). Later, Isaac's grandson, Joseph, rose from slavery in Egypt to become the pharaoh's right-hand man. He brought his father, Jacob, and his family to live with him in Egypt. What do the Egyptian hieroglyphs have to say about these events? Again, the answer is: 'Nothing!'

Silence about the patriarchs from all sources except the Bible leads some writers to conclude that the patriarchs never existed: they are inventions by

Jewish patriots exiled from their land, seeking to create a national history; or they are legendary men, figures of folk-lore without any reality at all. Arguments for views like these may follow several lines. Those who use archaeology as a platform for such a conclusion are, however, failing to look at the evidence properly.

To find Abraham's treaty with the king of Gerar, for example, would require archaeologists to locate the palace in Gerar and discover records which include that king's reign.

To find the treaty would require, first, that it was put into writing, then that it was written on a lasting material, stone, or a clay tablet. Yet Gerar was in the south of Canaan, near Egypt. So scribes who worked there are more likely to have written in the Egyptian way — on papyrus, which decays quickly — than in the Babylonian way on clay.

On top of this, the likelihood of archaeologists finding the right records is small. When a palace is dug out, as at Mari, the things found in it usually belong to the reigns of the last two or three kings who lived in it before it was abandoned. So the reign of Abraham's

ally would need to have fallen near the end of a period in the history of Gerar.

Even if all these demands could be met, there is no guarantee that every document buried in an archive survives intact and legible; exposure, damp, falling brickwork, careless excavation, can all destroy the writing on clay tablets.

The possibility of finding that treaty is remote. At present it would be an accidental and unexpected discovery, because no one can even be quite sure where Gerar is!

In Egypt the perishability of papyrus always presents a serious problem to historians (see *Any Sign of Moses?*). For the 500 years from 2000 to 1500 BC the monuments of kings in temples and tombs and the memorials of their servants are almost the only sources of information. Very few papyrus documents have escaped the rotting effects of damp. Fragments of one report on conditions in the south of Egypt, others deal with the affairs of a single town.

Once more, it is most unlikely any record will be found about Abraham or Joseph in Egypt. Unlike

other leading men, Joseph did not have a tomb in Egypt carved or painted with the significant moments of his career. Genesis 50 states that his embalmed body was to be carried back to Canaan.

Even though it provides no direct references to the patriarchs, archaeology may still offer help in studying the background to their lives. Are the stories in keeping with what we know about the period 2000 to 1500 BC in which the Bible seems to place them, or do they show signs of another era?

If they were written in the middle of the first millennium BC they might be aware of the Assyrian or Babylonian Empires, of the Arameans in Damascus, of the general use of iron and of horses. In fact these things are absent, except for Joseph's chariots in Egypt, presumably horse-drawn.

Other facts point to the earlier half of the second millennium as the most appropriate period. Egypt was then receiving a constant inflow of Amorites and others from Canaan, and some of them rose high in the pharaoh's service. In the end, some of these foreigners ruled Egypt for a

while (the Hyksos kings). Joseph's career and his family's emigration suit this time well.

Although the nomadic way of life (which the Mari tablets have documented) was widespread and common in more than one period, it certainly makes a dating for the patriarchs at 2000 to 1500 BC feasible.

Ancient Egyptian scribes copied out a story of an Egyptian who fled from the court and had many adventures in Canaan, eventually returning to honour and proper burial at home. The copies date from 1800 to 1000 BC. The story is set 150 years before the earliest copy. Egyptologists assert that it is based on fact and is in accord with the period it describes. The hero of the story, Sinuhe, had no national position. His tale was popular, it seems, as an adventure story.

In Genesis the Hebrew writers presented the stories of their nation's origin. Archaeology can shed light on their background. It cannot bring proof that they are true. Neither can it prove that they are baseless legends. What it can show is that similar stories were told, and appear to be reliable reports.

An Egyptian nobleman was proud of the day, about 1900 BC, when he introduced a party of foreigners to the Egyptian court. He had the scene painted on the wall of his tomb at Beni Hasan. A dark-skinned Egyptian scribe (to the right of the picture shown here) holds a placard announcing the visitors as

Asiatics from the region of Shut, bringing galena for the black eye-paint Egyptians liked. The leader is named 'foreign chief Abushar'. This group from Sinai or southern Canaan gives a visual description of the way the patriarchs could have appeared.

A PEOPLE REDISCOVERED
Who were the Hittites?

'Look, the king of Israel has hired the Hittite and Egyptian kings to attack us!'

This suspicion was enough to cause panic in the army of Damascus. The troops fled, suddenly releasing Samaria from a siege which had brought the city's inhabitants to starvation-point (the story is told in 2 Kings 7).

The ancient Egyptians have left too deep an imprint on humanity ever to be forgotten. But who were the Hittites? Until a century ago no one could answer that question. The Hittites, if they had ever existed, had vanished along with the Hivites, Perizzites, Girgashites and other peoples named in the Old Testament.

Yet although the Hittites are often mentioned simply as one of the list of nations which occupied Canaan — nations the Israelites were to destroy as they conquered the Promised Land —

Until late in the nineteenth century nothing was known of the Hittites outside the Bible. Their rediscovery is one of the most remarkable achievements of archaeology. This statue, from the eighth century BC, is of a late Hittite king.

the incident mentioned above and another, telling that Solomon sold horses 'to all the kings of the Hittites and the kings of Syria', suggest they were more important.

Nevertheless, because they were unknown and often classed with other unknown groups, some commentators believed that there must have been a mistake: at least in 2 Kings 7 the biblical historian was meaning the Assyrians.

In 1876, however, the rediscovery of the Hittites began, through the work of A.H. Sayce. An English scholar, Sayce spent much of his life travelling in Egypt and the Near East from his house-boat home on the Nile, returning to Oxford each spring to give the lectures his position demanded. Sayce realized that picture-writing on stone blocks reused in medieval buildings at Hama and Aleppo in Syria was the

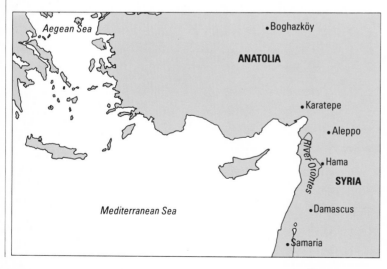

same as writing carved on rocks in Turkey. In 1876 he related these writings to the Hittites of the Old Testament and the 'Kheta' named in Egyptian texts.

From the Egyptian references there was no doubt the Kheta were a 'great power'; one of their kings made a treaty with Pharaoh Ramesses II as an equal. Explorers roaming Anatolia now began to pay more attention to these carvings and to the ruins of old cities scattered across the Turkish plateau.

Largest of all the ruins was a place called Boghazköy, about 160 km/100 miles due east of Ankara. Local people had sold pieces of clay tablets they found there to foreign visitors. The writing on the tablets was Babylonian, but the language was not. Two other tablets in the same language had come to light in Egypt in 1887, with Babylonian letters, including one from a Hittite king (see *Relatives of the Hebrews?*). But for a few years the language defied the scholars.

Boghazköy was the obvious place to learn more about the Hittites. In 1906 an expedition from Germany, led by H. Winckler, began to excavate the ruins. Success came immediately. In the burnt ruins of a range of store-rooms there were more than 10,000 pieces of cuneiform tablets, baked hard in the

Stone lions, about 3,500 years old, guard the gateway of the ancient Hittite capital, Hattusha, near Boghazköy in Turkey.

fire. Most remarkably, one of the documents proved to be a Babylonian version of the treaty between Ramesses II and the Hittite king. This, with other Babylonian texts, proved that Boghazköy was the capital city of a powerful kingdom. Its ancient name was Hattusha.

An outline of its history and the names of its kings for the period 1400 to 1200 BC emerged quickly from the Babylonian tablets. Hittite scribes had used that language for state records and international correspondence. They were able men, some of them specialist translators. In addition to Babylonian, six other languages are represented in the cuneiform texts. The most important is the one now called Hittite, written beside Akkadian in state documents, and used extensively for religious and administrative records.

Less than ten years after Winckler's discovery, study of the tablets led a Czech scholar, Bedrich Hrozný, to publish his conclusion that the Hittite language is a relative of Greek and Latin, French, German and English, a member of the Indo-European family of languages. Another scholar had suggested the same thing some years earlier, about the two tablets from Egypt. No one had believed him, and people were reluctant to believe Hrozný, but further research proved him right. Hittite now has a central place in the study of Indo-European languages and the history of the people who have spoken them.

The other languages used on the tablets at Boghazköy were one spoken by the pre-Hittite inhabitants, two related to Hittite (one of them, Luwian, used quite widely) and Hurrian which was current in eastern Turkey and northern Mesopotamia. Hurrian-speakers played a big part in the Hittite kingdom. A few phrases are all that remain of a seventh language, one connected to Sanskrit.

In variety of content and language the tablets from Boghazköy are unrivalled. Other discoveries in the city

disclose the culture and skill of the Hittites in numerous ways. (The excavations by Winckler lasted from 1906 to 1912; they were resumed under K. Bittel in 1931, interrupted in 1939, and have been continuing since 1952.)

The city of Hattusha covered more than 120 hectares/300 acres. A stoutly constructed wall of stone and brick defended the city, and instructions for the sentries are among the texts in the archives. At the east side is a high rock which was the fortified citadel.

In the city area five temples have been uncovered. The largest (64 × 42 metres/70 × 46 yards) was surrounded by rows of store-houses, doubtless to hold offerings brought to the god. A considerable organization was needed to staff the temples, and the texts give details of the rites and ceremonies the priests performed, some involving the king. Elaborate and lengthy services were carried out to consecrate a new temple or to purify people from sin.

It has been standard practice amongst Old Testament scholars to claim that the Hebrew laws of Exodus, Leviticus, Numbers and Deuteronomy are too 'advanced' or too complicated for so early a date as Moses' time, no later than 1250 BC. But the Boghazköy texts, and others from Egypt and from recent French excavations at Emar on the Euphrates, clearly dispute this: the ceremonies which Israel's Law prescribes are not out of place in the world of the late second millennium.

Beside the gateways of the city stood lions carved in stone, magical figures to keep enemies out. In a narrow gorge nearby a shrine was made for the gods and goddesses whose pictures are carved on the rock faces. Other rock-carvings and stone sculptures proclaim Hittite control in several parts of Anatolia.

The Hittites built their power from about 1750 BC. From about 1380 to 1200 BC the Hittite ruler was 'the Great King', overlord of numerous princes as far west as the Aegean and as far south as Damascus. Through this extensive empire the name of the Hittites was famous in antiquity. To control their subjects, the Hittite monarchs made treaties with the subject kings. Two dozen of these treaties, in whole or in part, have been pieced together among the tablets from Boghazköy. An analysis of them made in 1931 revealed their basic form, and this has provided a fruitful basis for investigating treaties in the Old Testament (see *Treaties and Covenants*).

On the Hittite sculptures, and on the seals impressed on the clay tablets, we can see the type of picture-writing known as Hittite hieroglyphs. These hieroglyphs look something like the Egyptian ones, and the Hittites may have taken the idea from Egypt, but the writing is not the same. In a few examples, mostly on the seals of the kings, the hieroglyphs stand in parallel with Babylonian cuneiform to spell the royal name and titles.

Using the Babylonian script as key, some of the values of the hieroglyphic signs became clear. The discovery in 1947 of much longer parallel texts, in Hittite and Phoenician, at a place called Karatepe, put understanding of the hieroglyphs on a firm footing.

Hattusha and the Hittite Empire came to an end soon after 1200 BC in the disturbances that afflicted many areas of the eastern Mediterranean (see *The Philistines*). Hittite traditions lasted longer. In small states in Anatolia and north Syria, local kings

On this relief carving of the eighth century BC from the Hittite centre at Carchemish is shown a baby prince in his nurse's arms, with a goat beside, perhaps to supply milk. The Hittite hieroglyphic writing gives the prince's name and title.

continued to have their inscriptions written in Hittite hieroglyphs and in the Luwian language as late as 700 BC (the date of the Karatepe inscriptions). Some of these kings may have traced their ancestry back to the Hittite Empire, some were not Hittite at all. But to other ancient nations, to the Assyrians and to the Hebrews, they were still Hittites.

At the time when the army of Damascus fled from Samaria, there was a strong 'Hittite' king a little further north, at Hama on the River Orontes. He could have been a threat to Damascus, especially if he was allied with other kings. This is the reality behind the biblical historian's report.

Rediscovering the Hittites is one of the notable results of Near Eastern archaeology.

TREATIES AND COVENANTS

Ancient kings were always suspicious of their neighbours. Would they attack to take over the kingdom? Or were they open to attack by more distant enemies? One way to get security was to make sure the neighbours were on good terms and did not threaten the frontiers or other interests. Strong kings might make treaties with each other as equals, by 'parity treaties', or they might persuade or force weaker kings to accept them as their overlords, by 'suzerainty treaties'.

Among the tablets discovered in the ruined Hittite capital city at Boghazköy are the texts of at least two dozen treaties, some very badly preserved. One of them is the famous agreement made between Ramesses II of Egypt and Hattusil III of the Hittites in 1259 BC. This is a parity treaty. The kings are brothers: they will respect each other's interests not fight each other, help each other against mutual enemies and send back fugitives.

In Egypt, the counterpart of this treaty was carved in hieroglyphs on the wall of a temple at Karnak. The Egyptian version even includes a detailed description of the silver tablet, engraved with the terms of the treaty and bearing the royal seal, which was shown on it. Men can never rely fully on one another, so formal curses were declared on any future Egyptian or Hittite king who broke the terms of the pact. The gods of both countries were called to witness and safeguard it.

Suzerainty treaties were more common. In return for the protection the Great King could offer, the junior king promised to be loyal, not to have any dealings with the Great King's enemies, nor with any foreign rulers unknown to the Great King. If the Great King went to war, the junior king would supply men for his army, and each year he would send a tax to the Great King. He was expected to send back any refugees from the Great King's realm, but the Great King could keep refugees from his land.

A careful analysis of these treaties was made in 1931. All followed the same basic pattern. After an introduction, there is an account of events leading up to the making of the treaty, then the requirements of the treaty, arrangements for its safe-keeping and public reading, the names of the witnesses, blessings on all who kept it and fearful curses on those who broke it. This was not a cast-iron pattern; some elements could be left out or put in a different order. It is, however, clearly the normal arrangement.

It was not until 1954 that an Old Testament scholar, G.E. Mendenhall, realized that the pattern also occurs in the Old Testament. Treaties as such are not quoted there, but they are reported at length. The accounts of the treaty, or covenant, which God made with Israel and which established the people as a nation under his care, are especially extensive. Parts of this appear in Exodus 20–31; and Deuteronomy presents a complete renewal. Joshua 24 also shows the basic elements of the treaty pattern, and they appear in Genesis 31:43–54 and in other passages.

What is significant about the emergence of this pattern in the Hittite and in the Hebrew texts is the dating. Shortly after 1200 BC the Hittite Empire ended. When other treaties become accessible to us, in Assyrian and Aramaic texts of the eighth century BC and later, the pattern has changed. At that time the introduction was followed by the names of the witnesses, then the requirements, and curses, with variations in order. The account of events leading up to the making of the treaty is missing (there is one very poorly preserved tablet that may have had it), and blessings are all but absent.

Despite various attempts to undermine it, the strength of the comparison between the Hittite treaties and those in the first five books of the Bible remains. It does not prove they were all written at the same period, but it makes it very possible. To suppose, as many commentators do, that the biblical texts did not come into being in their present form until 600 years later, requires the survival in Israel of an old-fashioned pattern, a pattern different from that of the treaties which Israelite and Judean kings accepted with the Aramaean kings of Damascus and with the kings of Assyria and Babylon. Still more research is needed on this subject, both with regard to the dating and to comparison of the patterns and the language.

RELATIVES OF THE HEBREWS?

An Egyptian peasant woman was busy grubbing in the mounds of earth near her village in 1887. She was looking for the marly earth that was good for enriching her field. The marly earth was the decayed rubbish and brickwork from an old town.

Sometimes, as the villagers dug into the mounds, they would find things left behind in the ruins which they could sell for a few pence to antiquity-dealers who would take them to Cairo for European collectors to buy. What they liked were carvings in stone, decorative glassware, metal statues, and the little beetle-shaped charms, 'scarabs'.

As the woman dug she came upon a lot of lumps of hard clay. They were of no use to her, and she had not seen anything like them before. A neighbour bought them from her for a few pence.

The lumps of clay were, in fact, cuneiform tablets, and there were 400 or more of them. Some were taken to Cairo, but no one there was sure whether or not they were really old. No cuneiform tablets had ever been found in Egypt before, so uncertainty and suspicion were natural.

For a few weeks Egyptian dealers hawked the tablets about the country, trying to get a good price. At the very end of 1887, Wallis Budge arrived from the British Museum with instructions to buy whatever he thought should be added to the museum's collections. He heard rumours about new discoveries of papyri and the unusual tablets, so he took the train south from Cairo, then transferred to a steamer at Asyut for the rest of the journey up the Nile to Luxor.

There, a dealer brought a few of the clay tablets to him. Budge could see they were not the sort of tablets familiar to him from Assyria and Babylonia, yet he was convinced they were not forgeries. When a second lot reached him he was able to recognize them as letters sent to kings of Egypt in the fourteenth century BC.

He bought eighty-two of them, which are now in London after being smuggled through Egypt. One hundred and ninety-nine tablets passed to the State Museum in Berlin, fifty stayed in Cairo, and a score or so came to rest in other collections. The total number known at present is 378.

Between the peasant woman's discovery and the safe housing of those tablets in museums some

Pictorial as well as written records have been discovered at El-Amarna, in Egypt.

damage occurred, and an unknown number were lost. There is a story about one very large tablet. Its owner was taking it to Cairo. As he climbed on to the train, hiding the tablet under his robe, he slipped, and the tablet crashed to the ground. He picked up most of the pieces, and they are now in Berlin. It is a list of treasures accompanying a foreign princess who went to marry the pharaoh.

Excavations carried out at the site of the discovery, El-Amarna, recovered a few more, broken, tablets. They had all been left behind when the Egyptian government moved back to the old capital under Pharaoh Tutankhamun. Apparently, they were unwanted files from the foreign affairs office.

Kings and princes all over the Near East wrote to the pharaoh, and he sometimes replied in Babylonian. Kings of Assyria and Babylonia wrote, so did princes of Syria and Canaan, rulers of cities like Tyre and Beirut, Hazor, Gezer and Jerusalem. They speak of international affairs, of local problems, of the loyalty of the Canaanite kings. Those who proclaim their faithfulness to pharaoh most vigorously are the ones who accuse their neighbours of disloyalty!

A problem these rulers faced was the menace of foreigners who roamed the

Tablets from El-Amarna, written by Canaanite kings to the Egyptian pharaoh, mention the problem of attack from roving bands of foreigners — the 'Habiru'. Were these the Hebrews of the Old Testament?

From earliest times the River Nile has been the great highway of Egypt, forming a fertile corridor through the deserts which lie to the east and west.

countryside, attacking the towns. They were bandits, criminals, fugitives of all sorts. They were not normal tribes of nomadic shepherds. The letter-writers called them Habiru. When this word was read in the Amarna Tablets a debate began which has not yet ended. Were these Habiru, who fought the Canaanites, the Hebrews of the Old Testament?

If the Israelites moved into Canaan in the thirteenth century BC as most people think, the Habiru of the Amarna Tablets could not be them, because they belong in the century before. If, on the other hand, the date of the exodus is put about 1440 BC, as some prefer, the Habiru *could* be the same as the Hebrews.

No connection can be established between the events and people mentioned in the letters and those in the Old Testament. Although the places are well known, the kings and princes in each source are different. There is a different background, too, for all the letters from Palestine are from rulers subject to Egypt, which is not the background we find in the books of Joshua and Judges.

Since the Amarna Tablets brought the Habiru to prominence, many more texts have come to light which refer to them. The Habiru appear in Egyptian, Hittite, Ugaritic (see *Conquered Cities of Canaan*) and Babylonian records. In large numbers they could be a threat; as individuals they were unimportant. Egyptian generals took

them prisoner in Canaan and they hauled stones or served wine as slaves in Egypt. In Babylonia they could sell themselves into slavery in return for food and shelter.

They are most common in documents written between 1500 and 1200 BC, but they appear 2–300 years earlier in Babylonia. All these texts combined indicate that Habiru became a name for homeless people, displaced persons.

Abraham and his descendants fall into that category; the name Hebrew is used mainly in the early part of Israel's history, down to the reign of Saul. The Habiru were not Hebrews, but they help to explain what the Hebrews were!

TUTANKHAMUN'S TREASURE

Lord Carnarvon was an extremely wealthy man, but he had paid for 200,000 tons of Egyptian sand and stone to be shifted and after six seasons of digging they had still found nothing. It was a waste of effort to carry on. He decided to end the work. He called Howard Carter to his country home to tell him. It was Carter who had proposed and directed the excavation beause he was convinced there was one royal burial place still to be found in the Valley of the Kings. Tombs existed there for all the rulers history suggested should be there, except for one — Tutankhamun.

Carter persuaded his patron to support one final attempt. Hardly an inch of the valley floor remained to be cleared of rubble. Just one area, which had been left so that tourists could visit another tomb easily, was still unexplored. Surely it would be worth

In November 1922 Howard Carter broke through the sealed door which stood between him and the richest treasure trove of all. Tomb robbers of past centuries had failed to find the burial chamber of King Tutankhamun of Egypt. Holding a candle to the opening Carter could see 'wonderful things' within. It was the only shrine of a pharaoh ever to be found intact.

clearing that, too! So, in November 1922, Howard Carter returned to his task — and to his triumph.

The workmen cleared away the stones and the ruins of huts which builders of another tomb had made. Beneath them, cut in the rock, was a staircase leading downwards. After sixteen steps there was a sealed doorway, and some of the seals bore Tutankhamun's name. Although in ancient times thieves had broken through, the royal cemetery-keepers had filled up the hole they made. Had the thieves left anything of value behind?

Beyond the door was a passage about 9 metres/30 feet long, then another sealed doorway.

On 26 November Lord Carnarvon, his daughter and an assistant pressed round Carter as he made a hole in the blocking and held a candle inside. What could he see?

'Wonderful things', he replied.

Carter was looking into the largest of four underground chambers. Three proved to be packed with objects, the equipment the king would need in his next existence. The fourth chamber housed the body of the king.

The robbers' hole, and the disturbance they had made searching in the tomb for precious things they could carry away, show how Tutankhamun's treasure was almost destroyed centuries ago, just after it was buried. The vigilance of the ancient guards foiled their attempt. Soon after, the entrance disappeared under the rubble of the valley floor, and the later workmen's huts hid it completely. That is how the tomb of an unimportant pharaoh escaped the looting which all the tombs of Egypt's greatest kings suffered.

Tutankhamun's tomb gives a glimpse of the glory that Egypt's kings enjoyed when the nation's power was great. Gold flowed into the treasury as booty or tribute from foreign countries, and from gold mines in the south of Egypt. Tutankhamun's tomb shows how the gold was used to honour the king.

The bird with its clutch of eggs is another of the treasures from Tutankhamun's tomb.

King Tutankhamun, the young Egyptian pharaoh of the fourteenth century BC, is known today by the spectacular gold mask made for the royal mummy, one of the treasures from his tomb.

A dog, representing Anubis, the Egyptian god of mummification and rebirth guarded a doorway in the tomb of King Tutankhamun.

What Carter saw in his first glimpse included a gilded wooden bed, a gilded statue and may other pieces of furniture decorated with gold. As they gradually emptied the tomb, the archaeologists were constantly amazed at the variety of the objects they found, the high quality of workmanship and the high level of art.

There is, for example, a wooden throne, the legs ending in lions' claws, and topped at the front by lions' heads, the whole encased in gold. The arms are carved as winged serpents, protecting the king, and the gold plating of the back shows the queen attending the seated king. The sheen of the gold is relieved by details picked out in silver and glass, coloured blue, green and reddish-brown.

Four chariots had been dismantled and laid in the tomb. The wooden body of one was cased in gold, beaten and engraved with pictures of Egypt's enemies tied together. The dead king owned many pieces of fine jewellery, too, of gold and semi-precious stones. He had a dagger of solid gold, and a more effective one with a blade of iron, a rarity at that time. Twenty-nine bows lay in the tomb, some of them bound or plated with gold. The catalogue of precious possessions seems endless.

Most magnificent of all, and most well known, are the solid gold coffin and the golden mask that enclosed the pharaoh's body. Inside the four shrines (see *Tutankhamun, the Tabernacle and the Ark of the Covenant*) was a yellow stone coffin. Within this coffin was another, mummy-shaped, of wood covered with gold leaf. A second gold-plated wooden coffin fitted inside the first and, when it was opened, the astonishing gold coffin was revealed. The metal is 2.5 to 3 mm/$\frac{1}{8}$ to $\frac{1}{10}$ in. thick, beaten to the shape of the body and inlaid, like the second one, with coloured glass and stones. The body had been mummified and on it, between the layers of careful bandaging, were dozens of amulets and jewels in precious metal.

In effect, the royal tomb was furnished with all the king had needed or used in his life-time, so that his spirit could maintain the same life-style in the next world. To ensure the welfare of the spirit, various magic texts were engraved in the tomb, and carved figures of gods and goddesses were placed in it. Great care had been given to do everything that was right and would benefit the dead Tutankhamun.

He had died about 1350 BC, within 100 years of Moses' lifetime. In the treasures of his tomb, therefore, we can see the style of the Egyptian court where Moses was educated, and the luxury that surrounded him. Although the ordinary Egyptians would not have shared in these riches, various discoveries make it clear that a considerable number of royal officials, soldiers and administrators did.

From those people, in the main, we may assume, the Israelites 'borrowed' the gold and silver they took when they left Egypt after the tenth plague.

Exodus 12 records: 'The Israelites had done as Moses had said, and had asked the Egyptians for gold and silver jewellery and for clothing. The Lord made the Egyptians respect the people and give them what they asked for. In this way the Israelites carried away the wealth of the Egyptians.'

Later, in the wilderness, according to Exodus 38, the Israelites gave nearly thirty talents of gold for decorating the Tabernacle (see *Tutankhamun, the Tabernacle and the Ark of the Covenant*) and making its equipment. Taking the talent as about 30 kg/66 lbs, this amounts to about 900 kg/1,980 lbs.

Some people are sceptical of so large an amount, yet it gains plausibility in the light of Tutankhamun's treasure. His solid gold inner coffin weighs about 110 kg/243 lbs, rather more than three and a half talents, and there are numerous other objects in his tomb which are made of gold or overlaid with gold. It is impossible to weigh the gold plating, but if 180 kg/400 lbs is a reasonable guess for the total weight of

The inside of the back of King Tutankhamun's throne shows the king with his queen. The throne is of wood overlaid with gleaming gold, silver, blue faience, calcite and glass. It is one of the richest treasures of Egypt.

A wooden chest from King Tutankhamun's tomb at Thebes is painted with scenes from life. The king in his chariot rides out against his enemies. On the lid he is shown hunting.

gold in the tomb, then it was about one fifth of the amount the Israelites carried off.

Tutankhamun's treasure is the most spectacular of all archaeological discoveries. Although there is no direct link between this discovery and the Old Testament, it illustrates the wealth of Egypt and the background for the Exodus story. It also demonstrates the quantity of gold available and how it was used.

TUTANKHAMUN, THE TABERNACLE AND THE ARK OF THE COVENANT

Tutankhamun's treasures help us understand more clearly two things which are described in the Bible. Both belong to the time of the Exodus, that is, within a century of Tutankhamun's burial.

The first is the Tabernacle, the sacred tent-shrine where God was present. This was a prefabricated structure that could be dismantled, carried in pieces from place to place, and reassembled. Its walls were a series of wooden frames linked together by cross-rails running through rings on the vertical posts.

All the wooden parts were covered with gold, and the posts stood on silver sockets. A set of ten curtains, brilliantly embroidered, hung round the sides and over the top of the framework.

To make it weather-proof, a covering of skins was stretched over the whole thing.

Egypt's craftsmen had been making prefabricated portable pavilions and shrines for many centuries. One lay in the tomb of a queen from the time of its burial, about 2500 BC, until its excavation in 1925. A gold-plated wooden frame provided a curtained shelter for the queen on her journeys.

In Tutankhamun's tomb four gold-plated wooden shrines protected the king's body. The largest is 5 metres/18 feet long, 3.3 metres/12 feet 9 ins wide and 2.3 metres/7 feet 6 ins high. A second shrine fitted inside the first, a third inside the second, and a fourth inside again. Each side was made of a wooden frame fitted with carved panels, covered with thin sheets of gold.

The undertakers had brought the parts separately along the 1.6 metre/5 foot 3 inch-wide entrance passage of the tomb, then fitted them together in the burial chamber. In their haste they had not matched all the parts correctly!

Covering the second shrine was a linen veil decorated with gilt bronze daisies representing the starry sky. The roofs of two of the shrines reproduce a very ancient form. They are made in wood with gold covering but, long before, at the beginning of Egyptian history, the shrine of a leading goddess had a light wooden frame roofed with an animal skin, and it is this that these two shrines reproduce in more splendid materials.

None of these things is identical with the Israelite Tabernacle. All of them show that the idea itself and the methods of construction used in making it were familiar in Egypt at the time of the Exodus.

The second thing which Tutankhamun's tomb illustrates is the ark of the covenant. This was a box holding the basic deeds of Israel's constitution, the laws of God which his people promised to obey, and was kept in the inner room of the Tabernacle. A gold ring was fixed at each corner for poles to be inserted for carrying.

Also amongst Tutankhamun's possessions was a wooden chest, a beautiful piece of joinery, which had poles for carrying it. Probably it was made for heavy royal robes. There were four carrying poles, two at each end, and

when the box was at rest they slid in rings underneath it, so that they did not project at all. Each had a collar at the inner end so that no one could pull it out from the base of the box. Although this was a little more sophisticated than the ark, it shows a similar pattern of construction.

A wooden box with rings and carrying poles, found in King Tutankhamun's tomb, illustrates the biblical 'ark of the covenant', the sacred box in which God's laws were carried.

In King Tutankhamun's tomb, four gold-plated shrines protected the embalmed body, each fitting inside the other, and all made to take apart — like the Israelite Tabernacle.

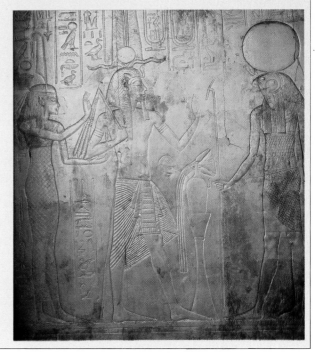

IN THE BRICKFIELDS OF EGYPT

Visitors to Egypt stand in amazement before the great pyramids near Cairo, then travel over 322 km/200 miles south along the Nile to gaze at the great temples of Karnak. These tremendous monuments are built of stone. Gangs of men were organized to quarry the stones in the hills at the edge of the Nile valley and bring them by sledge and by boat to the building site. There the masons would trim and shape them ready for use.

Although the stone structures still stand to impress the tourist (and there have been tourists visiting them for a very long time — the Sphinx and the pyramids were already an attraction in the time of Moses), bricks were the usual building material in ancient Egypt.

Each year the River Nile rises about 7.5 metres/25 feet to flood its valley. The flood begins in July and the waters gradually subside from the end of October. As the river rushes down from the mountains of Ethiopia, it brings tons of mud, suspended in the water. This rich black soil settles on the ground as the water moves more slowly across Egypt, leaving a new deposit to make the earth very fertile for farming. With mud all around them, it was natural for the Egyptians to use it for building.

Their earliest shelters may have been simply reeds woven and plastered with mud. Buildings of this sort were made for a long while, until the people discovered the advantages of bricks, some time before 3000 BC. The idea may have reached them from Syria or Palestine where bricks were common much earlier, as they were in Babylonia.

Making bricks was simple. Labourers dug out suitable mud and carried it to a yard where they mixed it with water, treading it in or turning it with a hoe to get the right consistency. Mud alone will make a brick, but adding chopped straw gives strength and makes the substance less crumbly. Nowadays, about 20 kg/44 lbs of straw are needed for every cubic metre of mud, and sand is often included as well.

After mixing and kneading, men carried the brick-earth to the brick-makers. They pressed it into rectangular wooden frames held flat on level ground. Then they lifted the frames off and left the bricks to dry. After two or three days in the hot sun, the bricks were hard and ready for the builder.

The work was messy, even when the bricks were dry. An ancient Egyptian scribe praised his own profession above all others. The builder, he said, had a miserable time: 'The small builder carries mud . . . He is dirtier than . . . pigs from treading down his mud. His clothes are stiff with clay . . .'

Bricks found in Egypt often show the pieces of straw still in their make-up. When they were soft, bricks destined for a special building might be marked with a stamp. Cut in the wooden stamp would be the name and titles of a pharaoh or a high official (see also *The Glory that was Babylon*). The bricks for houses measure about 23 × 11.5 × 7.5 cm/9 × 4½ × 3 ins. For bigger buildings they might be

Models found in ancient tombs show Egyptians making bricks nearly 2,000 years before Christ.

larger, up to 40 × 20 × 15 cm/16 × 8 × 6 ins.

Several records present accounts of brick-making for official purposes. They list gangs of twelve workmen, each under a foreman. In one case 602 men produced 39,118 bricks. That is only sixty-five each; the modern rate for a group of four men is 3,000 bricks each day. Other accounts give the numbers of bricks of various sizes — 23,603 of 5 palm-breadths, 92,908 of 6 palm-breadths — in all, 116,511 bricks. A detailed account from the thirteenth century BC lists forty men with the target '2,000 bricks' opposite each. Then the actual numbers delivered are entered, one being 'total 1,360; deficit 370'. We are not told the penalties for failure!

All this produces the same picture as the Bible gives in Exodus (chapters 1 and 5), describing Israelites making bricks for pharaoh before the Exodus.

'The Egyptians put slave-drivers over them to crush their spirits with hard labour. The Israelites built the cities of Pithom and Rameses to serve as supply centres for the king. But the more the Egyptians oppressed the Israelites, the more they increased in number and the further they spread through the land. The Egyptians came to fear the Israelites and made their lives miserable by forcing them into cruel slavery. They made them work on their building projects and in their fields, and they had no mercy on them.'

'Moses and Aaron went to the king of Egypt and said, "The Lord, the God of Israel, says, 'Let my people go, so that they can hold a festival in the desert to honour me.'" "Who is the Lord?" the king demanded. "Why should I listen to him and let Israel go? I do not know the Lord; and I will not let Israel go." Moses and Aaron replied, "The God of the Hebrews has revealed himself to us. Allow us to travel for three days into the desert to offer sacrifices to the Lord our God. If we don't do so, he will kill us with disease or by war." The king said to Moses and Aaron, "What do you mean by making the people neglect their work? Get those slaves back to work! You people have become more

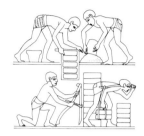

Stamped into the top of the mud-brick (top) is the name of Pharaoh Ramesses II, on whose great building projects it is likely that the Israelites slaved.

Painted on the walls of tombs from ancient Egypt are scenes of brick-making. A mixture of mud and straw is placed in the wooden moulds. They are dried in the sun, then carried to the building-sites. Brick-making was dirty work — an obvious for slave labour.

A modern brick 'factory' outside Cairo still uses the age-old methods and materials: mud from the Nile, and the hot sun to bake the bricks.

numerous than the Egyptians. And now you want to stop working!"

That same day the king commanded the Egyptian slave-drivers and the Israelite foremen: "Stop giving the people straw for making bricks. Make them go and find it for themselves. But still require them to make the same number of bricks as before, not one brick less. They haven't enough work to do, and that is why they keep asking me to let them go and offer sacrifices to their God! Make these men work harder and keep them busy, so that they won't have time to listen to a pack of lies."

The slave-drivers and the Israelite foremen went out and said to the Israelites, "The king has said that he will not supply you with any more straw. He says that you must go and get it for yourselves wherever you can find it, but you must still make the same number of bricks."

So the people went all over Egypt looking for straw. The slave-drivers kept trying to force them to make the same number of bricks every day as they had made when they were given straw. The Egyptian slave-drivers beat the Israelite foremen, whom they had put in charge of the work. They demanded, "Why aren't you people making the same number of bricks as you made before?"

Then the foremen went to the king and complained, "Why do you do this to us, Your Majesty? We are given no straw, but we are still ordered to make bricks! And now we are being beaten

and you are responsible." The king answered, "You are lazy and don't want to work, and that is why you ask me to let you go and offer sacrifices to the Lord. Now get back to work! You will not be given any straw, but you must still make the same number of bricks." The foremen realized that they were in trouble when they were told that they had to make the same number of bricks every day as they had made before.'

Here are the mud and straw, the moulds, the foremen and the taskmasters, and the daily quotas. The biblical narrative illustrates the human suffering and toil behind the figures of the Egyptian accounts. No wonder the people of Israel wanted to escape!

Their demand was for permission to leave to worship their God. That was in order; notes about workmen carving the tombs of the pharaohs in the Valley of the Kings report many men taking days off for religious festivals and worship.

Straw made better bricks: the Israelite labourers had to find their own, after their petition to pharaoh. An Egyptian official in a remote border-post complained, 'there are no men to make bricks, and no straw in the region.'

For thousands of years men have made bricks in Egypt; the Exodus record and the Egyptian sources give vivid pictures of the processes and hardships involved in the second millennium BC.

THE STORE-CITY OF PHARAOH RAMESSES II

When Egyptian kings wanted to honour their gods and preserve their own fame by some great building work, they always built in stone because mud-brick buildings did not last nearly as long. The stone had to be quarried in the hills and brought to the towns.

This was a very costly business for any buildings sited in the Nile Delta, in the north of Egypt. So, when one of the pharaohs ruling at a period when the country was weak, about 900 BC, wanted to build in two Delta towns, he could not afford fresh stones. Instead, his men took the stones they needed from the ruins of earlier palaces and temples.

The new buildings were put up at Tanis and at Bubastis. Excavations at Tanis, now called San el-Hagar, uncovered large quantities of carved stonework in the buildings of Osorkon II (about 874–850 BC). On many of the blocks are the names and titles of the great Pharaoh Ramesses II, who ruled 400 years earlier.

When they were first discovered, the excavator jumped to the conclusion that Ramesses himself had erected these important temples and palaces. He was known to have built a new city in the Delta, named after him, Pi-Ramesse, and believed to be the 'Ramesses' which the Israelites toiled to build (see Exodus 1:11; the identity of the other place, Pithom, is uncertain).

But Ramesses' stone-work at Tanis is clearly not in its original position. Some of the inscriptions are

Stone blocks inscribed with the name of Ramesses II were transported to Tanis and reused there, to the confusion of archaeologists trying to identify the site of pharaoh's store-cities.

built in the walls upside down, or facing the interior of the wall. Nowhere on the ground at Tanis were there any foundations of Ramesses II's buildings, or any blocks in their proper places.

Since the excavations at Tanis, other work has been done at a place 30 km/ 18 miles to the south, now named Qantir. Today there is almost nothing to be seen there above ground.

From time to time, brightly glazed bricks and tiles came out of digging done in the area. Some had decorated a summer palace that Ramesses' father, Seti I, had had constructed. Much belonged to a great reconstruction of the palace for Ramesses. His name and titles stood out in blue on white and white on blue, with scenes of his victories in other colours, and figures of defeated foreigners on the steps of the throne. Obviously, this had been an elegant palace, making up in decorative brick-work for the lack of the carved stone featured in palaces further south.

Study has disclosed that the palace at Qantir was part of a city — the city called Pi-Ramesse. There were temples for the chief

gods, and one for the Canaanite goddess Astarte, houses and offices for the government staff, and military barracks. Small houses and workshops accommodated large numbers of servants, craftsmen and labourers.

A canal led water from a branch of the Nile at one side of the river to join it at the other, so setting the town on an island. Ships from the Mediterranean could easily sail to the port created on the canal. Store-houses were built to contain goods imported and exported, and to hold the taxes the pharaoh's customs' men exacted.

All this was Ramesses' work, some of it done hastily. An ancient town, Avaris, lay beside the new one, so Ramesses had pillars carried from older temples there to complete one of his new ones, just as a later king, in turn, took Ramesses' stone blocks and pillars for his buildings at Tanis.

Pi-Ramesse was plainly a commercial centre. It was also a well-located military centre. Under Ramesses II, Egypt kept control over Canaan and part of Lebanon. After twenty years of battles and cam-

paigns in Syria-Palestine, Ramesses made a peace-treaty with the Hittite king whose army had marched as far south as Damascus (1259 BC).

From Pi-Ramesse there was easy communication with Egyptian governors in Canaan by land and sea, and the Nile led on through Egypt, giving access to the old capitals at Memphis and at Thebes, far up-stream.

No Egyptian accounts for the construction of Pi-Ramesse are known. The extensive, labour-intensive works would need many gangs of men, clearing sites, making bricks, and raising the walls. A large alien community living in the neighbourhood would be an ideal pool for the essential man-power. And that is exactly what the book of Exodus describes.

Even without precise details of the labour-force from Egypt, we can see how the discovery of Pi-Ramesse illuminates the biblical record, and endorses it. From Pi-Ramesse the oppressed Israelites did not have to go far to cross the frontier and escape into the Sinai Desert.

The head of Ramesses II, the pharaoh whose image dominates so many of the great ruins of ancient Egypt.

A colossal statue of Ramesses II lies among the palms at Memphis.

ANY SIGN OF MOSES?

One of the most important events in the Bible story is the Exodus of Israel from Egypt. Without it there would have been no nation of Israel, and so no Bible. And without a great leader to guide and encourage them, the escaping slaves would not have united to survive the desert and force their way into another country.

Moses, the book of Exodus relates, was brought up in the royal household of Egypt as an Egyptian. He fled from the country after he had murdered an Egyptian who was beating one of Moses' people, the Hebrews.

After a long absence, he came back, took the leadership of his people and tried to persuade the pharaoh of Egypt to let the Hebrews leave the land.

When the pharaoh refused, Moses, as God's agent, brought a series of plagues, the tenth one killing the oldest son of every Egyptian family. The pharaoh relented and the Hebrews left, but they were not out of Egyptian territory before he changed his mind and sent his army to stop them.

As the chariots appeared on the horizon, the waters of the Red Sea parted. The Hebrew tribes crossed safely; but as their enemies chased across the sea-bed after them, the waters ran back and drowned the Egyptians.

We might expect sensational events like these to leave their marks in the archaeological evidence. For a century or more people have been looking for them. They have made various claims.

The body of one pharaoh was said to be covered with salt, the result of his drowning in the sea. But this was soon seen to be a chemical salt produced during the embalming of the pharaoh's body.

Great brick buildings have been enthusiastically identified as the 'store-cities' where the Hebrews laboured before the Exodus, but nothing has been found to prove the bricks were made by Israelites rather than any other workmen.

Various pharaohs have been put forward as the oppressor of the Israelites because they were not followed on the throne by a first-born son. But in days when many babies died, it would not be unusual for a first-born child to die before its father, so that cannot identify the pharaoh of the Exodus.

When we look for information in the thousands of Egyptian inscriptions that survive, again, there is nothing known that can be related to Moses and the Exodus.

Since so rich and well-known a land as Egypt has failed to give us anything that can be clearly associated with the biblical story, some people suppose the story has no historical basis. They find it inconceivable that such disasters could have struck so well-organized a people as the Egyptians without their writing about them.

Great pharaohs carved their deeds on the walls of the temples, their servants had their biographies written in their tombs. Stewards and treasurers kept accounts of income and expenditure for the palaces and temples, and secretaries made lists of workmen, noting their days of work, holiday, and illness. So it certainly does seem odd, at first, that there is nothing in all the surviving records of Egypt about the events of Exodus.

But it is wrong to jump to the conclusion that the lack of evidence from Egypt implies the Bible story is baseless. What it really shows is how little we know about that country's history, and how small an amount of ancient writings actually survives.

Kings had their titles cut in stone, lists of conquered enemies, accounts of the battles they won. Some of these still stand, but many have been knocked down by later kings.

This was the fate of a great palace which Pharaoh Ramesses II built at Qantir, in the west of the Nile Delta (see *The Store-city of Pharaoh Ramesses II*).

Very many royal inscriptions have disappeared in this way. Yet even if we recovered every one, we would not expect to read in any of them how the army of Egypt was overwhelmed in the sea. The pharaohs, not surprisingly, did not present descriptions of their defeats to their subjects or to their successors!

If the royal monuments cannot help, the disruption Egypt suffered through the plagues and the loss of a work-force could result in administrative changes. Like any centralized state, Egypt's government consumed vast quantities of paper, papyrus, and much of its documentation was stored for reference. But this does not help either, for, as we have seen, the documents have virtually all perished and the likelihood of recovering any that mention Moses or the affairs of the Israelites in Egypt is negligible.

Once we understand the reasons, therefore, the complete absence of Moses and his people from the Egyptian texts is not surprising. Certainly it does not give any ground for arguing that he did not exist.

Indeed, famous leaders in the early history of many peoples are known, like Moses, only through documents handed down in native tradition, but more and more historians are treating them as notable men. The very sceptical attitudes formerly held are giving way to a more positive approach to what those traditions say, whether there is archaeological support for them, or not.

KING HAMMURABI'S LAW-CODE AND THE LAW OF MOSES

French archaeologists digging in the ancient city of Susa in western Persia in 1901–1902 made a surprising discovery. Amid ruins of buildings abandoned at the end of the second millennium BC they found finely carved stone monuments made hundreds of years before. They were not local Elamite sculptures, they were memorials that famous kings of Babylon had set up in their own cities.

In a short-lived moment of triumph, a king of Susa had raided Babylonia, carried away these pieces as trophies, telling about his victory in his own inscriptions, and writing his name on some of the prizes. The stones were shipped to Paris where they now adorn the Musée du Louvre.

Chief among these monuments is a black stone pillar. It stands 2.25 metres/7 feet 5 ins high and has a carving 60 cm/2 feet high at the top. Hundreds of lines of cuneiform writing are carefully engraved over the rest of the stone. Details of this discovery, with a translation of the text, were issued within a year, and so the world came to know about the Laws of Hammurabi.

There was great excitement, for here was a series of laws very much like the 'Laws of Moses' in many respects. Here are translations of paragraphs which find their closest similarities in Exodus 21–23.

'If a son has struck his father, they shall cut off his hand.' (no. 195)
'Whoever hits his father or his mother is to be put to death.' (Exodus 21:15)

The stela of Hammurabi of Babylon is inscribed with the king's laws. Although he lived several hundred years before Moses, the two law-codes invite comparison. The differences are as remarkable as the similarities.

'If a citizen steals a citizen's child, he shall be put to death.' (no. 14)

'Whoever kidnaps a man, either to sell him or to keep him as a slave is to be put to death.' (Exodus 21:16)

'If a citizen has hit a citizen in a quarrel and has wounded him, that citizen shall swear "I did not strike him intentionally," and he shall pay the doctor.' (no. 206)

'If there is a fight and one man hits another with a stone or with his fist, but does not kill him, he is not to be punished. If the man who was hit has to stay in bed, but later is able to get up and walk outside with the help of a stick, the man who hit him is to pay for his lost time and take care of him until he gets well.' (Exodus 21:18,19)

'If a citizen has hit a citizen's daughter and she has a miscarriage, he shall pay ten shekels of silver for her miscarriage. If that woman dies as a result, they shall put his daughter to death.' (nos. 209, 210)

'If some men are fighting and hurt a pregnant woman so that she loses her child, but she is not injured in any other way, the one who hurt her is to be fined whatever amount the woman's husband demands, subject to the approval of the judges. But if the woman herself is injured, the punishment shall be life for life, eye for eye, tooth for tooth, hand for hand, foot for foot, burn for burn, wound for wound, bruise for bruise.' (Exodus 21:22–25)

'If a citizen has put out a citizen's eye, they shall put out his eye. If a citizen has broken a citizen's bone, they shall break his bone. If a citizen has knocked out his equal's tooth, they shall knock out his tooth.' (nos. 196, 197, 200)

'Eye for eye, tooth for tooth, hand for hand, foot for foot.' (Exodus 21:24)

'If an ox has gored a citizen while going along the road and has caused his death, there shall be no penalty in this case. If the ox belonged to a citizen who had been informed by the authorities it was likely to gore, and he has not removed its horns or kept it under control, and that ox gored a citizen to death, he shall pay half a mina of silver (30 shekels).' (nos. 250, 251)

'If a bull gores someone to death, it is to be stoned, and its flesh shall not be eaten; but its owner is not to be punished. But if the bull had been in the habit of attacking people and its owner had been warned, but did not keep it penned up – then if it gores someone to death, it is to be stoned, and its owner is to be put to death also. However, if the owner is allowed to pay a fine to save his life, he must pay the full amount required. If the bull kills a boy or a girl, the same rule applies. If the bull kills a male or female slave, its owner shall pay the owner of the slave thirty pieces of silver, and the bull shall be stoned to death.' (Exodus 21:28–32)

'If a citizen has stolen an ox, or a sheep, or an ass, or a pig, or a boat, if it is the property of the temple or of the crown, he shall give back thirty-fold, but if it is the property of a dependant he shall give back ten-fold. If the thief has no means to make repayment, he shall be put to death. If a citizen has committed a robbery and is caught he shall be put to death.' (nos. 8, 22)

'If a man steals a cow or a sheep and kills it or sells it, he must pay five cows for one cow and four sheep for one sheep. He must pay for what he stole. If he owns nothing, he shall be sold as a slave to pay for what he has stolen. If the stolen animal, whether a cow, a donkey, or a sheep, is found alive in his possession, he shall pay two for one. If a thief is caught breaking into a house at night and is killed, the one who killed him is not guilty of murder. But if is happens during the day, he is guilty of murder.' (Exodus 22:1–4)

Hammurabi was king of Babylon about

1750 BC, several hundred years before the time of Moses. His laws deal with many of the same offences because Babylonians were mostly farmers living in small towns, as the Israelites were to be. Some of the similarities are so striking that there is little doubt the Hebrew laws draw on a widely known tradition.

This is most apparent in the laws about the dangerous ox. Another collection of Babylonian laws, slightly older than Hammurabi's, has a ruling he does not include, yet which is close to a biblical command: 'If an ox has gored another ox to death, the owners of the oxen shall divide between them the value of the living ox and the body of the dead ox.' ('Laws of Eshnunna', no. 53)
'If one man's bull kills another man's bull, the two men shall sell the live bull and divide the money; they shall also divide up the meat from the dead animal.' (Exodus 21:35)

The differences between these Babylonian laws and the biblical ones are just as striking as the similarities.

In the Babylonian laws property and possessions are as important as people. Crimes to do with either have the same range of punishments.

In the biblical laws only crimes against the person carry physical penalties, offences over possessions are penalized in money or goods.

The fate of the thief who cannot make repayment under Hammurabi's law (no. 8) is death, whereas Exodus 22:1–4 requires him to be sold as a slave. The Hebrew laws set a higher value on man than the Babylonian.

Hammurabi's laws, as far as can be discovered, were never exactly enforced. Although Babylonian scribes were still copying them in Nebuchadnezzar's time, well over a thousand years after Hammurabi, no Babylonian reports of legal cases refer to them. Their influence may have lain in their principles rather than their practice.

In this, too, they are interestingly like the Old Testament laws. Although they are recorded as given by Moses, scholars commonly claim there is little trace of them in the history books of Samuel and Kings. They could have existed for centuries, as Hammurabi's did.

This famous monument shows that Hebrew laws shared many concerns with the older Babylonian ones. The Hebrew laws may have inherited certain solutions for particular problems from the Babylonians. The comparisons also point to deep-seated distinctions in concepts of human life and values, drawing attention to an aspect of Hebrew thought which still influences modern civilized society.

UNDER THE PLOUGH
The Buried City of Ugarit

A farmer ploughing his field hit a large stone. When he heaved it out of the way, he saw a passage leading to an underground room. It was an ancient tomb, with the belongings of the dead man still in it. The farmer took them out and sold them to an antiquities dealer.

News of the discovery leaked out, reaching the government's officer in charge of ancient monuments, who sent one of his staff to inspect the tomb. His report, older studies of the area, and local stories that a great city stood there once upon a time, led to the decision to excavate.

This is the classic way for a great discovery to be made — and it was.

The country is Syria; the site is on the Mediterranean coast, north of the port of Latakia; the year of discovery was 1928. The French controlled Syria at that time, so it was a French team, led by Claude Schaeffer, that began excavations in 1929. With an interruption from 1939 until 1948, there has been work in the neighbourhood almost every year, and it still continues.

Under the farmer's field spread the ruins of a harbour town. Here were the houses and work-places of merchants, with their tombs beneath the floors, the factories and warehouses of a busy port. Hundreds of pottery bowls, jars and vases lay in them, including some foreign pieces imported from Cyprus, Crete, or the Greek islands. Contacts with Egypt were evident in styles of bronze axes and ivory cosmetic boxes. The whole place had been deserted suddenly, the buildings crumbling over

the centuries to be hidden by a few inches of earth. From the styles of pottery, Schaeffer could date the life of the port to some time between 1400 and 1200 BC.

In this site there was plenty to be found and studied but, after only five weeks' digging, Schaeffer took his men to a *tell* 1,200 metres/three-quarters of a mile inland, overlooking the harbour. At this place, local people told him, golden objects and tiny carved stones had been found. The *tell* is a big mound, up to 18 metres/60 feet high, spreading over an area of over 20 hectares/50 acres. Its modern name is Ras Shamra.

Starting at the highest point of the mound, the excavators soon cleared the walls of a large building. Carefully-cut stone blocks formed the walls, and inside were pieces of stone sculptures. On one was the name of an Egyptian pharaoh, on another was a dedication, written in Egyptian, to a god, 'Baal of Saphon'. Near the building had stood a stone slab bearing a picture of the storm-god Baal. These objects, together with the plan of the building, indicated that it had not been a house or a palace, but a temple, presumably for the worship of Baal.

At a short distance to the east were the walls and pillars of another building. This was a fine house, with a central court open to the sky, and paved rooms leading from it. A stone staircase suggested there had been an upper storey. Under a doorstep in this house was a hoard of seventy-four bronze tools and weapons, swords, arrowheads, axes, and a tripod decorated with pomegranates, each one swinging from a loop (like the ornaments of the Israelite high priest's dress, described in Exodus 28:33,34).

It was in a room of this house, in 1929, that Schaeffer made the most significant discovery. Tumbled on the floor were a quantity of clay tablets bearing cuneiform writing. Happily, the director of the ancient monuments service, Charles Virolleaud, was an expert in Babylonian. He was able to see at once that some of the tablets were the lists of words belonging to Babylonian schools. But not all the tablets were written in Babylonian.

The cuneiform writing on forty-eight of them was of an unknown kind. Virolleaud quickly made drawings of them which were published less than a year after the discovery, so other scholars were able to puzzle over them. The honour of deciphering the newly-found script belongs to Virolleaud, another French expert, E. Dhorme, and a German, Hans Bauer.

Between them, working independently but with Virolleaud receiving the results of the other two, they were able to work out the values of the thirty different signs used in the script. They thought the language was a Semitic one, so they then sorted out

The harbour town of Ugarit, on the Syrian coast, flourished in the years just before the Exodus. It was suddenly deserted and completely disappeared. Claude Schaeffer began the excavations which yielded many remarkable discoveries. Among the finds was a gold bowl (left) with a design showing a wild-bull hunt.

The seated goddess from Ugarit, modelled in bronze (below), dates from about the fourteenth century BC.

The remains of the palace entrance at Ugarit give some hint of its former glory. Kings here lived in style, using beautiful furniture inlaid with carved ivory, brought by foreign princesses as part of their dowry.

A clay tablet (below) shows the alphabet in the Ugaritic script. Fifteen hundred tablets using this form of writing have now been discovered.

the most common letters used to start or end words in West Semitic languages such as Hebrew. Their scheme gave translations that were sensible (a vital test!), and worked with other tablets found later.

Virolleaud had charge of the tablets and quickly translated them as they were unearthed. The language they preserve is known as Ugaritic, for they showed that the name of the city was Ugarit. In almost every season of excavation more tablets have come to light, so that now over 1,500 are known in this Ugaritic writing and language, and there is a large number in Babylonian (see *Canaanite Myths and Legends*).

With the appearance of the documents, the history and culture of the city began to come to life. Enthusiastically, Schaeffer opened trenches in other areas of the mound. Everywhere, the ruined buildings lay immediately below the surface of the soil.

In one place were houses and workshops of weavers, stone-workers, smiths and jewellers, with many of the tools and products left just where their owners had dropped them as enemies set fire to the city. In other parts there were grander houses for the wealthy men of Ugarit. Some had their own archives of cuneiform tablets.

The fabled treasures of local tradition became real, too. Gold and silver jewellery, copper statuettes of gods and goddesses, plated or decorated with gold, were hidden in several houses. One trench, dug in 1933, produced a dish and a bowl of gold with elaborate designs hammered in relief. Bowls of silver and gold also came out of excavations in the 1960 season.

By far the most impressive of the

buildings at Ugarit was the royal palace. Like the rest of the city, it had been burnt. Although the timbers disintegrated, the stone walls still stand 2 metres/6 feet or more above the ground.

A stepped entrance with two pillars supporting the lintel led to a small vestibule, then a large courtyard. Here, a well supplied water so that visitors could wash before entering the king's presence. A stone slab set in the floor was where they stood to have water poured over their hands and feet; a drain carried the water away.

King after king had added new courts and suites of rooms during the two centuries or so in which the palace existed. The archaeologists have detected twelve stages of building. Quite late in this process a garden was planted in one court, and in another was set a large, shallow pool where we may imagine fish were bred. Several rooms had been stores for palace records.

Cuneiform tablets in Babylonian and Ugaritic reveal the business of day-to-day government. Some report foreign affairs, treaties with neighbour kings, or imposed by the Hittites, even the case of a foreign princess who was married to the king of Ugarit being executed, probably for adultery.

Foreign princesses brought rich dowries with them, duly listed on certain tablets. In the palace were pieces of some of the furniture they describe. A bed had a head-board of ivory, carved with animals and hunting scenes and with pictures of the king and queen embracing, flanking a figure of the mother-goddess suckling two young gods. A round table had an elaborate inlay of ivory carvings of fantastic animals, sphinxes and lions with wings.

Other pieces of furniture had legs and feet of ivory in the shape of lions' legs and paws. Quite exceptional is a piece of elephant tusk cut as a support for a piece of furniture and carved as a human head, perhaps the likeness of a king or queen of Ugarit.

Ugarit's wealth came from trade. The city stood at the end of a road from Babylon, up the Euphrates and across to the Mediterranean. From Ugarit ships sailed to Cyprus and Crete, to the southern coast of Turkey, and down the coast of Canaan to Egypt. Not surprisingly, influences from all these regions appear in the art and culture of Ugarit.

They are most obvious in writing, for beside Babylonian and Ugaritic, Hittite and Hurrian were also written in cuneiform, Egyptian appears on metal and stone (and surely was more common on papyrus), while the Hittite hieroglyphs and a syllabic script from Cyprus are also found at Ugarit.

The peasant's plough opened an inexhaustible store of treasure in the ruins of Ugarit. Although the city lies outside the borders of Canaan, it gives a rich picture of the life that flourished in Canaan before the arrival of the Israelites. It was a society of wealthy land-owning kings and courts, and a host of peasant farmers.

CANAANITE MYTHS AND LEGENDS

The books people read and the songs they sing often reveal their hopes and beliefs. In biblical times only a few people's ideas were written down, and even fewer survive.

From the people who lived in Canaan before the Israelites there is almost no information of this sort at all, probably because they used papyrus as their writing material (see *The Alphabet*).

To the north, at Ugarit, clay tablets were more commonly used. Many have survived, and some contain stories about gods and heroes, rituals and prayers for the worship in the temples.

Although Ugarit is outside the boundary of Canaan, the people there revered the same gods and goddesses. Local variations may have existed in their beliefs, but it is safe to assume a general similarity.

El, the chief god (his name means simply 'god'), was thought of as an old man — helplessly drunk on one occasion — whose place as the vigorous, active god was taken by Baal.

Baal was god of rain and storm. He had two rivals.

One was Yam, the sea. Yam had a palace, but Baal did not. One of the myths gives an account of how Baal got a fine palace, perhaps after he defeated Yam.

Baal's sister, Anat, was his main supporter. At one stage she slaughtered the people of two towns:

'Lo, Anat fought in the valley,
She fought between the two towns,
She smote the crowds by the coast (?),
She silenced the men of the east.
Under her feet heads were like balls,
Palms of hands were like locusts about her,
The palms of warriors like heaps of corn (?).
She hung the heads at her waist,
She bound the palms to her belt.
She plunged up to her knees in the blood of heroes,
The hems of her skirts in the warriors' gore.
She drove out the old men with her staff,
With her bow string . . .
. . .
She fought hard, then looked around,
Anat struck, and laughed,
Her heart filled with joy . . .'

When she had finished her fighting, Anat bullied El into allowing Baal to have a palace built where he could sit in state.

Baal had another enemy

Baal was the Canaanite god of rain and storm. In contrast to the chief god, El, he was vigorously active, challenging rival gods with the aid of his sister, Anat.

A tablet in the Ugaritic script contains a series of spells to charm serpents.

to face, Mot, 'Death'. A broken tablet tells how Mot gained power over Baal, who entered the under-world. Anat mourned her brother, found Mot, his murderer, ground him like corn, burnt him, and scattered him over the earth. Meanwhile, the goddess Asherah, El's wife, suggested that another god should take Baal's place on the throne. He did, but he was too small to sit on it properly!

Baal, at the entry to the underworld, mated with a cow who immediately gave birth to a boy. When Mot was dead, Baal reappeared, killed Asherah's sons, and took his throne again.

Seven years later, Mot reappeared to open another fight. Neither won, for El stopped them, leaving Baal as king.

Gods like these do not commend themselves to people today. As far as the Israelites were concerned, they were a dangerous distraction from their one God. Canaanite gods had no moral scruples. They behaved and acted just as they pleased.

Followers of Baal performed all sorts of rituals to win his favour, usually through offering sacrifices. A prayer for a time of danger is preserved on one tablet:

'If a powerful enemy attacks your gate,
If a mighty one attacks your walls,
Lift your eyes to Baal:
''O Baal, drive away the powerful one from our gate,
The mighty one from our walls.
We consecrate a bull for you, O Baal,
We offer to you, O Baal,

what we have vowed,
We consecrate a bullock for you, O Baal,
We offer a sacrifice, O Baal,
We pour drink-offerings, O Baal,
We go up to your temple, O Baal,
We come along the paths to the house of Baal.''
Then Baal will hear your prayers;
He will drive away the powerful one from your gate,
The mighty one from your walls.'

Among the heroes of old in the legends of Ugarit was a King Keret. He lost his wife and family, and was mourning them when the god El, 'father of mankind', came to him in a dream to solve the problem.

Keret was to gather an army to march to the city of a king who had a beautiful daughter and demand her hand in marriage. After a long journey and a long conference, the wedding was arranged. In due course the princess bore many sons and daughters.

Yet all was not well. Keret fell ill, and his land suffered a drought. Eventually El intervened again, to cure him, or at least to give him a longer life.

Keret's son had hoped to be king, so he tried to persuade his father to retire because he was no longer capable of ruling: 'You do not judge the widow's case, nor do you give justice to the oppressed.' But Keret had enough spirit left to curse his son and keep his throne.

These stories, and several more, express the problems of life. Baal, Yam, and Mot personify the

forces of nature. Baal's death signifies the annual disappearance of rain and water in the summer's heat, to return in the autumn rains.

Directions on the tablets prove that they were read aloud, perhaps in annual festivals, to ensure that Baal would return.

Keret's story shows how the god cares for the king, and how the prosperity of the land depends on his health and success. Family rivalries and the problem of old age also play a part, although the end of the story, which may have told how they were solved, is missing.

This summary gives a small taste of Canaanite literature. Even to read all that survives can only bring partial knowledge, for many tablets were destroyed in ancient times, and a lot of the stories would have been kept alive by word of mouth alone, never being written down.

Still, there is sufficient for us to see the sort of beliefs the Israelites met in Canaan.

The records that survive have a value for Hebrew studies in another way. Their language is similar to Hebrew, and has helped us to understand more clearly some words and passages in the Old Testament.

The form of the poetry, with pairs of lines, the second almost repeating the first, is common in both literatures, showing how Hebrew poets took up the styles that were well known when they wrote psalms and hymns for their God.

The figure of Baal is made of bronze and dates from about 1400-1200 BC.

THE ALPHABET

The majority of languages written in the world today are written with an alphabet. Only those using Chinese and Japanese characters and their imitations are not. At first sight it is hard to believe that the Roman alphabet, the Hebrew alphabet, the Arabic alphabet and the Ethiopic alphabet are connected. Yet they are all descended from one parent. One of the contributions of archaeology in the regions of Palestine and Syria is the discovery of the early history of the alphabet.

In the hills on the south-western side of the Sinai Desert the ancient Egyptians had mines where they dug out a blue stone, turquoise, which they used in their jewellery. (It is still a favourite today, as a 'lucky' stone to ward off 'the evil eye'.) Egyptians were responsible for the production of the turquoise. The labourers in the mines were local nomads or men brought from Canaan. Both the supervisors and the workmen made offerings to the mother-goddess and other divinities. They commemorated special moments with inscriptions on stone.

Egyptian inscriptions follow the standard patterns. Beside them are others which, when Sir Flinders Petrie found them in 1905, no one could understand at all. In them were about thirty different signs, each a picture like the Egyptian hieroglyphs, but not the same as them.

The inscription on the stone sphinx from the Sinai desert is an example of early alphabetic writing.

After some years, the eminent British Egyptologist Sir Alan Gardiner perceived that these characters were a sort of alphabet. He was able to progress further by making the assumption that each sign stood for the initial sound of its name. Children learning the alphabet said, 'A is for apple, D is for dog'. Gardiner reasoned that the signs he studied were created on the reverse of this principle, that is to say, 'apple is for A, dog is for D'.

In 1915 Gardiner announced he had worked out the values of nine of the signs. Less cautious scholars rushed ahead, one claiming that there were links between the inscriptions and Moses. Even the most distinguished expert who attempted to read all of them found his results received with great scepticism. It is still not possible to read what the writings say, mainly because they are all very short. They are clearly dedications to the goddess and other religious records.

Finding these inscriptions, about thirty of them, in the Sinai Desert was an archaeological accident. When the mines were abandoned there was nothing but the weather and occasional visitors to damage them. The same sort of writing was used in Canaan itself, a meagre handful of examples assure us. One or two may be older than those from the Sinai, others slightly later. From such meagre sources

the early history of the alphabet can be deduced, at least in general terms.

Between the years 2000 and 1500 BC strong cities arose all over Syria and Canaan, usually on the ruins of those destroyed late in the third millennium. With the cities came a growth in trade all over the Near East, with contacts renewed between people speaking many different languages. Babylonian cuneiform and the Egyptian scripts were the normal forms of writing for inter-national communications. Both were complicated, with hundreds of signs, some with more than one meaning.

The coast of Syria-Palestine was a meeting-place for all these languages. It was there, perhaps at the busy port of Byblos, that a scribe hit on the idea of the alphabet. He was a genius, who saw a way to write which was very simple and very adaptable. His invention also displays an advanced attitude to his language. Babylonian scribes examined their language to make lists of syllables and the forms of verbs. The unknown originator of the alphabet separated each distinct sound in his language for which he could draw a picture on the 'dog is for D' pattern.

His language was a West Semitic one, probably a form of Canaanite which developed into Phoenician. In that language no word began with a vowel, so he

			Name	(Meaning)	Value
			'aleph	ox	'
			beth	house	b
			resh	head	r
			'ayin	eye	'

(1) (2) (3)

Signs in forms found in the Sinai mines (1) and in Canaanite writing of the thirteenth and twelfth centuries BC (2 and 3).

			Semitic value	Greek name	Greek value
			'	alpha	a
			b	beta	b
			r	rho	r
			'	omicron	o

(1) (2) (3)

Signs in forms found in Phoenician about 1000 BC (1), in Moab (2, Mesha's stone, see No Hidden Treasure), and in early Greek about 700 BC (3).

The Gezer calendar is the oldest continuous text written in the alphabet found in the land of Israel. It probably dates from the time of King Solomon.

did not make signs for the vowel sounds. They had to be supplied by the reader after each consonant, according to the sense. This is still the case in two descendants of that alphabet today. In Arabic and in Hebrew the vowels are either not written, or are marked by extra signs above and below the letters.

If this account is right, the clever scribe was most likely already an expert at writing Egyptian with a pen and ink on papyrus. That would explain why the new script ran from right to left: it was the Egyptian way (as it still is for Arabic and Hebrew). That also explains why so few specimens of the alphabet in its early stages survive. They were almost all on papyrus, so any left in ruined buildings in Canaan will have rotted away.

At Ugarit, the Babylonian system of writing on clay was

common; papyrus had to be imported from Egypt, which made it more costly. When knowledge of the early alphabet spread, a scribe trained in the Babylonian tradition saw its advantages and created an imitation, using wedge-shaped strokes on clay tablets. The tablets that survive at Ugarit bear witness to the way scribes there were ready to use this cuneiform alphabet for every form of record. There is no reason to doubt that the original alphabet was used with equal freedom in Canaan to the south.

As Israel gained control of Canaan, the alphabet was taking on a settled form, so that it could be understood wherever it was used. The oldest texts, apart from the very short ones of 1600–1200 BC, are Phoenician ones. They were engraved in Byblos on stone slabs, statues, and a coffin about the time David

and Solomon were ruling Israel. From that time onwards a number of inscriptions on stone, metal, and pottery enable us to trace the rise of local forms of the alphabet: Aramaic, Hebrew, Moabite, Phoenician.

The advent of the alphabet did not bring literacy to everyone, but it did make reading and writing easier and so available to far more people than the specialist scribes who wrote cuneiform and Egyptian.

In the centuries after 1000 BC the Greeks adopted the Phoenician alphabet. Their language has many words beginning with vowels and so they needed to write the vowels as well as consonants. To do that, the Greeks took letters for Phoenician sounds they did not need and used them to denote the vowels they did need (for example, the Phoenician gulping sound

named 'ayin was taken for 'o'.)

From this Greek alphabet, through the Romans, come the modern roman letters used throughout the Western world today.

CONQUERED CITIES OF CANAAN

Digging into the ruin mounds of Palestine, archaeologists have hit a level of buildings destroyed by fire. At site after site their reports are the same: 'a thick layer of ashes showing the level was brought to an end by a great fire . . . before the close of the thirteenth century BC' or '. . . the fortress . . . was completely razed by fire. The thickness of the destroyed layer was 1.5 metres/5 feet. The city was apparently destroyed in the second half of the thirteenth century BC.'

A number of cities destroyed about the same time points to a widespread enemy attack. The date fits the time when the Israelites are most likely to have entered Canaan. Many have drawn the obvious conclusion: the Israelite soldiers burnt these places.

Unfortunately for archaeologists, enemy armies left the smoking ruins and moved on. They seldom left a notice or a monument declaring, 'We, the Israelites, destroyed this city called Bethel', or anything like that. So it is impossible to be certain these ruins were made by Joshua's tribesmen. There is also another complication; beside the Israelites, there were Philistines trying to gain control of Canaan from the coast and Aramaeans from Syria in the north. Any of these people may have attacked the Canaanite towns and cities. Nor should the Egyptians be forgotten. Pharaoh Merenptah's forces were active at the end of the thirteenth century BC (see *Record of Victory*). Without written evidence we cannot place the blame on one group rather than another.

The pottery styles and a few objects inscribed with names of Egyptian kings give the clues to the dates of the destructions. These cannot be very precise, for a fashion may last longer in one place than in another, and some evidence may be missed.

The picture emerging at present is of several attacks on the Canaanites, some overwhelming several towns at once, some taking place occasionally at intervals of several years. This is in keeping with the age of disruption which the biblical book of Judges describes. Different armies, Israelite, Philistine, and others, would raid and burn a city here and a city there.

At the time of their first invasion, the Israelites did not burn the Canaanite towns wholesale. They needed them to live in! According to the Bible, only Jericho, Ai and Hazor were burnt by Joshua.

In the ashes and the ruins many possessions lie where their owners left them. Pottery is always the most common. The Canaanite potters made a variety of bowls and dishes, mugs and jars. Although by the thirteenth century BC their wares were not as good as they had been a few centuries earlier, the potters still enjoyed themselves painting animals and birds on some of the pieces they made.

One type of two-handled jar, about 57 cm/2 feet high was used to export Canaanite oil and wine. These jars were taken in trade or tribute to Egypt, and as far as Mycenae and Athens in Greece. Typical pottery from those countries came to Canaan in return.

Most striking are the pots painted with horizontal stripes of red or brown, produced by the potters of Greece. They were fashionable among well-to-do Canaanites, and so local potters made rather second-rate copies for poorer people. The fashions in this imported Mycenaen ware are a major key to the dates of the places where they are found, because the shift from one fashion to another can be linked to the reigns of certain pharaohs.

Canaanite craftsmen were skilled in casting and engraving metals — silver and gold for jewellery, copper and bronze for tools and weapons and other utensils. As at Ugarit, there were some who carved ivory with great skill, and a few who engraved stones as seals. In their art the Canaanites display their magpie instincts, mixing ideas from Egypt and Babylonia, from Turkey and Syria.

A similar mixture of local with foreign ideas is also seen in Canaanite religion. Small figures of gods may wear Egyptian crowns; the goddesses may have the curls of the Egyptian mother-goddess, Hathor. At the same time, Canaanite priests tried to tell the future in the Babylonian way, looking at the livers of animals they sacrificed. Clay models of livers, used to teach them how to do this, have been found.

The temples where sacrifices were made, and the gods worshipped, have been uncovered at several sites. At Lachish, a small shrine outside the city wall was rebuilt three times. Each new temple buried the old one and anything left in it. Scores of bowls in and around the temple had held offerings, probably of flour baked into bread in the ovens standing nearby. A bin to the left of the altar was full of animal bones, the sacrifices given to the god and his priests. Almost all were the bones of the right foreleg of a sheep or goat, the shoulder which was the priest's part of the Israelite peace-offering (described in Leviticus 7:32). This shrine and the city were burnt, perhaps a few years after 1200 BC.

Another Canaanite city burnt by enemies was Hazor. The destruction there may be dated a little earlier. Yigael Yadin's excavations from 1955 to 1958 cleared several temples used during the Late Bronze Age and violently destroyed. One was a single room with a recess opposite the doorway. Entering the shrine, the worshipper would see facing him a rough stone slab serving as a table for offerings. Behind it, in the recess, were a seated stone statue of a man, and ten stones stood upright in a row. On the middle one was carved a crescent moon and a disk, with a pair of hands reaching up to them. These seem to be symbols of the moon god and his wife.

The other stones may be memorials to dead people, or to great events. Pillars had this purpose in many periods and places, from Jacob's 'pillow' (in Genesis 28) to the present day. For the Canaanites they had become objects of worship, so Israel was told to destroy them: 'Do not bow down to their gods or worship them, and do not adopt their religious practices. Destroy their gods and break

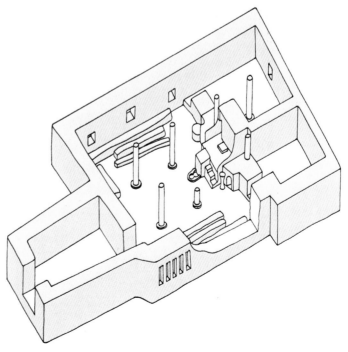

At Lachish a small temple building was discovered. It was burnt, with the rest of the city, probably a little after 1200 BC.

Yigael Yadin's excavations at Hazor revealed a Canaanite shrine. The carvings on the central standing stone are thought to be symbols of the moon-god and his wife. Temples in use during the Late Bronze Age had been violently destroyed.

God promised his people a land 'flowing with milk and honey' — the land of Canaan. From Mt Tabor the view extends over the fertile Valley of Jezreel.

down their sacred stone pillars.'

A much larger temple had three main rooms, a porch, a middle room and a sanctuary, an arrangement which parallels Solomon's temple, although the proportions are different. Strewn among the ashes on the floor of the sanctuary were stone tables with hollows for liquid offerings, an altar for incense, basins, a number of stone seals and bronze figures, a small stone statue of a seated man, and part of a larger statue of a god. Professor Yadin identified him as the god of the storm, Hadad or Baal to the Canaanites.

In these Canaanite cities, where new buildings were put up above the ashes of the destructions, they were usually very different from the old ones. Only in Egyptian garrison towns at Beth-shan and Megiddo did life continue much as before well into the twelfth century.

Whoever came to live on top of the ruins did not care for the old religion.

The temples were not rebuilt, and the Canaanite figures of gods and goddesses made of metal or pottery soon disappear entirely.

Canaanite pottery styles were carried on, with less skill, but the buildings were very much poorer, sometimes little more than squatter huts, with many pits 2 metres/6 feet deep or more, used for storing foodstuffs. Eventually these poor levels give way to better-made houses with finer pottery.

Setting all this archaeological evidence beside the biblical records, there seems little room for doubt that some of these changes, at least, mark the arrival of the Israelites. They were less accustomed to town life, and were supposed to have a very different religion from the Canaanites, with only one God and no local temples. There was no place for separate city-states when a single nation had control of the land.

This bronze plaque of a Canaanite was found at Hazor.

AND THE WALLS CAME TUMBLING DOWN

CANAAN

Jericho•

•Jerusalem

Dead Sea

Ancient walls serve as a reminder that Jericho is one of the oldest cities in the world going back to before 6,000 BC.

The Bible tells us that, at the time of the Israelite conquest of Canaan, Joshua's soldiers marched round Jericho, and when the walls fell flat they killed the inhabitants, took everything worth having, and set the city on fire. If any event in Israel's history can be traced by archaeology, surely this one can!

Jericho was one of the first places in Palestine to attract the early archaeologists. The first team sent from London by the Palestine Exploration Fund, a group of Royal Engineers led by Charles Warren, dug shafts deep into the ruin mound in 1868. Everyone was hoping for great stone carvings like those recently brought back from the Assyrian palaces. Finding nothing but earth and mud bricks, the diggers decided there was nothing worth searching for, and moved on.

Forty years passed before more excavations were made at Jericho. In the interval there was some progress towards a better understanding of the ancient cities in Palestine. German archaeologists, directed by E. Sellin, uncovered part of the city wall and houses within it during the years 1907–1909. They found nothing they could say was the result of Joshua's attack.

That was left to the third expedition, from 1930 to 1936. Led by John Garstang of the University of Liverpool, the excavators had the search for remains of Joshua's Jericho as a major aim. After digging for a few weeks, Garstang amazed the world. He pointed to masses of mud-bricks

and the stumps of walls. These, he claimed, were the very walls that fell before Joshua and his men. Garstang's discovery was accepted by other archaeologists and became a stock example of how archaeology 'proves' the Bible's record true.

There were two walls, parallel, with a space of 4.5 metres/15 feet between them. Buildings had rested across the tops of these walls. A violent destruction by fire had overtaken the city. According to Garstang this happened about 1400 BC, a date he reached on the evidence of Egyptian scarabs from tombs he opened around Jericho. None of the scarabs was later

than the reign of Pharaoh Amenophis III, then dated about 1411–1375 BC. This date is in agreement with the earlier of the dates proposed for the Exodus (see *Relatives of the Hebrews?*).

In addition to this city belonging to the Late Bronze Age, Garstang's work proved that Jericho had been an important place at much earlier periods, in the Middle Bronze Age, in the Early Bronze Age (about

3000–2300 BC), and in the Neolithic Age, before man used metal. It was about this very early time that the fourth series of excavations at Jericho had most to reveal, but they also related to the question of 'Joshua's Jericho'.

In 1952 Miss Kathleen Kenyon of the University of London opened new trenches at Jericho. She wanted to clear up some problems about Garstang's

The great mound, all that is left of ancient Jericho, shows clearly from the air.

conclusions. Other excavations in Palestine had produced results which did not agree entirely with Garstang's, quite apart from the question about the date of the destruction of the city. Very few scholars accept the date Garstang used, about 1400 BC, preferring the late date in the thirteenth century.

Kathleen Kenyon examined the walls and houses Garstang found, and was able to show he had dated them wrongly. By minute, painstaking study of the layers of earth running beneath them, up to them, and over them, and of the broken pottery in those layers, she demonstrated that the walls were about 1,000 years older than Garstang had thought. Earthquakes had made them tumble long before Joshua's day. The rubbish of later buildings piled up over the ruins and Garstang's excavations failed to separate them.

Kathleen Kenyon found the same evidence for destruction by fire as Garstang had done. With better knowledge of the pottery fashions, the fruit of an extra twenty years' research by many archaeologists, she demonstrated that the fire happened

some decades before 1500 BC. After that, Jericho lay desolate until about 1400 BC or soon after.

What buildings existed then, and how long they stood, is very hard to say. Certainly there was never a great city at Jericho again. Over many centuries, wind and rain have scoured the mound, washing away the ruined mud-brick walls. The city which was burnt before 1500 BC had a great rampart all round it with a brick wall on top. Erosion had taken away every part of that wall, except at one corner, and there only the foundations had escaped. At other points up to 6 metres/20 feet of the height of the sloping rampart had vanished, too. In the light of this evidence, Kathleen Kenyon could suggest that erosion had removed almost all traces of the lost Jericho.

However, she found a small part of a building which she dated before 1300 BC, and Garstang had found pottery belonging to the same time or a little later. There is enough to show there were some people about at Jericho somewhere near the time of

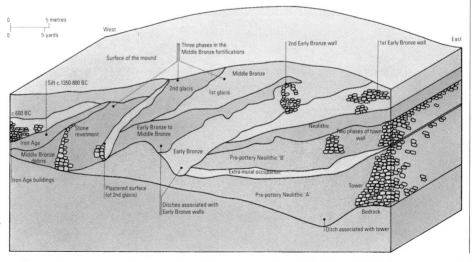

Kathleen Kenyon's main excavation at Jericho is shown in the cross-section. Erosion has removed almost all traces of the lost Jericho.

THE PROBLEM OF AI

After the fall of Jericho, the biblical book of Joshua recounts the Israelites' march against Ai, and their capture of the city after an initial failure.

In 1838 Edward Robinson, the American pioneer of exploration in Palestine, suggested Ai might be an imposing mound called Et-Tell, although he preferred another place.

Another great American scholar, W.F. Albright, argued in favour of Et-Tell in 1924, and his arguments have convinced most people.

A French team dug into the mound from 1933 to 1935, and an American team from 1964 to 1970. Both excavations found remains of a large town

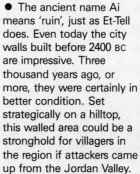

with a strong city wall still standing 7 metres/23 feet high at one point. Inside the town was a fine temple, houses and a reservoir. Its life began about 3000 BC and it was finally destroyed about 2400 BC. Neither expedition found any pottery or buildings that they could date between then and about 1200 BC.

Here archaeology presents a problem to the historian: how is he to explain the ancient record? Three answers are possible.
● Et-Tell may not be ancient Ai. There are no inscriptions to prove its identity. Yet attempts to find another site which fits the biblical description of Ai as well have not succeeded so far.
● The story may be a

legend, a popular explanation for the people living there after 1200 BC of how the great old walls they could see were broken down. This overcomes the archaeological difficulty, but denies the Hebrew narrative any factual basis.
● The ancient name Ai means 'ruin', just as Et-Tell does. Even today the city walls built before 2400 BC are impressive. Three thousand years ago, or more, they were certainly in better condition. Set strategically on a hilltop, this walled area could be a stronghold for villagers in the region if attackers came up from the Jordan Valley.

To the present writer this last is the most satisfactory explanation of the problem of Ai.

Joshua's attack. But what the place was like cannot be discovered.

Jericho is a good example of the limitations archaeologists may face. The excavations have revealed nothing that really agrees with the biblical history. The best one can say is that erosion has obliterated the ruins of Joshua's Jericho. But the absence of ruins is taken by some Old Testament scholars to support their view that the biblical account is a piece of legend or folk-lore, a story which need have no factual content at all.

In the case of Jericho, archaeology

can contribute nothing for or against this view. For a historian, however, it is most unsatisfactory, for it opens the way to treating ancient records in any way the individual pleases. He may even remodel them to suit his own theories.

The book of Joshua preserves the story in its ancient form. Like any other ancient record it deserves serious historical consideration. The fact that archaeological discoveries have been reinterpreted warns us against treating them as crystal clear evidence.

RECORD OF VICTORY
The 'Israel Stele'

'Canaan has been plundered in every evil way,
Askelon has been brought away captive,
Gezer has been seized,
Yenoam has been destroyed.
Israel is devastated, having no seed,
Syria is widowed because of Egypt.
All lands, they are united in peace,
Everyone who roamed, he has subdued him,
By the king of Egypt . . . Merenptah.'

These words stand at the end of an Egyptian inscription on a stone slab. The monument was found in 1896 at Thebes where it had stood in the temple honouring the Pharaoh Merenptah. From the appearance of 'Israel' in it, the stone is called the 'Israel Stele'.

Merenptah was a son of the great Pharaoh Ramesses II, and followed him on the throne of Egypt about 1213 BC. He was not as great a soldier or builder as his father, and although Egypt had enjoyed several years of peace there were still enemies abroad.

The Libyans threatened Egypt from the west, and Merenptah defeated them. This inscription celebrates that decisive victory, won in the fifth year of his reign. At the end come the lines quoted, as a final note of praise to the king, naming an earlier victory.

The name of Israel is clearly recorded on a stone slab (right) found at Thebes which records the military triumph of Pharaoh Merenptah. It is the oldest evidence for the existence of Israel outside the Bible.

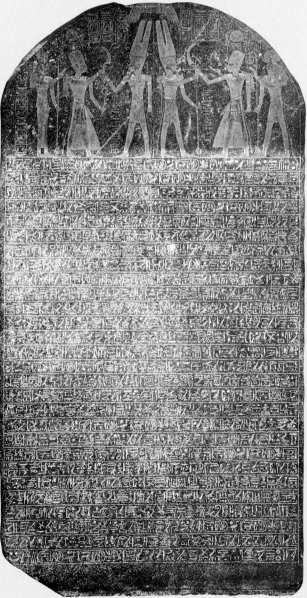

That the name 'Israel' is on this slab is beyond doubt, despite an attempt to disprove it. Also beyond doubt is the fact of military action between Merenptah's forces and peoples and places in Canaan, although some scholars have tried to argue there was none. In a separate inscription the same pharaoh is given the title 'he who binds Gezer'.

The 'Israel Stele' is valuable because it gives the oldest evidence for the existence of Israel outside the Bible. The next inscriptions to mention Israel are Assyrian and Moabite, written nearly 400 years later (see *No Hidden Treasure, The Price of Protection*). Without the Old Testament, the history of Israel in those four centuries would remain unknown.

Here is an example of the chance element in archaeological discovery; without the 'Israel Stele', and apart from the Old Testament, there would be no evidence that Israel existed as early as 1200 BC.

The words of the stele do not make it quite clear whether the name Israel applied to a people settled in a definite territory, or to a nomadic group. Israel is clearly in Canaan, and it is most satisfactory to set the conflict in the period when Israel was settling their Promised Land, after the death of Joshua. The phrases 'destroyed, is devastated, having no seed' are part of the usual way of claiming a complete victory. They should not be interpreted literally.

In fact, Merenptah's reign lasted only ten years, and then Egypt's power grew weaker, so the success did not have lasting effect as far as Israel was concerned. That may be one reason why the biblical writers did not report this incident. It may have been a single battle in which the Egyptians drove Israel out of part of Canaan for a short time.

There is one other point arising from the 'Israel Stele'. If Israel was in Canaan by 1213 BC or soon afterwards, the Exodus from Egypt clearly happened earlier.

Before the stele was discovered some historians had claimed the Exodus took place in Merenptah's reign. Unless the Bible's timing is wrong, or its picture of Israel moving in a single body from Egypt to Canaan is wrong, Merenptah could not be the pharaoh of the Exodus. There is a strong possibility that this pharaoh was in fact Merenptah's father, Ramesses II.

Pharaoh Merenptah or his father, Ramesses II, storms the fortress of Ashkelon in the south of Canaan. It is typical of the strong, fortified cities faced by Joshua and his army.

THE PHILISTINES

The head of a Philistine soldier was carved at Thebes in Egypt. It dates from the twelfth century BC.

Pharaoh Ramesses III was pleased. His army had won a great victory. For years there had been bands of strangers sailing across the Mediterranean to Egypt. Some had settled peacefully, some had joined Egypt's old enemies, the Libyans, to the west. The mighty Ramesses II conquered one attacking party at the very beginning of his reign and made some of them fight for him at the great battle of Qadesh, when he faced the Hittites in 1275 BC. After Ramesses, Merenptah also captured some of these foreigners.

Both kings tell us the names of tribes or parties of these people: there were Sherden and Sheklesh, Lukka and Aqaiwasha. They are all described as 'foreigners of the sea'. Unlike the Egyptians themselves, they were uncircumcised. Modern scholars refer to them as the Sea Peoples.

Ramesses III faced a bigger threat than earlier kings, so his success was greater. How many of the Sea People he killed or captured we do not know; Merenptah killed over 2,000, Ramesses III killed over 12,000 Libyans in a one-year war. It was in his fifth year, about 1175 BC, that he joined battle with the Sea People. They were arriving by ship in the Nile Delta and trekking overland along the coast of Syria and Canaan in ox-drawn wagons. More tribes came than before. Some were the ones already known, and there were Tjekker and Weshesh and Peleset. The Egyptians probably did not really know who all these people were. To them they were aliens and enemies, and we know little more today. The only name we

can identify for certain is the last one in the list, the 'Peleset', who were the Philistines of the Bible.

Even though these were strange and despised enemies, the Egyptians took note of their appearance and their equipment. Ramesses wanted a record of the triumph, so he had pictures of the battle carved on the walls of this temple. Visitors to Medinet Habu, on the opposite bank of the Nile to Luxor, can view them still.

One scene depicts the land battle. Many Sea People lie dead or dying beneath the feet of their fellows who are vainly fighting the ranks of the Egyptian infantry. Here and there in the battlefield are the Egyptian light chariots and horses and the heavy wagons and oxen of the Sea People.

Pharaoh's artists took care to make the differences between the Egyptian soldiers and their foes clear. Egyptian soldiers carry oblong, round-topped shields, heavy tipped clubs and short daggers; the chariots carry archers. In contrast, the Sea People have spears and long, tapering swords, round shields, and head-dresses of feathers or hair standing straight up on their heads. One group, fighting on the Egyptian side in these pictures, wears helmets with a pair of horns on top.

Another scene illustrates the war at sea. Egyptian archers, in ships with oars and a sail used for moving up and down the Nile, shoot at Sea People in sailing ships. One of those has overturned, and the water is full of drowning Sea People with both kinds of head-gear — but not one Egyptian.

The sculptures of Ramesses III and their captions state plainly that the folk with the horned helmets were the Sherden, whom some writers link with Sardinia. Wearers of the plumed hat included the Philistines.

After their defeat, the Sea People evidently broke up. Egyptian army units absorbed some, as they had done earlier, and they may have been posted to Canaan where, it appears, other Sea People clans had settled. The Old Testament refers to the presence of the Philistines in the south-west of Canaan, on the coast, and the very name 'Palestine' is proof that they were once present there in force. At about 1100 BC an Egyptian traveller found members of another group, the Tjekker, a little further up the coast, at Dor.

There could hardly be better evidence for the arrival of the Philistines and their occupation of part of Canaan. For a long time archaeologists have related these events to a series of discoveries in sites all over the eastern Mediterranean area.

In Turkey, the empire of the Hittites collapsed, attacked by enemies from the west and east. At Ugarit, letters written just before the city was burnt speak of all the ships going west to help the Hittites, and of the damage a few enemy vessels had done. From

The Bible makes frequent mention of the Philistines as the enemies of Israel. They were one of the 'Sea Peoples' who invaded Egypt itself. Captured Philistines, wearing feathered head-dresses are shown on an Egyptian relief which records the pharaoh's victory.

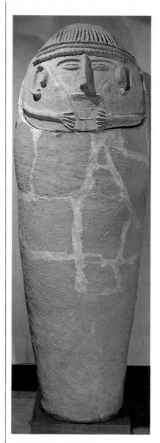

Towns flourishing before the destructions had imported older styles of this pottery. Now there was much more, and the local copies were almost as good as the originals. A particular pattern featuring a bird was popular, and has become the characteristic by which this pottery is recognized. The pottery is found mainly in the region in which the Bible places the Philistines, and so it is named Philistine pottery. This is one of the few cases where a particular type of pottery can be associated with a specific people.

That unusual fact almost exhausts archaeological knowledge of the Philistines. They left no recognizable writings, and too little has been found in their towns to build a picture of their culture. One other type of object found in the Philistine area and commonly called Philistine is a clay coffin with face and hands modelled in relief. Above the face are horizontal bands with vertical lines rising from them which echo the Sea People's head-dress. Examples from Transjordan and southern Egypt could be relics of Sea People squadrons in Egyptian garrisons. These clay coffins obviously imitate Egyptian mummies.

According to the Israelite historian, the Philistines controlled iron-working in the land, and it may be that they introduced this skill. The time of their arrival, and of the destruction of so many cities, coincides, in archaeological terms, with the end of the Bronze Age and the beginning of the Iron Age.

An anthropoid clay coffin (above) found at Bethshean, Israel, seems to wear a similar head-dress to the Philistines on Egyptian reliefs.

The characteristic style of pottery illustrated by the jug (right) is associated with the Philistines.

Ugarit southwards, at place after place, heavy deposits of ash and hastily evacuated buildings support the remark in Ramesses III's Egyptian text that the Sea People destroyed the Hittites, Carchemish, Cyprus and the Amorite land.

Ugarit and some other places did not recover. Where towns did rise from the ruins there is often confirmation of a change in population. The buildings have different plans and, most noticeably, there are new fashions in pottery. They are closely connected to styles of pottery current in Greece, Crete and Cyprus.

A GOLDEN TEMPLE

The Temple built by King Solomon as a house for God in his capital city, Jerusalem, was not very big, but it was certainly spectacular. For, inside, everything was gold. There were dishes and bowls, lamps, lampstands and tongs of gold. The door fittings were gold, and so was the table for the sacred bread.

Gold has always been one of the things people have given to their gods. Cathedrals in Europe and South America, temples and shrines in Asia, still display chalices and lamps and other equipment for worship made of solid gold.

But Solomon's Temple had more than a wealth of golden furnishings. The priests, mounting the steps to go inside, would see nothing but gold — and a rich curtain at the far end.

The biblical description in the first book of Kings, chapter 6, says: 'Solomon built the Temple . . . he lined its walls inside with cedar boards . . . he overlaid the whole interior with gold . . . he also covered the floors of both the inner and outer rooms of the temple with gold.'

A golden temple! The idea is breathtaking.

Building temples or renovating old

King Solomon's Temple, like this miniature shrine of King Tutankhamun, was a glory of gold.

An artist's reconstruction of King Solomon's Temple, based on the measurements and description given in the Bible. The building was quite small — just 27 × 9 × 13.5 metres/ 89 × 30 × 44 feet inside. It was intended as a house for God, rather than a great cathedral in which his people could meet.

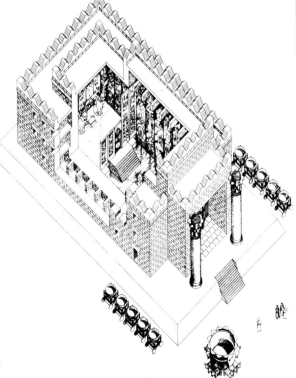

Are the nail-holes in these stones evidence of sheets of gold once pinned to temple and palace walls, so that they shone like the sun?

ones was a regular activity for ancient kings. They wanted to win the favour of their gods and popularity with their people, and to win fame for themselves. The stronger and richer they were, the more lavishly they decorated the buildings they put up.

Over the centuries local people have pillaged the ruins of these great temples for bricks and stones. And long before that all the moveable furnishings of any value had been carried off. Yet still today, when only the basic walls remain, visitors to the temple-towers in ancient Babylonian cities such as Ur, or to the Egyptian temples at Karnak, cannot help being impressed by their grandeur of size and design.

Sometimes the kings who had these temples built left inscriptions telling of their work. When we read them, we have to remember that they were written to impress their readers, in particular to tell future generations how great and how pious their ancestors had been. They may have exaggerated in some cases, or claimed more than their due, but there is no good reason to doubt them over all.

We need not doubt the word of kings of Assyria and Babylonia when they boast of covering the walls of temples with gold like plaster, or of plating them with gold so that they shone like the sun; nor of the pharaohs who told how they put sheets of gold on the walls of their temples in Egypt.

From Egypt there also appears to be some physical evidence of the gold sheets covering parts of temples. One temple built by Pharaoh Tuthmosis III, about 1450 BC, bears inscriptions that record its splendour: certain doorways, shrines and pillars were plated with gold.

When an eminent French Egyptologist closely examined the ruins of the building he noted unusual narrow slits in some of the stone columns, the bases on which they stood, and the capitals that crowned them. These slits are too narrow to be of any use in the construction, and they add nothing to the carved decoration. Their function, the Egyptologist deduced, was to take the edges of sheets of gold hammered over the stonework and folded round into the slits to hold them in position. Other stone blocks have rows of small holes which could have held nails fixing the golden sheets to the flat walls.

What the Egyptian inscriptions describe appears to be supported by the stones of the temples; the gold was there, adorning their walls, not as gilding to highlight parts of the design but as sheets covering whole surfaces.

So there is good contemporary evidence that the Bible's account of King Solomon's golden Temple is no mere invention, or even exaggeration. It falls into the known pattern of ancient practices.

SOLOMON'S BUILDINGS

The most remarkable of the buildings assigned to Solomon's time are the gateways leading through the walls of three cities. There are no foundation stones or documents to say who built them. But the pottery found there can be dated to Solomon's reign, showing that the buildings were certainly in use at that time.

One was discovered at Gezer in excavations from 1902 to 1909, another at Megiddo in 1936–37, and the third at Hazor in 1955–58.

Progress in the techniques of excavation and better knowledge of pottery types led Yigael Yadin to assign the gate he excavated at Hazor to Solomon's time. He then took a further look at the ruins at Gezer and especially at Megiddo, which the original excavators had not associated with Solomon at all.

Yadin was able to show that all three gates have a nearly identical plan and very similar dimensions. The pottery fragments belonging to the moment when the gates were constructed and in use belong to Solomon's time — the middle of the tenth century BC.

Yadin turned his attention to Gezer and Megiddo after the Hazor gateway had come to light because he recalled a passage from the Bible that relates Solomon's building activities at important towns in his kingdom. 1 Kings 9:15 records: 'King Solomon used forced labour to build the Temple and the palace, to fill in land on the east side of the city, and to build the city wall. He also used it to rebuild the cities of Hazor, Megiddo, and Gezer.'

In addition to the uniform plan of the gateways in each city Yadin found that the adjoining city walls were also of identical design. They were what is called 'casemates' — that is, a double line of wall with cross-walls making a series of long narrow rooms.

At each site the stone-work of the walls above floor level was of very high quality. The blocks in each face of the walls were carefully squared and laid, giving an imposing solidity to the structures.

The similarities between these three gateways, and the quality of their masonry, suggest they were built to a design circulated by a central authority with considerable resources at its disposal. The evidence of the pottery indicates a tenth century date for the building work.

When these points are placed beside the biblical report, the conclusion that these gateways are indeed Solomon's work becomes almost inescapable. Short of inscriptions on the stones themselves, it would be hard to make a stronger case.

At Megiddo there were traces of extensive buildings within the city belonging to the same date. Unfortunately, their stone-work was so good that later builders demolished the walls to re-use the blocks, with the result that the palaces, offices and houses of the time are little known.

At Gezer and at Hazor, too, very little could be learnt about the Solomonic cities because later occupants had disturbed and destroyed their ruins.

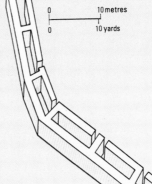

0 ———— 10 metres
0 ———— 10 yards

The Bible says that King Solomon rebuilt three cities — Gezer, near Jerusalem, Megiddo and Hazor. Yadin discovered that all three cities had identical gates and casemate walls. The plan of Hazor clearly shows the distinctive structure, also visible in the photograph of Megiddo.

A FORTUNE IN SILVER AND GOLD

Pharaoh Shishak invaded Judah and plundered the Temple at Jerusalem. This bracelet belonging to the pharaoh's son may have been made from the Temple gold.

Soon after King Solomon died, the Bible book of Kings reports, 'Shishak king of Egypt attacked Jerusalem. He carried off the treasures of the temple of the Lord and the treasures of the royal palace. He took everything . . .'

This is the earliest incident in Israel's history which documents outside the Bible also reflect.

Shishak was the founder of a new dynasty of kings in Egypt, the twenty-second. In previous years the land had been divided among kings, local chieftains, and priests. The new pharaoh united Egypt under his rule, then set out to gain control over his neighbours Judah and Israel, which had once been

the Egyptian province of Canaan.

As long as Solomon was on the throne, Israel was probably too strong for Shishak to attack. Once Solomon's kingdom had split in two, with Judah ruled by Solomon's son Rehoboam, and Israel under the rebel Jeroboam, it was too weak to defend itself.

Shishak's men marched through the land, visiting, sometimes destroying, as many as 150 towns and villages. Returning home victorious, Shishak set about building temples at Memphis in the north and Thebes (Karnak) in the south. Only the Theban one survives.

There, a length of wall still stands around a great

courtyard. Near one gateway the stones are carved with a huge picture of the pharaoh in triumph. Beside him are the names of the towns and villages he conquered in Israel. He claimed he had brought them back under Egyptian control, as they had been 200 years before. To remind the conquered people of his victory, Shishak had a stone slab set up in Megiddo with his name and titles engraved on it. A small piece of this was found in the ruins of Megiddo, happily a piece bearing Shishak's name to guarantee its identity.

Shishak died a year or so after his victory. His son was not strong enough to follow his example as a conqueror. One damaged inscription details the gifts Shishak's son gave to the gods of Egypt. They amounted to much more in gold and silver than any other pharaoh records giving. By weight they totalled to about 200,000 kg/200 tons of gold and silver.

Study of other Egyptian documents shows no reason to suppose these amounts are exaggerated. Other pharaohs also gave magnificent presents to their gods, even if none were as large as this.

Nothing tells where this wealth came from, but it seems reasonable to suppose that much of it was the gold which Shishak carried away from Solomon's Temple and palace in Jerusalem.

IVORY PALACES

We knelt on the dry, dusty soil, working slowly with penknives and paintbrushes. Embedded in the mud on the floor of a palace store-room were scores of pieces of carved ivory. They had grown brittle, lying there for nearly 3,000 years, and the weight of fallen brickwork had cracked them. Each one had to be lifted separately in the block of earth around it. But as we carefully cut one free others would appear beneath or beside it. So the task took a long time.

In the expedition house we gently chipped away the mud with scalpels and needles, and sponged it off the smooth surfaces with moist cotton-wool. We watched with amazement as superb miniature works of art emerged from the dirt. The pieces were creamy-white, cut and polished smooth. Some were inlaid with stones or glass coloured red or blue. A few still had pieces of gold foil stuck to them.

What were these ivory carvings?

Another store-room made the answer clear. There, fifteen or more chairbacks stood in rows across the floor. Great panels of ivory had been fixed to the wooden frame or backing, so that the woodwork was invisible. The furniture appeared to be made of ivory.

Some parts were simply strips of

Ivories carved with sphinxes show the influence of Egypt.

Furniture inlaid with carved ivory was carried as booty to Assyria. It was high fashion among the wealthy in Israel, whose extravagance and exploitation of the poor called down the wrath of God's prophets.

The ivory of a woman at a window is typical of the Phoenician style.

ivory cut and polished to give a smooth surface at the edges of beds and chairs. Some pieces were solid blocks of ivory carved or turned on a lathe to make decorative supports and finials.

Most of the pieces were plaques that fitted into a frame to make a decoration. The majority of these were carved in relief. Their designs were chosen for their magical and symbolic values, as well as for their beauty. Figures grasping a plant or tree represent fruitfulness. The winged disk of the sun shows divine care. Men fighting dragons depict the triumph of order over chaos.

Very often the carvings show clear signs of Egyptian influence. There are sphinxes and palm-fronds and lotus flowers, and there are unmistakably Egyptian gods and goddesses. But the pieces we dug out did not lie in the ruins of an Egyptian palace, they were in an Assyrian city.

It was clear that most of the ivory furniture came to Assyria as booty, or as tribute from countries the Assyrian armies had conquered. The soldiers sent the furniture home for their kings to use. The royal apartments were adorned with many of these costly products. In fact there was so much that it also filled several palace store-rooms.

Assyrian kings have left records of this conquered city or that subject prince sending ivory beds and chairs to them. Hezekiah of Judah was one, according to Sennacherib (see *'Like a Bird in a Cage'*). Ivory furniture was obviously expensive, a luxury item for the houses of the very rich, a status symbol that an enemy would want to take away.

That is how it appears in the Old Testament. King Solomon fetched ivory to Jerusalem when his ocean-going 'ships of Tarshish' went on their voyages (recorded in 1 Kings 10). He used the ivory to make a throne. This would be a wooden frame sheathed entirely in ivory.

Two hundred years later, ivory furniture was fashionable among the nobles of Samaria. They would squeeze every penny out of their debtors, and more, in order to spend all their money on ostentatious extravagance.

'Woe to those who loll on beds of ivory,' shouted Amos, the shepherd-turned-prophet from Judah, 'they'll be left with only the corner of a couch or the leg of a bed,' useless relics of their squandered wealth.

Israel's rulers, one of them at least, encouraged the fashion. 1 Kings 22 reports that King Ahab made an 'ivory house'. This may mean a house panelled with ivory, or more probably a house provided with ivory furniture. The discoveries in Assyria illustrate the sort of decoration, intricately-carved ivory panels, some enriched with coloured stones and covered with gold foil.

To modern eyes the effect might be rather bright and gaudy, but that was

what the ancient people liked. In the Song of Solomon a girl describes her lover as having a body of ivory inlaid with blue stones.

At Samaria, ruins of the Israelite palace were unearthed. In them, smashed and scattered on the ground were over 500 fragments of ivory, more than 200 of which were carved. Some scholars think they belong to the reign of Ahab, about 860 BC. Others date them a century later. Whether or not they are from Ahab's time, they show the sort of furniture he would have had, and it is just like many examples found in Assyria.

Phoenician craftsmen set the chief style for ivory-carving. And Ahab's wife, Jezebel, came from the Phoenician city of Sidon. It was in Phoenicia that local Canaanite concepts were mixed with some from Egypt and other places to produce the designs on the ivories. Imported into Israel, these pagan patterns can hardly have helped God's people to remember the commandment not to make carved images.

When invaders ransacked the palaces of Samaria, and later of

Assyria, they smashed the ivory furniture. They could not carry away large numbers of couches and chairs, so they stripped off the gold overlay and left the wood and ivory parts behind. What the archaeologist now finds is, in Amos's words, just 'the corner of a couch or the leg of a bed'. Yet even these are enough to show how splendid this furniture was when it stood in all its beauty in Ahab's 'ivory house'.

An ivory bed-head from Nimrud vividly recalls the words of Amos, the shepherd-prophet who pronounced God's judgement on Israel. 'Woe to those who loll on beds of ivory.' When the kingdom fell to the Assyrians it was seen as God's punishment.

THE ENGRAVER OF SEALS

Israelite craftsmen were kept busy meeting the needs of the ordinary people. There were carpenters and blacksmiths, weavers and dyers, potters and masons. Their work was essential, but in almost every case it has disappeared because of destruction either by man or by nature. Only the potter's products are still plentiful.

Along with ordinary pieces of craftsmanship, the work of the experts also disappeared. Hardly any Israelite jewellery has come to light, perfumes and cosmetics vanished long ago. But one sort of object made by experts does survive in fairly large numbers: the seal-stone.

Before the Babylonians created their cylinder seals, people had carved designs on small stones as a mark of personal identification so that they could make an impression on a piece of clay to seal a box or jar. In Egypt and Canaan this shape of seal was normal, and the Israelites also adopted it.

Anyone with the money could buy a seal from the jeweller. It would be a small stone, perhaps a gem-stone — amethyst, agate, or cornelian — hard and with a pretty colouring. Cheaper seals were made of local limestone.

The engraver, or his apprentice, would polish the stone, cut it to give an oval or round shape at one end, and smooth that end until it was almost flat. Through the middle of the stone, or at the other end, he would drill a hole so the seal could hang from a necklace or be fixed into a ring.

Now the stone was ready for the engraver. He had to work on a polished surface normally less than 2.2 cm/1 in across. With fine drills and tiny wheels with sharpened edges he would cut into the stone the chosen design.

The customer wanted a design he and other people could recognize as his, distinct from anyone else's. So the engraver would offer a choice. Would his client like a picture of a griffin, or a sphinx, or a scarab beetle in Egyptian style, or a plant, or a person in an act of

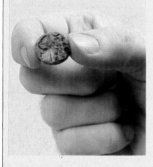

The author's hand gives an idea of the size of the tiny seals on which the ancient engravers worked with such skill.

Seals dating from the eighth to sixth centuries BC are inscribed in the ancient Hebrew script, many of them made from semi-precious stones. They carry the owner's name and were used to impress the lumps of clay which sealed containers and papyrus scrolls. Several of these sealings are shown on the right.

worship, or a god or goddess? All of these can be seen among the hundreds of seals in modern collections.

Some people wanted a seal that was theirs only, that no one else could use. For that they had to have their name inscribed on the stone, assuming they could read.

So far almost a thousand seals have been discovered which carry their owners' names in the old 'Phoenician' alphabet, seals made between the tenth and fourth centuries BC. The seals belonged to members of all the nations in the area, Arameans and Phoenicians in Syria and Lebanon, Ammonites, Edomites and Moabites in Transjordan, Israelites and Philistines in Palestine.

Often the seal-engraver would add a person's name in a space around the design, and so the majority of the seals have a picture or pattern and an inscription.

The majority of the seals which we can identify as Hebrew are different. They bear an inscription only. Although there are Aramaic seals without designs, and several from Transjordan, the proportion is far higher for the Hebrew seals. The

reason could be an attempt to follow the command recorded in Exodus 20, 'You shall not make an image.'

Usually the seal bore its owner's name and his father's name. Sometimes a title follows the owner's name, 'servant of the king', 'steward of X'. The few seals engraved for women have the same pattern, 'daughter of X' or 'wife of Y'.

How can we decide whether or not a seal is Hebrew? Study of the writing can give a clue, but the names themselves are the best guide. Israel and her neighbours worshipped God as El ('god'), using his name to make their own: for example, 'Ishmael', meaning 'God heard', 'Elnathan', 'God gave'. Names like these could be Hebrew or could belong to a neighbouring nation.

When the personal name includes the special name of the national deity, the origin of the seal's owner is clear. 'Chemosh-sedek' and 'Chemosh-nathan' were evidently Moabites, for Chemosh was the chief god of Moab. Seals of 'Jeremiah', 'Jehoahaz', 'Gedaliah', equally clearly belonged to Hebrews, whose God's name was shortened to

'-iah' or 'Jeho', or 'Yaw'.

In these seals, more than in any other excavated objects, we are brought into touch with the men and women of ancient Israel. The engraver's skill has kept their names alive.

Seals were hung from necklaces, or set into rings. The ring seal (top) belonged to a man named Shaphat.

One seal which has survived (above) belonged to 'Nehemiah, son of Micaiah', names familiar from the biblical records and obviously common at the time.

PRIVATE HOUSES

The luxurious 'ivory houses' of kings produce exciting discoveries, which catch the imagination and bring fame to those who dig them up. Less sensational, but just as valuable for our knowledge of ancient times, are the ruins of houses which once belonged to ordinary townspeople.

Excavators have uncovered the remains of houses built during the days of the kings at many places in Israel. These round out the information supplied by written records and, together with observation of recent country life in the Near East, give us a picture which is surprisingly complete.

In most towns Israelite houses were built to the same basic plan, but the arrangement of the rooms naturally depended on the shape of the building plot. It is those whose work brought them an adequate livelihood, making them moderately prosperous, who lived in the typical 'Israelite' house. (The poor lived in one- or two-roomed hovels which have left little trace.)

The entrance opened from the muddy, unpaved street on to a small courtyard, perhaps cobbled. On one side a row of roughly squared stone pillars supported a low roof, forming a byre where animals might be tethered at night. (They could not be left unguarded in the fields in case wolves, bears, or other wild animals savaged them.) Another row of pillars might stand opposite, with stones or bricks between them to make a wall, or there might simply be a wall, with a doorway into the long narrow room.

At the end of the courtyard the space across the width of the house was enough for two more rooms. These were the main living and sleeping quarters. All the rooms could be divided by inserting cross-walls.

In the courtyard, the householder could arrange a hearth and an oven as he wanted. Ovens were often built of mud bricks, plastered smooth inside. Flat cakes of moist dough, stuck on the inside walls of the oven, were cooked by the heat the walls absorbed from a fire lit in the bottom.

Baking was a daily task in every household. Most would have their own stores of grain, kept in small pits in the floor, lined with stones or basketry. A stone quern or mill was all that was needed to grind the barley or wheat into flour.

Other basic supplies were stored in the houses, too. Large jars set into the floor, or standing on special brick

The typical Israelite house consisted of rooms built around a central courtyard. A flat roof with a parapet gave extra space.

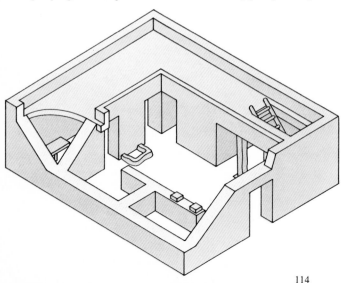

114

pedestals, could hold oil or wine or water, or be used for dry goods. Oil was crushed from olives in special stone pressers.

A group of these in one town suggests that a particular household supplied several of its neighbours. Other people spun thread from wool or flax, and wove it into cloth. Clay weights for the spindles and for holding threads taut in the looms have been found lying on the floors.

The roofs of the houses were flat. Tall trees were uncommon, so the roof beams were quite short, making the rooms fairly narrow, rarely much more than 2 metres/6 feet 6 ins wide. Branches and twigs were laid over the beams, then several layers of mud plaster were packed on top and made solid by pressing with a stone roller.

Mud plaster was also used on the stone and brick walls. A fresh coating was applied each summer to help make the building water-proof. It also gave a surface that could be decorated, or at least whitewashed (this is referred to in Ezekiel 13). The mud bricks were not baked in a kiln, only dried in the sun, and without proper care they soon crumbled, and the wall collapsed. A well-tended house could stand for thirty years or more.

In the summer, the flat roofs were convenient for all sorts of domestic activities. Joshua (chapter 2) records that in Jericho Rahab laid the flax there. On warm nights the family often slept on the roof. A wise law (recorded in Deuteronomy 22) demanded that every house have a parapet around its roof to prevent anyone moving about at night from falling off.

Rooms could be built on the roof to provide extra accommodation, but some houses did have an upper storey, perhaps set above the rooms at the end of the courtyard. Stairs led up to these

rooms from the courtyard, or, occasionally, from the outside of the house. It was a room of this sort that a well-to-do lady prepared for the prophet Elisha (the account is in 2 Kings 4). She furnished it with a bed, a table, a chair and a lamp, which was probably as much furniture as any room would have.

The lamps were shallow pottery dishes, pinched at one place on the edge to make a lip. A wick of rush or rag would lie in the lip, drawing fuel from the pool of oil in the dish. The pottery was simply earthenware or terracotta. Glazes were not in use, but the better quality wares were given a high polish before they were baked. This resulted in a very smooth surface which was easy to keep clean.

The potters made bowls and basins of all sizes; large deep ones for cooking, small, open ones for eating. They made a great variety of jugs for oil, wine, and water, and small ones for the perfumes needed frequently in the hot weather. Although the pottery was plain, it was expertly made, and the simple shapes have real elegance.

Although no one can claim, 'This was Elisha's house', or 'This was Jeremiah's', the ruins that have been found remind us that the Old Testament describes the deeds of real people who were once alive, and show us the sort of houses they lived in, and how their basic needs were met.

Every home had its simple pottery lamp (above) filled with olive oil.

Houses line a narrow street in Iron Age Beersheba (left).

IN THE DAYS BEFORE COINAGE

To buy something in ancient Israel you had to have something else to give in exchange because there was no coined money (see *Jewish Coins*). Even if a shop-keeper set his prices in silver shekels, he might take a sheep or a shirt of the right value instead.

For paying in silver people needed scales and weights to check the amounts. The silver could be scraps of metal, or rings and other pieces of jewellery. So it was necessary to have a system of weights that everyone would know.

In Jerusalem, and other towns, numbers of ancient weights have been found. These weights are mostly of stone, cut and carefully smoothed to a rounded shape with a flat base and a domed top. Tiny fractions of a shekel may be only

1 cm/ ½ in in height and diameter, weighing 2 or 3 gms/0.06 or 0.09 ozs, while in contrast weights of 4,500 gms/10 lbs may represent 400 or 500 shekels.

Although the weights look well-made, even those which ought to weigh the same vary. As a result, the exact weight of the shekel is not certain. It was probably 11.4 gms/0.34 ozs.

In order to identify them easily, the smaller weights were often inscribed with their value. This might be a number with a sign for 'shekel', or it might be the name of a smaller weight. The writing was probably the work of the seal engraver.

Apart from the shekel, two other weights mentioned in the Old Testament are identifiable among those found. The

first is the *beqa'*, the half-shekel which each adult Israelite paid as a tax to God's shrine.

No one knew the second weight until examples came to light and were related to a biblical verse. On these weights is engraved the word *payim*, meaning 'two thirds' of a shekel. In 1 Samuel 13:21 this word stands in the Hebrew text, but no one had understood it. The Authorized Version and the Revised Version translate it as 'a file', with a note of doubt.

When the passage was read with knowledge of these weights it became clear, so translations now read, 'the charge was two thirds of a shekel' imposed by the Philistines on the Israelites for repairing their iron tools.

Before there was coined money, payment in silver was made by weight. This meant a system of weights that everyone knew. The bronze lion-weights from Assyria (top) are inscribed with the name of the king for whom they were made.

The value of the weights (above) is marked on them in Hebrew. The second from the right is a payim weight.

NO HIDDEN TREASURE
The 'Moabite Stone'

Sheep — hundreds and hundreds of sheep! The king's secretaries had been sent out to check that the right number had arrived. Now they reached the total: 100,000 sheep. Besides the sheep, there was wool from another 100,000 rams. The king of Israel was pleased. All this was tribute from his subject, the king of Moab.

Naturally the Moabites resented this tax. They resented Israel's control. Eventually the moment came when they could reject it.

The man who had put Moab in this position was Omri, the king of Israel who had built the new capital of Samaria. Ahab, his son, maintained control, but at the end of his reign he joined with other kings in an inconclusive battle against the Assyrians, and soon afterwards he was killed when fighting the king of Damascus. The son who followed him fell from a window and died.

Here was an ideal opportunity to assert Moab's independence. Mesha, king of Moab, rose in rebellion. Ahab's second son Joram, now king of Israel, led a campaign to put down the revolt. Although his army reached the Moabite capital, they withdrew without taking it. Moab was free.

The Bible and Assyrian records give us this information. More comes from the Moabite side.

Mesha, king of Moab, was able to throw off Israel's rule, win back some

Moabite territory and rebuild some of its towns. He was so proud of his deeds that he had the story engraved on a stone slab. He then erected this stela in the citadel at Dibon, his home town.

Like many other ancient royal inscriptions, it starts by introducing the king: 'I am Mesha, son of . . . ,

king of Moab, the Dibonite.' The recital goes on almost entirely in the first person. 'I fought, I killed, I took, I built.'

But the king did not believe he won entirely by his own power. He explains that he built the high place where the stela stood for Chemosh, the national god of Moab. The king was

Thinking it must contain treasure, local people used fire and water to break open the 'Moabite Stone'. But the 'treasure' was the Stone itself and the inscription.

In ancient times it was often the job of the scribes to count and record tribute. These two scribes come from Assyria.

honouring his god 'because he delivered me from all kings and because he let me have victory over all my enemies'.

He says that Israel ruled Moab as a consequence of Chemosh being angry with Moab in time past. Now Chemosh had told him to fight Israel and so re-establish Moab. In particular, he told Mesha to capture the town of Nebo from Israel. Mesha went at night, fought all morning, took the city and slew 7,000 people. He devoted it as an offering to his god. Objects in it belonging to Yahweh, Israel's God, Mesha carried off to present to Chemosh. He conquered other places and the prisoners he captured were set to work on the citadel at Dibon.

The inscription is written in old Phoenician letters, also used for writing Hebrew. Its language is very much like the Hebrew of the books of Judges, Samuel, and Kings. Ideas in it are similar to ideas the ancient Israelites held.

When their God was angry with them, enemies such as the Philistines attacked and ruled them. Then he inspired leaders to free his people — the Judges, Saul and David.

Like Mesha, Israelite kings also set enemy prisoners to work on their buildings. As Mesha devoted the town of Nebo to Chemosh, so Joshua set Jericho apart. Everything in it belonged to God.

Mesha's inscription presents some problems for the modern interpreter. This is not uncommon when we read ancient texts and compare two accounts of events written from different points of view. Mesha did not name the king of Israel at the time of his victory. To the annoyance of historians, his words are vague: 'Omri took possession of the territory of Madeba and (Israel) lived there during his days and half the days of his son, forty years.' Omri reigned for twelve years (about 884–873 BC), his son Ahab for twenty-two (about 873–853 BC) — much less than forty years altogether. Should we understand 'forty years' as a round number, or as a 'generation'? Do the words 'son' and 'half' mean simply 'descendant' and 'part'?

In fact, forty years from some time in Omri's reign end in the reign of Joram (about 852–841 BC), Ahab's son who failed to reconquer Moab. Mesha could have had his monument made soon after that.

Mesha's monument, now known as the 'Moabite Stone', stands in the Louvre in Paris. Originally it was over 1.15 metres/3 feet 9 ins high, and 68 cm/27 ins wide at the foot. Now it is a battered group of fragments of black basalt. Yet when it was found it was nearly complete. The story of its discovery illustrates the dangerous life of many ancient monuments.

In 1868 a German missionary saw the stone at the ruins of Dibon. It had probably been incorporated into a later building. The next year a French scholar in Jerusalem had an Arab copy some lines of the writing. These made him realize how important the stone was. Next he had a paper squeeze or impression made of the whole stone, and set about trying to buy it.

To the local people, it was only a stone. The writing meant nothing to them. There must be treasure inside it, they thought. So they heated the stone over a fire, then poured cold water over it. It shattered, as they intended, but there was no hidden treasure.

The Frenchman, Clermont-Ganneau, determinedly collected all the pieces he could, buying them from the villagers. Although he recovered only about three-fifths of it, he was able to restore the missing parts from his paper squeeze, and so read the story of Mesha's triumph.

The 'Moabite Stone' is the only monument of its kind known to survive from Israel, Judah, Edom, Moab, or Ammon. If there were others, which is likely, they are either still buried or destroyed, as Mesha's so nearly was.

THE PRICE OF PROTECTION
The 'Black Obelisk'

The excavation had gone on for days. Nothing of interest had come to light. It was November 1845. Henry Layard, who was directing the work, had to leave the ruin-mound on an errand.

Before he left he talked with the workmen. They had dug a trench more than 15 metres/50 feet long. The soil was hard and dry, they were dispirited. Layard told them to dig for one more day, until he returned. Then he rode away.

He was hardly clear of the mound when a panting workman overtook him. Something had been found in the trench. He should stop to see it.

Layard rode back, dismounted, and climbed down into the trench. There at the bottom lay a block of polished black stone, carved and inscribed. As Layard watched, eager hands hauled it out with ropes. It was a four-sided pillar or obelisk, 2 metres/6 feet 6ins high, with five panels of small pictures on each face, and line upon line of finely engraved cuneiform signs.

Layard himself made careful drawings of the pictures and the writing, and had it packed and sent off to England. Today it stands in the British Museum in London with other monuments Layard unearthed.

If he had listened to his men and stopped the digging before he left that day, the 'Black Obelisk' might still be buried in the ruins of the ancient Assyrian city of Calah (now called Nimrud).

When the obelisk came to light, Layard could not read the inscriptions, nor could anyone else. He had the drawings printed quickly, and sent them to scholars who were trying to decipher the cuneiform writing. At almost the same time two of them were able to read some of the words on the stone.

The first was a shy Church of England rector, Edward Hincks, who lived in Ireland. He studied quietly in his rectory, and occasionally at the British Museum. His parishioners were probably quite unaware that their rector, who spent so much time with large books in foreign languages, was unlocking one of the long-closed doors of ancient history. Hincks and Layard were friends, and it was Hincks who was able to tell Layard the meaning of many of the inscriptions he found.

The other great decipherer at this time was Henry Rawlinson (see *Secrets from the Rock of Behistun*).

Both men recognized that the 'Black Obelisk' records the triumphs of an Assyrian king, and that the writing above each row of pictures describes them.

As they worked through the text, the decipherers found that the first row of panels is labelled as the tribute of a king from north-west Persia. This king, or his ambassador, is shown kneeling in front of King Shalmaneser, whose officers stand behind.

On the other panels, attendants lead a horse and two camels, and porters carry other things as examples of the tribute this king is giving to Assyria.

The second line of pictures proved to be the most exciting. In the first panel another figure kneels to kiss the dust at the feet of the king of Assyria. Thirteen men follow the Assyrian courtiers bearing the tribute. Above the pictures the label reads, 'Tribute of Yaua son of

In 1845 men working for Henry Layard on the site of the ancient Assyrian city of Calah (Nimrud) uncovered a block of polished black stone, carved and inscribed. The 'Black Obelisk' records the triumphs of the Assyrian king, Shalmaneser.

The first panel in the second line of pictures (above, right) proved exciting. The text above the kneeling figure lists tribute brought to the king from 'Yaua son of Humri', that is, Jehu, who took the throne from a descendant of Omri, king of Israel. The Assyrian monument throws interesting light on the reign of a biblical king.

The 'Black Obelisk' is the only monument so far discovered which shows Israelites (pictured above) bringing tribute to an Assyrian king.

Humri: I received silver, gold, a golden bowl, a golden beaker, golden goblets, golden pitchers, lead, a royal staff, a javelin.'

It was not hard to identify the name of the king who sent these presents. Yaua is the Assyrian writing of Jehu, king of Israel, and Humri is Omri who set up the Israelite capital at Samaria.

Here is an important link between an Assyrian monument and the Bible — a fact that Hincks and Rawlinson realized immediately.

Before we look further at this matter, we should notice the other pictures. No more kneeling envoys appear, but there is a variety of tribute. Row three has two camels, three horned creatures, an elephant, two monkeys and two apes. These came from Egypt, the horned creatures perhaps including a rhinoceros, and were intended for the royal zoo. The Assyrian kings loved to collect unusual animals and plants.

Following a scene of a lion felling a stag, the fourth row of pictures illustrates the tribute of a king living by the middle section of the River Euphrates. It is much like the first two sets of tribute, with the addition of folded clothes.

In the final row the procession of porters bears the tribute of a state on the coast of Syria, very similar to Jehu's tribute.

Assyrian stone-carvers may not have seen some of the animals sent from Egypt before, and so may not have cut their pictures very accurately in the stone. They did take care, on the other hand, to give each group of tribute-bearers different clothing, and it is likely they were trying to depict the various native costumes.

In the 190 lines of inscription at the top and bottom of the pillar, Shalmaneser relates his triumphs from the first year of his reign (857 BC) to the thirty-first (826 BC). It was in the sixteenth year, 841 BC, other records of Shalmaneser explain, that Jehu paid his tribute. Now Jehu was not a royal prince of Israel. He was a soldier who killed King Joram, a descendant of Omri. At the same time Jehu killed the king of Judah. The second book of Kings, chapter 9, tells the story.

Shalmaneser's other records and the biblical records, when taken together, indicate that Jehu's murder of the two kings, and his seizing the throne in Samaria, happened in the same year as he paid homage to Assyria. He may well have thought he could make his position more secure by having Assyrian protection. The Bible does not tell us about this aspect of Jehu's reign; it was not relevant to the Hebrew historian's purpose.

The 'Black Obelisk' remains the only monument with carvings of Israelites bringing tribute to an Assyrian king. From the time of the first studies by Hincks and Rawlinson it has held a major place among the Assyrian documents relating to the Old Testament, as well as being an important work of art in its own right.

'THE ASSYRIAN CAME DOWN...'

In a British Museum show-case in London stands a hollow brown clay prism. On each of its six faces is line after line of neat cuneiform writing. This dull-looking piece of pottery, almost 37.5 cm/15 ins high, is one of many inscriptions recording the successes of King Sennacherib who ruled Assyria from 705 to 681 BC. The British Resident in Baghdad, a Colonel Taylor, acquired this example at Nineveh in 1830 and it entered the museum in 1855, to be known as the 'Taylor Prism'.

Assyrian kings had such records written to bury in the foundations of the temples, palaces, and city-gates they built or repaired. They hoped their successors would find them in due course, read them and realize what great men they had been. In this way the memory of a king such as Sennacherib would be kept alive. That explains the tone of the inscriptions. They sound very boastful and conceited, telling of nothing but the king's prowess and the victories he won, the enemies he executed and the loot he took home.

A closer study suggests that these kings were not quite such blatant, bullying imperialists as they seem at first sight. They justified their wars quite often with the claim that their national god commanded them to fight. Often, too, they fought to put down rebellious subject kings. That is the reason for all the wars of Sennacherib which the 'Taylor Prism' describes.

Among those Sennacherib attacked was Merodach-baladan, king of Babylonia. After earlier battles, he had accepted the Assyrian presence in Babylonia, but when Sennacherib became king he had made an alliance with enemies of Assyria to the east. He also tried to win support from other subjects of Assyria, including King Hezekiah of Judah, far to the west.

The biblical book of Kings tells how Hezekiah received Merodach-baladan's messengers with honour, and it may be that their visit was one of the reasons for Hezekiah's rebellion against Assyria. For Hezekiah did rebel and, after dealing with the Babylonian

In the time of King Hezekiah of Judah, the Assyrians hammered at the gates of Jerusalem itself. The capital did not fall — but Lachish, to the south, was taken after a siege. King Sennacherib decorated his palace walls in Nineveh with scenes of the dramatic finale. Here the inhabitants leave as missiles fall.

The ambassador of King Merodach-baladan of Babylonia (the king pictured below) was made welcome at King Hezekiah's court. A century later Babylon, not Assyria, was the chief threat.

trouble, Sennacherib marched west.

The Assyrian king reports how he moved down the Mediterranean coast in 701 BC, meeting various local kings who bowed before him. Eventually he reached Philistine territory, south-west of Israel and Judah.

One king, the king of Ashkelon, refused to submit, so Sennacherib deposed him and packed him off to

The might of proud Assyria is expressed in this statue of King Ashurnasirpal II, from the ninth century BC.

Assyria with all his family. A man who had ruled Ashkelon previously, under Assyrian protection, was made king.

Another Philistine city, Ekron, was also in revolt. Some of the leading citizens had tied up their king who was loyal to Assyria, and handed him over to Hezekiah, king of Judah, in Jerusalem. The rebels called on Egypt to help them, but the Assyrian army won the battle at Eltekeh, and Ekron was overwhelmed. Sennacherib executed the leaders of the rebellion, and took their supporters prisoner, but allowed the rest to go free. Then he set back on the throne the king who had been imprisoned in Jerusalem.

Although Sennacherib's inscriptions describe these events one after another, the release of the king of Ekron may have taken place only after the final stage of the campaign.

One rebel remained defiant.

Hezekiah of Judah, evidently a leader of the revolt, was holding out in his capital, Jerusalem. Sennacherib overran the whole of Judah and encircled the capital. His record tells the tale (see *'Like a Bird in a Cage'*).

There are several notable points. Although his troops surrounded Jerusalem so that no one could enter or leave the city, there is no account of an attack made on it as there is for the 'forty-six strong walled towns', or for other rebel cities. Sennacherib claims Hezekiah gave in to him, paying a heavy tribute, yet he makes no mention of his soldiers entering Jerusalem, or of meeting Hezekiah himself.

The most striking fact comes at the end. Hezekiah sent his messenger, and all the tribute, to Sennacherib 'later, to Nineveh'. The Assyrian army did not carry them home in triumph in the usual way.

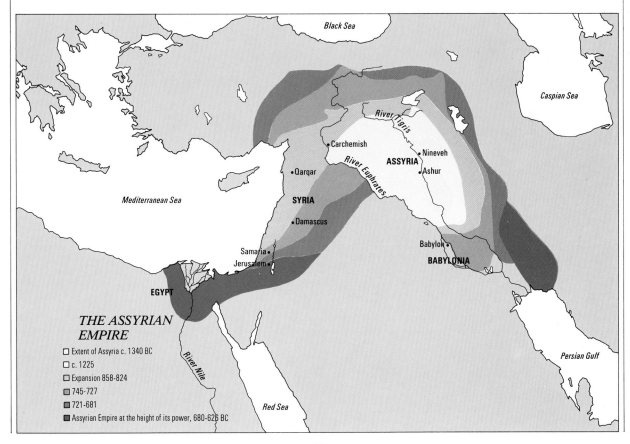

THE ASSYRIAN EMPIRE

☐ Extent of Assyria c. 1340 BC
☐ c. 1225
☐ Expansion 858-824
◼ 745-727
◼ 721-681
◼ Assyrian Empire at the height of its power, 680-626 BC

'LIKE A BIRD IN A CAGE'
Sennacherib Attacks Jerusalem

King Sennacherib's attack on Jerusalem is recorded on the 'Taylor Prism'.

This is a translation of the report Sennacherib left for later kings to read about his attack on Judah:

'As for Hezekiah, the Judean who did not submit to my yoke, I surrounded and conquered forty-six of his strong walled towns and innumerable small settlements around them by means of earth ramps and siege-engines and attack by infantrymen, mining, breaking through and scaling. I brought out from them and counted as spoil 200,150 people of all ranks, men and women, horses, mules, donkeys, camels, cattle and sheep. He himself I shut up in Jerusalem, his royal city, like a bird in a cage. I surrounded him with watchposts and made it impossible for anyone to go in or out of his city. His cities which I had despoiled I cut off from his territory and gave to Mitinti king of Ashdod, Padi king of Ekron, and Sil-Bel king of Gaza, so reducing his realm. I added to their previous annual tribute a tribute gift befitting my lordship and imposed it on them. Fear of my lordly splendour overwhelmed that Hezekiah. The warriors and select troops he had brought in to strengthen his royal city Jerusalem, did not fight. He had brought after me to Nineveh, my royal city, 30 talents of gold, 800 talents of silver, best antimony, great blocks of red stone, ivory-decorated beds, ivory-decorated armchairs, elephant hide, tusks, ebony, box-wood, valuable treasure of every sort, and his daughters, women of his palace, men and women singers. He sent his messenger to pay tribute and do obeisance.'

This episode is known to us from the Old Testament, too. The story is told at length twice, in 2 Kings 18 and Isaiah 36 and 37 (and in summary in 2 Chronicles 32). Reading the biblical accounts beside Sennacherib's shows that there are many differences. Yet both clearly deal with the same events.

The differences are not surprising since the accounts come from opposing sides. In addition, none of them necessarily follows the actual order in which the events took place.

According to the Hebrew writers, Sennacherib threatened Jerusalem, tried to persuade the citizens to open the gates, and tried to bully Hezekiah into surrender, but failed. Jerusalem remained intact. Hezekiah had assurances from God, through the prophet Isaiah, which encouraged him to resist. And he did not fall!

A famous verse states the Hebrew historian's interpretation: 'the angel of the Lord went out, and smote in the camp of the Assyrians an hundred fourscore and five thousand: and when they arose early in the morning, behold, they were all dead corpses. So Sennacherib, king of Assyria departed, and went and returned, and dwelt at Nineveh' (2 Kings 19:35,36, in the Authorized Version).

What exactly happened we cannot

discover. There is no good reason to doubt this report of a catastrophe cutting short the Assyrian campaign. Understandably, Sennacherib would not record such a disaster for his successors to read, for it would discredit him.

A sudden sharp drop in the strength of his army, leading to a quick withdrawal, would explain why Sennacherib does not claim to have captured Jerusalem, and why he received Hezekiah's submission by messenger, in Nineveh.

One other fact suggests Sennacherib failed to capture Jerusalem. In his palace at Nineveh one room was decorated with carved stone slabs illustrating the campaign in Judah. They are concerned with the capture of one city, and that is not Jerusalem, but the stronghold of Lachish to the south. If the Assyrians had captured Jerusalem, that could be expected to feature on the palace walls. But it did not. Lachish was given the prominence.

Sennacherib's 'Taylor Prism', and its parallels, give the most extensive example of a piece of Hebrew history told from the enemy's point of view. It is very valuable as an aid to understanding the biblical texts, and in the way it corresponds to them.

In this scene from the time of Assyria's greatest influence, King Ashurbanipal leads the lion-hunt.

KING HEZEKIAH'S TUNNEL

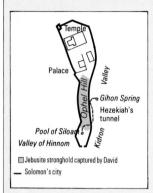

The tunnel wriggles its way through the rock from Spring to Pool.

In 1880 a boy noticed some writing scratched on the wall of the tunnel which led to the Pool. It records how two gangs of workmen, starting from opposite ends, broke through the rock to meet deep underground.

For years women of Jerusalem had washed their clothes in the pool at the south of the city. Water came into the pool from a tunnel and the children used to splash in the water. Some of the boys crept a little way into the dark passage.

One day in 1880 one of them, holding a light, went further than usual. By the flickering flame he noticed some writing scratched on the rocky wall. He came out to describe his discovery.

Nobody had seen this inscription before, so soon it was studied carefully. Water running down the tunnel wall had left deposits of lime over the writing, but when they were cleaned off, six lines of clear Hebrew writing appeared.

They describe how two gangs of men cut a tunnel through the rock. The gangs began work at opposite ends and eventually met deep underground. The text says one gang heard the sound of the other hacking at the rock, so they knew which way to go.

The tunnel runs to the pool from a spring on the east side of the city, in the Kidron Valley. People had known about it for a long time when Edward Robinson, a famous American explorer of Palestine, made the first accurate survey of it in 1838. He demonstrated that the water ran from the Virgin's Fountain to the pool, not the other way as some had thought.

With his friends, he managed to make his way through the whole length of the tunnel. At some places it was 4.5–6 metres/15–20 feet high, at others it was so low the explorers could only wriggle through, lying at full length and dragging themselves along on their elbows. Since that time the silt has been cleared from the bottom and it is not as difficult to walk through.

Robinson had expected the tunnel to be about 366 metres/1,200 feet long on an almost direct line. So he was surprised when his measurement reached 534 metres/1,750 feet. The reason is clear. The tunnel bends like an S. There is another double bend near the middle which is evidently where the two gangs of tunnellers met. Had they not heard each other's pick-axes, the plan suggests they might not have met at all!

Why the tunnel has so twisting a course is not certain. Despite their lack of compasses, the ancient engineers could have kept a straight line by sighting from the ends. Possibly they followed an underground stream and faults in the rock for parts of their work.

The tunnel was dug to take water from one part of the city to another. That is obvious. The inscription which the local boy found nearly fifty years after Robinson's survey points to the time when the tunnel was made and the reason for making it then.

The engraving is a fine example of the ancient Hebrew handwriting current before the Exile. From the time of its discovery, scholars have linked it with King Hezekiah of Judah, just before 700 BC. In recent years the recovery of other early Hebrew documents has shown that the shapes of the letters belong to this date. Among them is an impression on clay of a seal owned by one of Hezekiah's officers, 'Jehozerah son of Hilkiah, servant of Hezekiah'. (Hilkiah is mentioned in 2 Kings 18.)

The link with Hezekiah follows from records in the Old Testament about Hezekiah making a reservoir and a canal in Jerusalem. 2 Kings 20:20 records: 'Everything else that King Hezekiah did, his brave deeds, and an account of how he built a reservoir and dug a tunnel to bring water into the city, are all recorded in *'The History of the Kings of Judah.'*

2 Chronicles 32:3–4 says:
'he and his officials decided to cut off the supply of water outside the city in order to prevent the Assyrians from having any water when they got near Jerusalem. The officials led a large number of people out and stopped up all the springs, so that no more water flowed out of them.'

Verse 30 adds: 'It was King Hezekiah who blocked the outlet for the Spring of Gihon and chanelled the water to flow through a tunnel to a point inside the

walls of Jerusalem. Hezekiah succeeded in everything he did.'

Today the pool is open to the sky, and lies outside the Turkish wall of Jerusalem. When Hezekiah's men dug it, the pool may have been open, reached by steps cut around the sides, or it may have been entirely underground. At that time it was within the walls of the city, for the oldest part of Jerusalem was built above the Virgin's Fountain, the Gihon Spring of the Old Testament, which provided the citizens with water.

A Greek who hoped to become rich by selling the inscription chopped it out of the rock in 1890 and broke it. The Turkish authorities, who then ruled Jerusalem, confiscated it, and it is now on exhibition in the antiquities museum in Istanbul.

The pool is called the Pool of Siloam, but it is not certain if this is the pool mentioned in the Gospel of John, chapter 9, as the one Jesus sent the blind man to wash in. That could be another pool, slightly to the south.

To safeguard Jerusalem against siege, King Hezekiah had a tunnel cut through solid rock to bring water from the Spring of Gihon (above, left) within the city walls. The Spring was then sealed off.

The tunnel now channels water to the Pool of Siloam (above).

'WE CAN'T SEE THE SIGNALS'

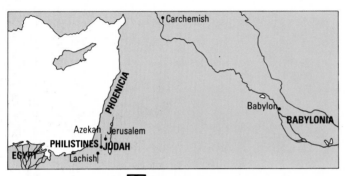

The tiny kingdom of Judah was in trouble. Her pious old king Josiah had been killed in a battle he should never have fought. His conqueror, the king of Egypt, put Josiah's son on the throne as his subject king.

Only four years later the army of Babylon defeated the Egyptians at Carchemish, far to the north. The Babylonians then moved on south to take control of the cities of Phoenicia, the Philistines, and Judah. So Judah's king was now subject to the king of Babylon.

Although its armies were strong, Babylon was far away. Egypt, on the other hand, was next door to Judah. After the Babylonians had gone home, Jehoiakim, king of Judah, listened to the pharaoh's messengers as they urged him to break the treaty that bound him to Babylon and join the Egyptian side again. In Jerusalem, the prophet Jeremiah tried to persuade him not to agree, without success. The Egyptian alliance was renewed.

As the prophet had warned, King Nebuchadnezzar of Babylon took swift action. He sent local forces to bring the rebel to heel. When their attacks had no lasting effect, the Babylonian army marched to Jerusalem to set matters right.

Jehoiakim died in Jerusalem, and his son Jehoiachin became king. He had ruled for only three months when the Babylonians captured him and his capital. They took the young king and his leading men captive to Babylon, and set his uncle, Zedekiah, on the throne.

Incredibly, Zedekiah did just what Jehoiakim had done. He joined Egyptian intrigues and the Babylonians were roused again. Nebuchadnezzar could not allow the people of Judah to have a king of their own any longer. Their continual defiance must be ended.

His army laid siege to Jerusalem and took it. The soldiers broke down the city walls, ransacked Solomon's Temple, and set it on fire. They caught Zedekiah as he tried to escape, killed his sons as he watched, then blinded him. All the well-to-do and skilled people were taken in exile to Babylon, and a local governor was left in charge, under Babylonian supervision.

That is the history of the last twenty-five years of the kingdom of Judah as the Bible and Babylonian documents tell it.

Archaeology can add to their accounts. From 1932 to 1938 a team of Britons dug into an impressive mound between Hebron and Ashkelon. The ruins are believed to be those of the ancient city of Lachish (see also *'The Assyrian Came Down . . .'*). At one

place on the edge of the mound the spades quickly struck the stumps of stone walls. They were the remains of the city gate. The floor of the guard-chamber was covered with rubble and ash, evidence that they were destroyed by fire. The fire had also ravaged some poorly-built houses nearby.

From the style of the broken pots lying in these gateways it is almost certain the destruction was the result of one of the Babylonian assaults on Judah. Most archaeologists believe it was the last one, when Jerusalem was sacked. The burnt walls and broken vessels are a reminder of the disaster such an invasion brought to the ordinary people of Lachish. Their homes were never rebuilt.

A few potsherds found in the gatehouse bring the situation to life. A junior officer in the Judean army

On this 'tell', the ruins of ancient Lachish, burnt walls and broken vessels are a reminder of the disastrous attack its people suffered at the hands of the Assyrians.

On pieces of broken pottery found in the gatehouse are reports from a Judean soldier to his commanding officer at Lachish. News was sent by smoke signals.

mention of a prophetic warning that had come by letter, which the writer is forwarding.

There are eighteen letters, some of which are very poorly preserved, the ink has faded or been washed away. One may come from the last moments of the garrison. The officer reports he had put down all he was instructed on a writing-tablet or a column of a scroll, a certain man has been taken to the city (perhaps Jerusalem) as a prisoner, and ends 'we are watching for the beacon from Lachish, following the signals you, sir, gave, but we do not see Azekah.'

These last words apparently refer to a system of sending news from place to place by smoke signals or bonfires. Azekah is identified as a place about 15 km/9½ miles north of Lachish. The officer was at a place where he could see both. Smoke signals would be especially important as a warning of invasion. (A chain of beacons was set up in Britain to serve exactly the same purpose if Napoleon invaded in 1803.)

The prophet Jeremiah warned King Zedekiah to change his policies at a moment 'when the army of the king of Babylon was fighting against Jerusalem and against all the cities of Judah that were left, Lachish and Azekah, for these were the only fortified cities of Judah that remained.'

It is tempting to think this insignificant-looking piece of pottery carries a message from those last days as the Babylonian forces closed in.

had sent reports from his outpost to his commander in Lachish. They were short messages written in ink on pieces of broken pottery. Their language is good Hebrew, just like the language of the Old Testament. Their writing shows how Hebrew appeared at that time. This is what the written prophecies of Jeremiah and Ezekiel would have looked like. Apart from a list of names discovered on a potsherd in Jerusalem, these were the first examples of ordinary ancient Hebrew writing unearthed in Judah. Others have been recovered since at different places.

The letters are simple. In one, the officer seems to say he is not as stupid as his commander suggested, he really is able to read! Another notes the arrival of a general on his way to Egypt, an echo of the intrigues between Judah and the pharaoh. There is also

'NEBUCHADNEZZAR, KING OF THE JEWS'

Excavators digging into the ruined palaces of Sennacherib and other Assyrian kings all tell the same story. The magnificent halls and courtyards lined with sculptured slabs of stone were looted and burnt, and left desolate. What the plunderers could not carry away, they left to wild animals and the elements. The glory of Assyria vanished.

In place of Assyria, Babylon rose to rule. A few Babylonian tablets, the Bible, and some Greek reports describe these events. After 640 BC Assyria grew weak. From the east, from the hills of Persia, Medes and their allies attacked. From the south came the forces of Babylonia, commanded by successors of Merodach-baladan, the king whom Sennacherib had defeated.

Following several battles, these forces joined to bring Assyria's power to an end by capturing Nineveh in 612 BC. The victors shared the Assyrian Empire, the Medes taking the hill-country to the east and north, the Babylonians holding Mesopotamia, Syria, and Palestine.

A third power, Egypt, tried to win some of the spoils, but the Babylonians thoroughly defeated the Egyptians at Carchemish, in 605 BC. Commanding the Babylonian army in that battle was Nebuchadnezzar. He became king of Babylon in the same year and reigned for forty-three years, until 562 BC.

Nebuchadnezzar did not leave long descriptions of his victories on the walls of the temples and palaces he built, as the Assyrian kings had done. The inscriptions he did leave speak almost solely of what he did for the gods he worshipped. As a result, the history of his reign is not very well known. Some inscriptions name places in his empire, showing how large it was, and two groups of cuneiform tablets supply more detailed information.

The first group is the Babylonian Chronicles. Two tablets cover events in the reign of Nebuchadnezzar's father, and two in his own reign (other tablets deal with earlier and later kings). The two tablets for Nebuchadnezzar, unfortunately, only refer to the first eleven years of his rule. The remaining thirty-two are almost entirely without record. It is possible other tablets will

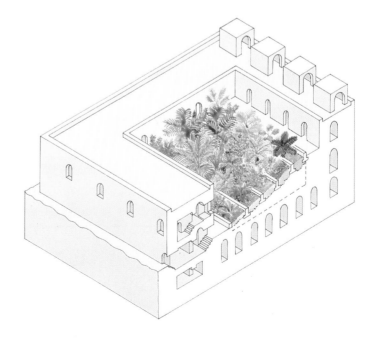

The 'Hanging Gardens' of Babylon were among the seven wonders of the ancient world.

be found one day. Those known at present were bought by the British Museum late in the nineteenth century, but the two about Nebuchadnezzar lay there awaiting publication until 1956.

Why the tablets were written is not explained; they seem to be extracts from a fuller account of each year's events. These chronicles are not boastful descriptions of bloodshed and victory, like the Assyrian kings' monuments. They are plain, factual, and, scholars agree, reliable. They tell us about the rise of Babylon to power and the fall of Assyria, of the battle of Carchemish and Babylonian successes in Syria and Palestine.

One short entry states: 'The seventh year, the month of Kislev, the king of Babylonia mustered his forces and marched to Syria. He encamped against the city of Judah and on the second day of the month of Adar he

took the city and captured the king. He appointed a king of his own choice there, took its heavy tribute and brought them to Babylon.'

Enough is known for these dates to be translated exactly. The month of Kislev in year seven was December 598 BC. The second of Adar was 15/16 March 597 BC. Here is the Babylonian report of the attack on Jerusalem which ended with Nebuchadnezzar making Zedekiah king in place of young Jehoiachin, whom he took prisoner to Babylon (see also *'We Can't See the Signals'*). These kings were under Nebuchadnezzar's control. He was really 'Nebuchadnezzar, king of the Jews', as the nursery rhyme says!

The Babylonian soldiers transported Jehoiachin and his courtiers to Babylon. There they lived under guard in the royal palace. During excavations in that palace some cuneiform tablets

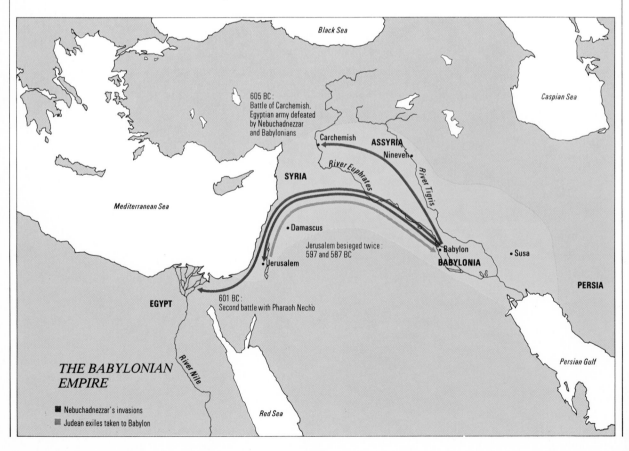

605 BC:
Battle of Carchemish.
Egyptian army defeated
by Nebuchadnezzar
and Babylonians

Black Sea

Caspian Sea

Carchemish **ASSYRIA**
Nineveh

River Euphrates *River Tigris*

SYRIA

Mediterranean Sea

• Damascus

Jerusalem besieged twice:
597 and 587 BC

• Babylon
BABYLONIA

• Susa

• Jerusalem

PERSIA

EGYPT

601 BC:
Second battle with Pharaoh Necho

River Nile

Persian Gulf

**THE BABYLONIAN
EMPIRE**

■ Nebuchadnezzar's invasions
■ Judean exiles taken to Babylon

Red Sea

came to light which list rations issued to all sorts of people living there. The tablets are dated by years of Nebuchadnezzar's reign, between 594 and 569 BC.

Among those who received grain and oil were Medes and Persians, Egyptians and Lydians, all with their own distinctive names. There were men from Phoenician cities — Byblos, Arvad and Tyre — from Philistine Ashkelon, and some from Judah. Most of them were officials or craftsmen, sailors, boat-builders, carpenters, and one Egyptian was a keeper of monkeys (see also *The Price of Protection*).

From Ashkelon there were sons of the king, but from Judah there was the king himself. Four tablets list rations for 'Jehoiachin, king of Judah', for his five sons and, probably, for four other Judeans — one a gardener bearing the good Hebrew name 'Shelemiah'.

Nebuchadnezzar kept Jehoiachin in his palace throughout his reign. His son, 2 Kings 25 relates, released him and gave him a privileged place at his table.

Nebuchadnezzar made Babylon a splendid city (see *The Glory that was Babylon*). He had a very large palace, heavily defended, at the north end of the city. Its main entrance opened into a great courtyard almost 66 metres/220 feet long × 42 metres/140 feet wide. At either end were rooms for guards and other personnel. Opposite the main entrance the visitor would pass through a hall into the second court, a rather smaller one with many rooms at the ends. A suite at the southern end may have served the highest officials under the king for receiving petitioners.

A monumental gateway led west from that courtyard into the main one, nearly 60 metres/200 feet long × 55 metres/180 feet wide. Bricks covered with blue glaze bearing tree and flower designs in yellow, white, red, and blue, covered the south wall of the main

courtyard. Below the trees ran a frieze of lions.

A central doorway led through this wall to the king's throne-room, a hall 52 metres/170 feet long × 17 metres/56 feet wide. The king's throne probably stood opposite this main door, partly recessed into the wall. This was presumably the room in which Belshazzar may be imagined sitting when the hand wrote his doom on the plaster of the wall. Beyond this central courtyard and throne-room lay two more courtyards with many more rooms. In some the royal women may have lived.

At the north-eastern corner of the palace was a structure with thick brick walls and long, narrow vaulted chambers. (The ration tablets of Jehoiachin were found here.) These may have been store-rooms, but the thick walls suggest this was a high building. The excavator proposed to identify it with the 'Hanging Gardens'.

Greek historians explain how a Baylonian king created a mountain-like garden to please his Median wife. She came from a hilly land and was homesick in the flat plains of Babylon. The vaulted rooms could have supported terraces of brickwork for these gardens.

Nebuchadnezzar had a long reign in which to enjoy his glory. Less than twenty-five years after his death the Persians conquered Babylon and the city gradually lost its importance.

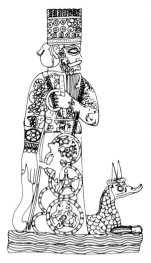

Nebuchadnezzar embarked on building work which made Babylon a splendid city. Even the bricks (above, left) were stamped with his name.

King Nebuchadnezzar paid due attention to matters of religion. He rebuilt several temples, including that of the god Marduk (above). This may be the god he honoured with a golden statue 27 metres/89 feet high, according to the book of Daniel.

THE GLORY THAT WAS BABYLON

For hundreds of years people living on the banks of the River Euphrates in Iraq had dug into the mounds of ancient Babylon for the hard baked bricks used in the old buildings. Most of the villages along that part of the river, and the town of Hillah, were largely built with Babylonian bricks. Yet, although the ruins were pillaged in this way, the city was so great that much remained.

Major excavations began at Babylon under German auspices in 1899. Robert Koldewey was in charge of the work, summer and winter, for eighteen years. His men uncovered city-walls, palaces, temples and houses. In them were pots and pans, metal objects, stone carvings and cuneiform inscriptions. Almost all belonged to the Chaldean period, 626–539 BC, when Nebuchadnezzar ruled.

The Ishtar Gate (left) stands as a memorial to the glory that was Babylon.

The plan (page 137) and artist's reconstruction of 'great Babylon' at the time of King Nebuchadnezzar give just a glimpse of its magnificence.

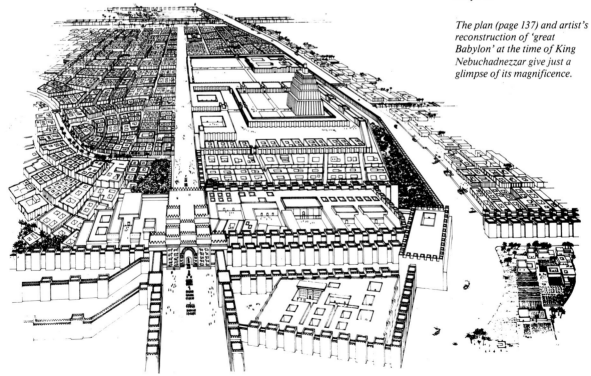

Ruins of earlier buildings lie below these, but the nearby river makes the water-table too high for them to be excavated properly. Consequently what visitors to the site see today is the work of Nebuchadnezzar and of later builders. It was his work that left its mark most strongly on Babylon.

When Nebuchadnezzar became king he pressed forward with the rebuilding his father had begun. Babylon stood on the east bank of the Euphrates, with a suburb across the river.

Two lines of walls protected it. The inner line was made up of two parallel walls 6.5 metres/21 feet and 3.72 metres/ 12 feet thick with a space between them 7.2 metres/24 feet wide serving as a roadway. These walls ran for about 6 km/3½ miles along the north, east, and south sides of the city, the river guarding the west side. Similar walls enclosed the suburb.

Outside the walls a moat some 80 metres/262 feet broad gave added protection. The outer walls were even bigger (7.12, 7.8 and 3.3 metres/23, 25 and 11 feet thick), with another great moat beyond. They enclosed an area of triangular shape occupied by suburbs and another royal palace. Their length was slightly over 8 km/5 miles.

Anyone entering the inner city

Over 200 animal-images decorate the great Ishtar gateway, faced with glazed tile, at the entrance to the processional way that led to the temples of the gods.

passed through impressive gateways in these walls. By far the most splendid was the Ishtar Gate, beside the palace at the north. This gate controlled a processional road leading to the main temple. Nebuchadnezzar rebuilt the Ishtar Gate three times. In each case the walls had a decoration of magical animals moulded in relief in the brickwork, but in the last stage the bricks were glazed, yellow and brown animals against a blue background.

Although brick-hunters had demolished all of the glazed walls, enough bricks remained loose on the ground for the reconstruction now standing in the State Museum in Berlin. The earlier, unglazed walls can still be seen at Babylon.

Flanking the street leading to the gateway, the walls were also covered with glazed bricks with lions moulded in relief. For the pavement of the road,

white limestone slabs were laid, each more than 1 metre/3 feet square, with red and white veined slabs along the sides. This road ran straight from the Ishtar Gate for almost 900 metres/half a mile to the temples of the god of Babylon. He was Marduk, commonly called Bel, 'Lord'.

Little could be discovered about the two central temples of Babylon. One was a tower built in diminishing stages. This great mass of mud-brick had been a rich quarry for the local brick-hunters. Nothing remains of the tower but a large hole in the ground and a few foundations. Its base was about 91 metres/100 yards square, with a long staircase at right angles on the south side for access to the upper stages.

Other information about the tower comes from Babylonian tablets which give measurements for each stage, and from Greek descriptions. The sides of

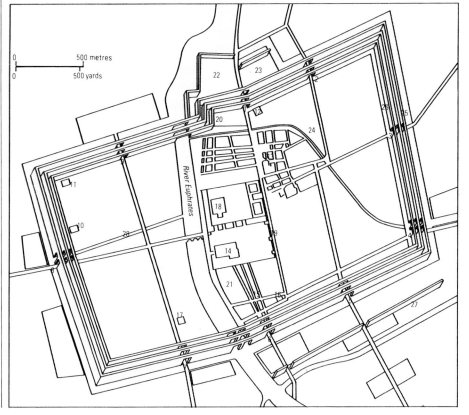

1	Ishtar gate
2	Sin gate
3	Marduk gate
4	Zababa gate
5	Enlil gate
6	Urash gate
7	Shamash gate
8	Adad gate
9	Lugalgirra gate
10	Temple of Adad
11	Temple of Belitnina
12	Temple of Ninmah
13	Temple of Ishtar
14	Temple of Marduk
15	Temple of Gula
16	Temple of Ninurta
17	Temple of Shamash
18	Temple tower
19	Processional way
20	Palace of Nebuchadnezzar
21	Esagila
22	Northern Citadel
23	Citadel
24	Southern Citadel
25	Outer wall
26	Inner wall
27	Nebuchadnezzar's outer wall
28	Canal

the stages were painted in different colours, the shrine at the top, perhaps 190 metres/300 feet above the ground, was covered with the blue glazed bricks. A great courtyard surrounded the tower, with dozens of rooms for priests and stores, and shrines for less important gods.

The second temple was named Esagila. Koldewey could not excavate it properly for it is buried under almost 21 metres/70 feet of debris, and a Muslim shrine stands on top of the mound. Nebuchadnezzar's own records and the report of the Greek writer Herodotus show it was a magnificent place.

The Babylonian king covered the walls of the holy place with gold and provided a great gold-plated bed and throne for the god. There were two golden statues of Marduk, Herodotus states, one sitting and one standing. Local priests told Herodotus that over twenty tons of gold had been used for the temple and its furniture.

Chiselled on the paving stones of the processional way and stamped on many of the bricks were inscriptions proclaiming, 'I am Nebuchadnezzar, king of Babylon, son of Nabopolassar, king of Babylon.' This is the claim echoed in the Bible book of Daniel, 4:30: 'Is not this great Babylon which I have built . . .?'

The ruins reveal the grounds for the king's boast. The period of madness which followed, does not appear in Babylonian records, but, as we have noted, hardly any exist to tell of Nebuchadnezzar's last thirty years' kingship.

THE WRITING ON THE WALL
Belshazzar — Man or Myth?

The book of Daniel is famous for its stories of heroes. They were men who stood firm for what they believed was right. They were protected by the power of God when the pagan kings persecuted them. Daniel himself was kept safe in the lion's den. His three friends stepped out alive from the burning fiery furnace . . .

A different story is just as famous — the story of the writing on the wall. It became so well known that the phrase 'the writing's on the wall' has gone into the English language.

Belshazzar, king of Babylon, held a feast for his courtiers. They ate and drank, using the gold and silver vessels brought from God's temple in Jerusalem.

As they revelled, a hand appeared.

The hand wrote on the wall in front of the king. The words it wrote did not make sense: MENE, MENE, TEKEL, PARSIN.

The king's scholars tried to find a meaning. They failed. Daniel was brought in. He saw at once what the words indicated, gave the king a warning, and told him his reign was about to end.

It seems the writing was the equivalent of 'Pounds, pence' - units of money or weight. Daniel's interpretation played on the meaning of each unit's name (as one might say 'pound' means 'beat, crush'). This was one of the methods Babylonians used for interpreting old books by which they tried to tell the future.

'Mene (number): God has numbered the days of your kingdom and brought it to an end.'

'Tekel (weight): you have been weighed on the scales and found to be too light.'

'Parsin (divisions): your kingdom is divided up and given to the Medes and Persians.'

The prophecy came true. The ancient historians record how Cyrus the Persian diverted the course of the River Euphrates and brought in his men along the river-bed to take the impregnable city of Babylon.

Belshazzar is remembered for his feast. Rembrandt and other great artists have painted pictures of it, and Sir William Walton used its theme for his famous modern oratorio 'Belshazzar's Feast'. Yet Belshazzar's name was not to be found outside the book of Daniel.

As a result, some scholars have promoted the idea that the whole story is fiction. It was made up, they argued, to give encouragement to Jews fighting for their independence in the second century BC. Indeed, they claimed, the whole book of Daniel was written then, and has no historical foundation. The supposed King Belshazzar was one of several historical mistakes the author made.

One eminent German wrote in his commentary on the book of Daniel that Belshazzar was simply a figment of the author's

imagination. That commentary was published in 1850.

In 1854 a British consul explored ancient ruins in southern Iraq on behalf of the British Museum. He dug into a great tower built of mud-brick at an ancient city ruin. The tower was part of the temple of the god of the moon, and dominated the city. Buried in the brickwork he found several small clay cylinders. Each one is about 10 cm/ 4 ins long inscribed with sixty or so lines of Babylonian writing.

When the consul took his finds to Baghdad, his senior colleague was able to read the inscriptions, for, fortunately, he was Sir Henry Rawlinson, one of those who had deciphered the Babylonian cuneiform script. Rawlinson immediately saw the importance of the clay cylinders.

The inscriptions had been written at the command of Nabonidus, king of Babylon, 555– 539 BC. The king had repaired the temple tower, and the clay cylinders commemorated the fact. The words they carried proved that the ruined tower was the temple of the city of Ur. The words were a prayer for the long life and good health of Nabonidus — and for his eldest son. The name of that son, clearly written, was Belshazzar.

Here was clear proof that there was an important Babylonian called Belshazzar, so at least he

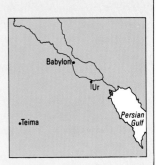

was not an entirely imaginary person. But this prayer spoke of him only as crown-prince. Since 1854 several more Babylonian documents have been unearthed that refer to Belshazzar. In every case he is the king's son or the crown prince; he is never given the title 'king'.

In fact, other records make it clear that Nabonidus was the last native king of Babylon. Belshazzar never came to the throne. So the majority of scholars concluded that the author of Daniel had still made a mistake in calling him king — although the mistake was not as bad as they originally thought.

Yet even that may not be right. Some writers have drawn attention to the reward Belshazzar offered to Daniel if he could interpret the writing on the wall:

'You will be clothed in purple, and have a gold chain placed around your neck, and you will be made *the third highest ruler* in the kingdom.'

If Belshazzar was king, why could not Daniel be given second place, like Joseph in Egypt? But if Belshazzar's father was king, Belshazzar himself would be second, and able to offer only the next place to Daniel.

The Babylonian texts support this idea. They reveal that Nabonidus was an eccentric ruler. Although he did not ignore the gods of Babylon, he did not treat them in the approved way, and gave a lot of attention to the god of the moon at two other cities, Ur and Harran.

For several years of his reign Nabonidus did not live in Babylon, but in the distant oasis of Teima in northern Arabia. During that time Belshazzar ruled in Babylon. According to one account of events, Nabonidus 'entrusted the kingship' to him.

That being the case, it is quite in order for him to be called 'king' in unofficial documents such as the book of Daniel. He acted as king, even if he was not legally king, and the distinction would have been irrelevant and confusing in the story.

The cylinders from Ur and other Babylonian texts do not tell us any more about 'Belshazzar's Feast'. But they do tell us about Belshazzar. They show that Daniel was not just telling

fables. And if he got these odd details right, perhaps we should listen to his message, too: God was in control. And even with kings, God knew the end from the beginning.

The records name as last king of Babylon Nabonidus, who is shown here. So was Belshazzar, who figures in the biblical book of Daniel, merely a myth?

PERSIAN SPLENDOURS

Three merchants from central Asia were travelling to India in May 1880. Coming into northern Afghanistan with bags of money to buy tea and other things in India, they were told the local chief was taking a heavy tax from all travellers. The chief wanted money to build up his army. (He got enough to do that, later becoming ruler of Afghanistan.)

But he failed with these merchants.

Someone told them there was treasure for sale, a treasure of gold and silver objects. The merchants bought those things and sewed them into packages to look like merchandise and so escape the chieftain's greedy eyes. All was well. They travelled across the country, through Kabul, and on. They were making for the Khyber Pass and Peshawar.

Then disaster fell on them.

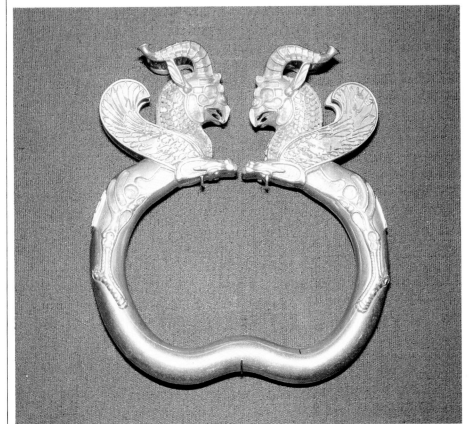

No one knows where the Persian 'Oxus Treasure' was found. The story of its discovery is one of high romance, involving chieftains and merchants and robber bands. Small wonder lives were lost in a struggle to possess such treasures as the beautiful gold bracelet (left).

Above the lines of human figures on the palace stairway at Persepolis are carved the symbols of religion. The bearded sphinx (below) was a frequent choice of sculptors.

Bearded bull-figures, in Assyrian tradition, guard the Porch of Xerxes (opposite) at the Persian capital, Persepolis.

Persepolis was sacked by Alexander the Great and left to decay. But it has yielded some treasures to the archaeologists, among them a silver goat (below, right).

The bowl of beaten gold (below) is another of the treasures from the Oxus. It dates from about the fifth century BC.

Somehow, rumours had spread about their load of gold. Robbers attacked, carrying off the merchants and their packages. But a servant escaped, made his way to a British political officer nearby, and reported the robbery.

Taking two men, the officer caught the bandits by surprise at midnight. They had been fighting over the share-out: four lay wounded on the ground. They handed over most of their loot to the Englishman. He heard of a plan to attack him, hid all night, went back to his camp, and threatened to lead his men to hunt down the robbers. Frightened, they brought more of the gold to him: only about a quarter was lost. He gave the treasure back to the three merchants, keeping one magnificent armlet which they could hardly refuse to sell to him in gratitude.

At length, the three men arrived in Peshawar, went on to Rawalpindi, and there sold the treasure to local dealers. From them, a British general and another collector bought all they could, and the treasure eventually came to the British Museum.

No one knows exactly where the treasure was found. The merchants said it came from a place where a river running into the great River Oxus cuts through the ruins of an ancient town. In 1877 the river's waters washed out the objects and the local people were delighted to find them scattered over the sand. How many pieces they found is also unknown. Some were lost, a few were cut up to be shared. What remains is called the 'Oxus Treasure'.

It is not a set of table-ware or jewellery, it is a mixed collection. Three gold bowls and a gold jug stand beside a gold dagger sheath, sixteen gold and silver figures of men and animals, thirty or so gold bracelets and collars, a series of gold sheets with human figures on them, and a number of other objects. The most likely source for such a collection is a temple. People would have left them as gifts to the god or goddess. Whatever their purpose, these objects display the skill of the goldsmiths who worked during the Persian Empire. There is no doubt all the pieces belong to the fifth and fourth centuries BC.

Other examples of Persian

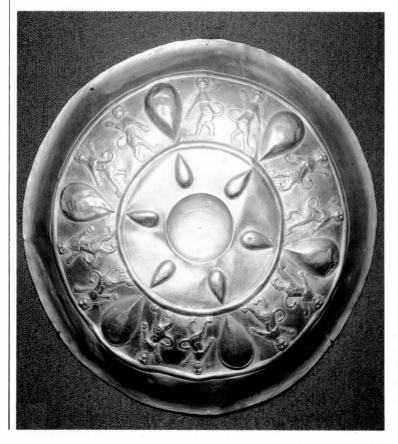

goldwork have come to light from time to time. They show clearly what the biblical book of Esther describes: 'drinks were served in golden goblets'. They illustrate the tremendous wealth of the Persian Empire. When Alexander the Great marched into Susa, one of the capital cities, Greek tradition says he took 40,000 talents of gold (that is about 1,200,000 kg or 1,180 tons). And there was more in other Persian cities.

Persian kings were great builders. Their empire stretched from India to Greece and south to Ethiopia, so they could draw on the skills and resources of every land. King Darius (522–486 BC) had an inscription written about the palace he built at Susa. Babylonians made the bricks, he said, men of Ionia and Sardis carved the stone, Assyrians brought cedarwood from Lebanon, gold came from Sardis and from the east, to be worked by Medes and Egyptians . . .

Little can be seen of the splendid palace of Susa. The description in Esther chapter 1 rings true in the light of what is known. The king is holding a banquet in the palace gardens: 'The courtyard there was decorated with blue and white cotton curtains, tied by cords of fine purple linen to silver rings on marble columns. Couches made of gold and silver had been placed in the courtyard, which was paved with white marble, red feldspar, shining mother-of-pearl, and blue turquoise.'

Much more survives of the new palace Darius began at Persepolis. He probably designed it as the centre

Privileged visitors seeking an audience with the Persian king at Persepolis climbed a great stairway lined with elaborate carvings. Persian guards lead the great procession to the throne.

Following the guards and nobles come representatives from all parts of the Persian Empire bringing tribute to the Great King.

Carved on the rock-face at Behistun is an awe-inspiring portrait of the Persian king, Darius I.

for the annual festival at the New Year. It was also a centre for administration and storing treasure. Once Alexander's soldiers had sacked it, it was left to decay until archaeologists began to study it. An important expedition from the University of Chicago worked there from 1931 until 1939, and further studies and restoration work have taken place since.

To achieve the greatest impact, Darius set his palace on a stone terrace partly cut in the rock, partly built artificially. Visitors would climb a wide stone staircase to a gateway, then pass into a great courtyard. Rising from this court was another stone platform 2.6 metres/8 feet 6 ins high which supported the audience hall. To reach it, privileged visitors climbed more stairs. These had elaborate carvings on the walls.

In low relief, long lines of men move towards the centre. They are the royal guards, horses and chariots, the nobles of the Persians and the Medes, and then representatives of all the provinces of the Persian Empire, each one carrying the special products of his land as tribute to the Great King. Arabs lead a dromedary, Ethiopians carry elephant tusks, an Indian bears jars probably filled with gold dust.

At the top of the stairs was a pillared porch leading to the audience hall. This was square, each side 60.5 metres/200 feet long, its roof held up by slender stone columns 20 metres/65 feet high, topped by elaborately carved bulls' heads.

Here the Great King sat in state, as a famous carving shows. The hall was bright with colour, paintings and woven hangings on the walls, carpets on the polished stone floors. The courtiers moved in ceremonial dramas, wearing heavily embroidered robes and massive gold jewellery. Seated on couches covered with gold, at banquets they ate and drank from dishes and flagons of gold and silver, like those of the Oxus Treasure.

Next to nothing remained of the treasure once housed at Persepolis. But the buildings themselves, and fine bronze work and stone vessels which the Americans found in their excavations, point to the high quality of everything made for the palace. They show why Persia represented the greatest degree of luxury for the ancient Greeks.

From the walls of King Darius' palace at Susa (Shushan) comes this Persian guard. The Persian Empire was vast — stretching from India to Greece, and south to Ethiopia.

THE KING'S ORDERS — IN EVERY LANGUAGE

Wherever the Persian king was, there was the government, for everything depended upon his decrees. What he said was law. So when he made an announcement it had to be carried to every part of his empire that was affected.

Routes used for centuries connected the ancient cities which Cyrus conquered from the Babylonians in 539 BC.

Couriers sped along the great roads of the Persian Empire taking the king's orders to every corner of his domain. The peoples he governed spoke many different languages. The stele from the temple at Xanthos (right) is inscribed in Greek and in the local Lycian language.

The tomb of Mausolos at Halicarnassus, decorated with fine sculptures, was one of the seven wonders of the ancient world. The figure pictured below may be Mausolus himself.

When he took control of western Turkey, the Persian surveyors mapped a new road from Sardis, the capital of Lydia, to Persepolis, covering some 2,600 km/1,600 miles. This was called the Royal Road.

Along these roads a well-organized messenger-service linked all the major cities. At regular stations 25–30 km/15–20 miles apart there were rest-houses with stables. Here, fresh horses awaited the couriers, so that they could speed on their way, or hand over their messages to a fresh messenger.

By this means, the Great King's orders could be made known throughout the empire. Equally, news of the state of affairs in each province would swiftly

reach the ears of the king. Agents throughout his empire kept him well-informed. They were known as 'the eyes and ears of the king'.

The Persian kings divided their great empire, which stretched from India to Greece, into provinces. A governor or satrap ruled each one. These men spent part of their time in their provinces and part with the king. When they were away with the king, more messengers had to travel between them and the provinces.

The king and the leading satraps were Persians, but they governed an empire containing a mixture of peoples speaking many different languages. There had always been

plenty of work for interpreters in the Near East. They are listed at Ebla as early as 2300 BC (see *Headline News: The Lost City of Ebla*).

In the Assyrian Empire the language problem was reduced with the spread of Aramaic. This language was current in Syria and spread widely as the Assyrians conquered small kingdoms such as Arpad, Hamath and Damascus.

2 Kings 19 records the Assyrian king's threatening words to King Hezekiah of Judah: 'My ancestors destroyed the cities of Gozan, Haran, and Rezeph, and killed the people of Betheden who lived in Telassar, and none of their gods could save them. Where are the kings of the cities of Hamath, Arpad, Sepharvaim, Hena, and Ivvah?'

Under the Persians, Aramaic became the ordinary language for the royal officials all over the empire. That is why letters to and from the Persian kings are recorded in Aramaic in Ezra 4–7.

A discovery made by French archaeologists in 1973 is a good illustration of the way Aramaic was used. The excavators were clearing a Greek temple at Xanthos in south-western Turkey. There, lying at the foot of a wall, they found a stone block carefully cut and finished. It is about 1.35 metres/4 feet 6 ins high, almost 60 cm/2 feet wide and nearly 30 cm/1 foot thick.

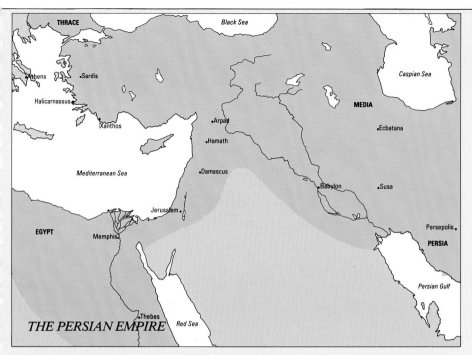

THRACE

Black Sea

Athens
Sardis

Halicarnassus

Xanthos

Mediterranean Sea

Caspian Sea

MEDIA

Arpad
Hamath

Ecbatana

Damascus

Babylon
Susa

Jerusalem

EGYPT
Memphis

Persepolis
PERSIA

Persian Gulf

Thebes   Red Sea

THE PERSIAN EMPIRE

Originally it had stood somewhere in the temple. On three sides of the stone there are finely engraved inscriptions.

On one of the wider faces the writing and language are Greek. The French scholars could understand it straightaway.

This stone was the foundation charter for the worship of two gods. The citizens of Xanthos agreed to build an altar for them, appoint one man and his descendants as priests for ever, and give property and an annual grant to maintain the shrine. They would sacrifice one sheep each month and one ox each year. The citizens swore to carry out their promises, and curse anyone who upset the arrangements.

On the opposite side of the stone the inscription is written in the local language, Lycian. Earlier discoveries gave examples of Lycian, mostly written on

tombs, but very little of the language was understood.

Reading this monument, scholars soon saw that the Greek and the Lycian texts say almost the same thing. As a result, the Lycian language is becoming less mysterious; it proves to be a lingering survival of the language the Hittites spoke (see *A People Rediscovered*).

This Lycian inscription appears to be the original agreement about the new shrine, afterwards translated for the sake of the Greeks living in Lycia.

Any new cult like this had to have permission from the Persian power. A public meeting-place, supported by public funds, could easily turn into a centre for troublemakers and rebellion.

So the citizens of Xanthos took their agreement to the Persian governor for his approval. He was not a Persian. He was a brother of Mausolos

whose famous tomb at Halicarnassus was one of the seven wonders of the ancient world.

Despite his local associations, the satrap was acting as the representative of the Persian king. He accepted the citizens' request, and so the new shrine was set up.

The satrap's approval is the third inscription on the stone from Xanthos. It is given in an Aramaic text set between the Greek and the Lycian on the narrower side of the stone.

It begins, 'In the month of Siwan year one of Artaxerxes, in the citadel of Xanthos, . . . the satrap said . . .'

A summary of the citizens' request follows, then the satrap's assent, 'This law he has written'. Eight lines of curses by the gods of Xanthos and other places warn everyone against interfering with the agreement.

This, the official Persian deed, is proclaimed in the official language of the empire, with due attention to local circumstances.

When the Jews were rebuilding the temple in Jerusalem in the reign of Darius, the governor Tattenai wanted to stop them. He asked Darius if the Jews had official permission, and the king replied that they had, ordering Tattenai to help in every way.

At the end of his letter, recorded in Ezra chapter 6, Darius curses anyone who hinders or destroys the work, and he calls on the God of Jerusalem: 'May the God who chose Jerusalem as the place where he is to be worshipped overthrow any king or nation that defies this command and tries to destroy the Temple there. I, Darius, have given this order. It is to be fully obeyed.'

Scholars could not accept that the Persian king should acknowledge the Jewish deity, and concluded that Jewish scribes had changed the text. The Xanthos decree shows that they were wrong.

At Xanthos the gods of that place were asked to protect their own interests; the king does precisely the same in Ezra.

FROM PERSIAN POSTBAGS

The Persian governor of Egypt was living in Babylon, but there were all sorts of problems in his province. He would have to send his officer to put things right.

It was a long journey and it could be dangerous. Ezra thought of asking the king for a guard when he went from Babylonia to Jerusalem. He says (chapter 8), 'I would have been ashamed to ask the emperor for a troop of cavalry to guard us from any enemies during our journey, because I had told him that our God blesses everyone who trusts him.'

The governor had three other members of his staff who ought to go to Egypt, so they would all travel together, with the officer's ten servants.

The governor wrote a letter to the officials in the main towns on the way. He ordered them to draw on his accounts to supply the party with food. They were to have flour, wine or beer, and a sheep each day. But if they stopped longer than one day anywhere, they could not draw extra rations.

We know about this because the governor's order was kept in a leather bag with some other letters, and an Egyptian found it somewhere, about 1930. The order, and fifteen or more letters, were written on leather in Aramaic, in Babylonia. The bag may have been the postbag in which the officer had carried some of them to Egypt, and then he or someone else used it for holding other letters as well.

In his letters the governor asked about the income from his estates, about the staff on them, and about a sculptor who was to carve a figure of a horse and rider.

These letters open a small window into the affairs of a Persian administration. They also show what sort of letters were written in Babylonia in the fifth century BC and what the Aramaic language spoken there was like. No leather letters buried in Babylonia's damp soil could last so long. Through these letters it is possible to picture the letters reported in the biblical book of Ezra.

Another collection of Aramaic letters and legal deeds adds to the picture. These are written on papyrus and were discovered, odd as it may seem, on an island in the middle of the River Nile.

The island is Elephantine, which lies opposite modern Aswan, 700 km/ 430 miles south of Cairo, just north of the famous High Dam. It was a frontier post throughout Egyptian history, guarded by troops drawn from many places.

During the sixth century BC, some of the garrison were Jews and Syrians, and their families lived there until about 400 BC. The papyrus documents

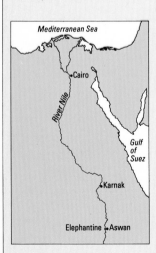

When there was trouble with the local Egyptians, Jews at Elephantine applied to the Persian governor for permission to rebuild their temple. Excavation is carried out on the site, in Egypt.

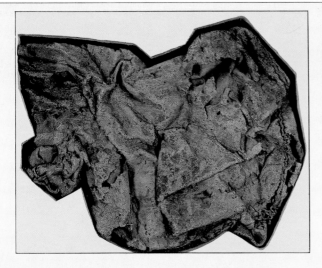

The leather postbag was once a diplomatic bag used for official communications in the Persian Empire.

Aramaic, the language in which the letter is written, was used by royal officials throughout the Persian Empire, a fact reflected in the way letters from the Persian king are recorded in the biblical book of Ezra.

belonged to them.

Deeds recording the sales of houses, marriages and marriage gifts, divorces, gifts and loans make up the majority of the collections found in the ruined houses. There are also letters and a few examples of literature.

Several of the Jewish people had names familiar from the Old Testament, especially with the name of God in them (see *The Engraver of Seals*).

Not all of the Jews at Elephantine were orthodox in their religious beliefs. They worshipped other gods, inherited from the Canaanites (the goddess Anath, for example), borrowed from other peoples, or invented by themselves.

Such situations aroused the prophet Jeremiah's indignation (chapter 44): 'They offered sacrifices to other gods and served gods that neither they nor your ancestors ever worshipped. I kept sending you my servants the prophets, who told you not to do this terrible thing that I hate.' Even so, the chief god was still the God of Israel.

What surprises the reader of the texts is to learn that these Jews in the south of Egypt had a temple where they worshipped Israel's God. They offered sacrifices, burnt offerings, flour offerings, and incense. It was a fine building with a cedar-wood roof, cut stone doorways, and gold and silver dishes, and they were proud of it.

The Jewish worship annoyed local Egyptians, and, in 400 BC, the priests of the chief Egyptian god of Elephantine, Khnum, destroyed the Jewish shrine and stole its treasures.

The attack was made when the Persian governor was away with the king. Clearly it was against official policy, but it took some years for the Jewish leaders in Elephantine to win permission to rebuild their temple.

They wrote to the Persian governor of Jerusalem about it and to the sons of Sanballat, governor of Samaria, as well as to the High Priest in Jerusalem.

After three or four years,

Sanballat's sons replied with advice on approaching the governor of Egypt. It would no longer be a temple that they had, but an 'altar-house' where they would offer flour and incense, no longer, it appears, burnt offerings.

The papyrus letters and draft letters which supply this history make an instructive parallel case to the history in Ezra.

Jews trying to rebuild Jerusalem's temple faced local hostility, and Sanballat of Samaria was a leading enemy. They had to petition the Great King, and he took the same attitude present in the Elephantine situation: local people should be allowed to worship peacefully as they wished, especially if they followed a good, well-established precedent. (Ezra 5:6−6:7 records the correspondence with the king.)

Another papyrus illustrates the same position. A problem arose in Elephantine about observing the Passover, perhaps a problem about the exact date. The letter reports the king's decision

about the question, giving the exact dates for observing both the Feast of the Passover and of the Unleavened Bread.

The words of the letter echo the words of Exodus 12-13 which records the institution of these festivals, and were evidently presented to the king for his approval, very much like the agreement at Xanthos (see *The King's Orders — In Every Language*).

From this it appears that for King Darius to write a letter about the Temple in Jerusalem, with the details which Ezra 6 contains, was not out of keeping with Persian practice.

Before the papyri were read, scholars had stated authoritatively that the documents quoted in Ezra were Jewish forgeries, or adaptations of Persian documents.

Now there is no reason to doubt that they are copies of the official letters.

THE WORK OF THE SCRIBE

Copies made by scribes were checked by counting the number of words or lines. Mistakes could then be spotted and corrected. In this Aramaic treaty engraved on stone, words that have been missed out are written in between the lines.

Being able to read and write was a rare qualification in the world of the Old Testament. Egyptian hieroglyphs and Babylonian cuneiform needed a long training and frequent practice if a boy was to become a scribe.

When the Phoenician alphabet spread (see *The Alphabet*), writing became simpler, easier, and more common. Still, there were large numbers of people, the great majority, who never learnt to read or write; they had no need to. If they wanted something read or written, they would call on a professional scribe.

So scribes were powerful men. You had to trust them to read or write correctly, for you could not check for yourself — and that applied to many kings as well as commoners.

Their skill gave scribes the opportunity to control affairs of state to a great extent, and their ancient role is reflected in the modern title 'Secretary of State'.

Such a scribe was Ezra, a Jewish employee of the Persian government who won King Artaxerxes' favour and led a major reform in Jerusalem.

According to Jewish tradition, Ezra carried out a major change in Hebrew: he encouraged the Jews to write their language in the letters used for writing Aramaic, instead of the old-fashioned Phoenician letters.

With Aramaic used all over the Persian Empire, his move made it easier for Jews everywhere to read their Scriptures. They no longer had to learn a different style of writing.

Recent discoveries in Israel display the change in process early in the fifth century BC. Over seventy small lumps of clay were found by accident and sold to private collectors.

On one side of each is the impression of a seal. The seals seem to have belonged to governors of Judah and their circle just before the time of Ezra. Old Hebrew writing is engraved on some, Aramaic on others.

In Samaria, to the north, the old letters of Phoenician type were still written. They present the name of Sanballat, governor of Samaria, on his son's seal, and they eventually became the distinctive script of the Samaritans.

In the Bible, Ezra is seen doing another duty of well-qualified scribes in most ancient empires. He translated or interpreted an old written text so that his hearers could understand it.

Aramaic spread as the official language, but the local languages also flourished, so royal decrees had to be translated and explained (see *The King's Orders — In Every Language*). People at Elephantine, far up the Nile in Egypt, read an Aramaic version of the inscription Darius set up at Behistun in three other languages.

Translating went further

than official documents, to include literature and religious books. At Elephantine, scribes read the wise sayings of Ahiqar, a member of the Assyrian court, in Aramaic and in Egyptian. In due course, the Jewish Law was put into Greek.

One of the important tasks of scribes was the accurate copying of old books and papers. It is surprisingly easy to make mistakes if you are copying page after page of a book. Scribes learnt this lesson very early in the history of writing, and soon accepted rules which could help prevent them making mistakes.

In Babylonia a scribe might check his friend's work, or he might count the lines in his copy to make sure it had the same number as the original.

Much later, Jewish scribes followed the same idea, counting the number of words in the originals and in their copies.

Unless extremely old copies of the Hebrew Scriptures are found, it is impossible to measure the accuracy of copyists who worked long before the Christian era. Several hints from the Old Testament itself and from other writings show that they tried to be accurate. Of course, there were bad, careless and lazy scribes. None was perfect. They did make mistakes.

Ancient manuscripts and writing carved on stone enable us to see some of the mistakes, and to see some of the corrections — for instance, words written above the line where they had been left out.

One manuscript which was quite heavily corrected is the famous scroll of Isaiah, found among the Dead Sea Scrolls (see *Dead Sea Treasure Trove*).

A rather obscure subject has proved that the Jewish scribes were very accurate in some cases. It is well known that names change when they are taken from one language to another. Often foreigners will alter them to suit the sound patterns of their own speech (compare, for example, Londres for London, Leghorn for Livorno).

Several non-Hebrew names in the Old Testament are known to us from documents written when the names were current. The documents written in the Aramaic alphabet are most helpful for comparison with the Old Testament because that is so close to the Hebrew script.

Scribes of Aramaic had to write foreign names with their alphabet, and it is clear they tried to represent what they heard. When we put the ways they wrote the names of Assyrian kings beside the writings of the same names in the Hebrew text, it is striking to see how similar they are.

In both, the names Tiglath-pileser and Sargon, for example, are written TGLTPLSR and SRGN (the vowels are not certain). In the dialect of Babylon the names were reflected in

ﬡ	ﬡ	ﬡ	'aleph
ﬡ	ﬡ	ﬡ	beth
ﬡ	ﬡ	ﬡ	resh
ﬡ	ﬡ	ﬡ	'ayin
(1)	*(2)*	*(3)*	

Letters in forms used in Hebrew handwriting about 600 BC (1) the Lachish Letters (see We Can't See the Signals*), and Aramaic writing on stone (2) and papyrus (3) of the fifth century BC.*

Aramaic documents as TKLTPLSR and SHRKN. Yet, according to common opinion, it was in Babylonia or under Babylonian rule that the Jewish books containing these names were edited later.

The evidence of the Aramaic sources shows that, whatever later scribes did to the texts handed down to them, they kept these names in the old-fashioned forms of the Assyrian dialect and copied them faithfully.

Faithful copying also characterized the Hebrew scribes who preserved the book of Esther.

Among the Persian names in the book are some which seem so strange to commentators (and copies of the ancient Greek translation of the Old Testament write them so differently) that their original forms are thought to have been lost through scribes' carelessness.

In fact, one of the suspect names, Parshandatha, a son of the evil Haman, is a perfect reflection of a good Persian

name. A seal, carved for a Persian citizen in the fifth century BC bears his name in Aramaic letters. It is PRSHNDT, identical with the name in Esther. The Jewish copyists did their work perfectly in this case.

Examples such as these have a very small place in the whole text of the Old Testament. Yet they are the only means of checking the scribes' work in the centuries before our oldest manuscripts were written. They prove that they could copy with great accuracy and, at least as far as foreign names are concerned, they often did.

The importance of God's law, safeguarded by the scribes, is vividly illustrated by the copies worn on forehead and arm by orthodox Jews. A Jewish boy at his Bar Mitzvah wears the small leather boxes (phylacteries) which hold copies of verses from the book of Deuteronomy.

ALEXANDER'S ADVENTURE AND THE GREEK IDEAL

Alexander, king of Macedon, was twenty-one years old when he led his 45,000 Greek soldiers across the Near East to conquer Persia. He marched on and on, and ended up at the Indus river. The brilliant young general was not only a conqueror, he wanted to spread Greek culture and thought. To do that he gave his veteran soldiers land in those distant places, urging them to settle, marry local girls, and build up societies based on Greek ideals.

Alexander's ambition was to a large extent realized. Greek became as widespread a language as Aramaic, city-states organized themselves on the pattern of Greek cities and many used Greek coin values. East of the Euphrates, local languages and customs reasserted themselves in many places within a century or so, but traces of the Greek influences still remained. In Syria and Palestine the impact of the Greeks was stronger. Alexander's generals, who ruled there after his death, sustained it until the Romans came.

Alexander's conquests eventually

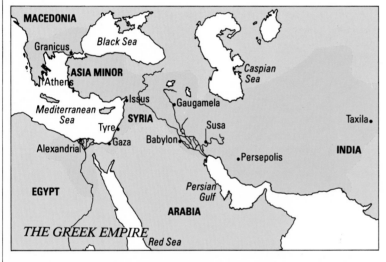

THE GREEK EMPIRE

MACEDONIA
Granicus
Black Sea
ASIA MINOR
Athens
Caspian Sea
Mediterranean Sea
Issus
Gaugamela
SYRIA
Tyre
Susa
Taxila
Gaza
Babylon
Alexandria
Persepolis
INDIA
EGYPT
Persian Gulf
ARABIA
Red Sea

left a stronger mark on the archaeological record than any other event, apart from the building of mosques after Islam swept across the Near East in AD 634. New approaches to art brought naturalism and individuality in place of formal and conventional styles. Coins carry fine portraits of kings; statues and other forms of art also characterize personalities. Above all, the Greek attitude reveals itself in towns planned on a regular, geometric pattern, the main buildings set up to Greek plans. These features began before the time of Roman rule in the Near East, and continued through it.

Excavations made over a few weeks in 1900 at Tell Sandahanna, between Ashkelon and Hebron, uncovered the whole of a small town destroyed about 40 BC. An inscription in a tomb near the site, and remarks in ancient books, prove that the name of the place was Marisa.

A city wall with square towers enclosed an area roughly 158 × 152 metres/170 × 165 yards. Dominating the eastern end was a large building thought to be a temple, and towards the centre, around two large courtyards, were what seem to have been a market-place and an inn. Other houses varied, from the large ones with central

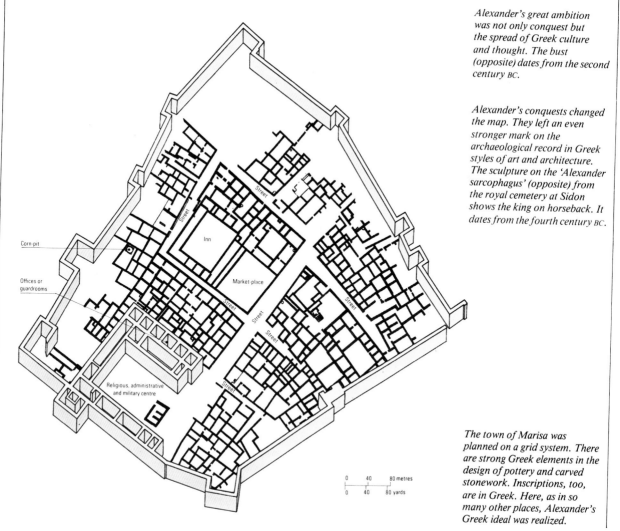

Corn-pit

Offices or guardrooms

Inn

Market-place

Street

Religious, administrative and military centre

Alexander's great ambition was not only conquest but the spread of Greek culture and thought. The bust (opposite) dates from the second century BC.

Alexander's conquests changed the map. They left an even stronger mark on the archaeological record in Greek styles of art and architecture. The sculpture on the 'Alexander sarcophagus' (opposite) from the royal cemetery at Sidon shows the king on horseback. It dates from the fourth century BC.

0   40   80 metres
0   40   80 yards

The town of Marisa was planned on a grid system. There are strong Greek elements in the design of pottery and carved stonework. Inscriptions, too, are in Greek. Here, as in so many other places, Alexander's Greek ideal was realized.

courtyards to small ones of a few rooms fitting into the space available. The town was clearly planned on a grid system, although in its later stages some of the streets were blocked by private buildings. Pottery and carved stonework have strong Greek elements in their designs, and most of the inscriptions are written in Greek. The most unusual finds were two groups of magic spells, and some richly decorated tombs.

Citizens of Marisa would commission small lead figures of their enemies. These were bent and tied, and left in the temple. On stone tablets they, or a magician, would scratch the words of a curse: 'May the god strike X and Y with dumbness and impotence because they caused A to lose his job.' Several dozen of these spells were found, and a few in Hebrew which are hard to read. Others are prayers to the gods for help.

The names of the people in distress display the variety in the city's population. Egyptian and Semitic names are joined by many Greek and some Roman. Such a mixture was probably normal in all the larger towns outside Judah. The pagan forms of magic were probably typical too.

There were some quite wealthy men in Marisa in the second century BC. Their wealth can be seen in their unique tombs. A long underground hall was hollowed in the rock and cut in its walls were horizontal shafts, each large enough to hold a coffin. Smaller chambers led from the hall to take more burials. On the rock walls were quite elaborate paintings. One depicts a man walking along, playing pipes, while a woman follows with a harp.

In the largest tomb is a long procession of animals, not only the local ones, but foreign and wild ones. A rhinoceros and a hippopotamus, an alligator and an elephant walk along, a wild ass fights a snake and a lion stalks its prey. Greek letters by some of the creatures spell out their names. So strange was the giraffe that it had a made-up name 'camel-tiger'.

In addition to these real animals there were imaginary ones, a griffin with a lion's body and eagle's wings, a lion with a human face, and Cerberus, the many-headed dog whom Greeks believed guarded the way to the Underworld. All these animals were painted in a fashion coming from Egypt but inspired in the first place by the Greek philosopher, Aristotle. Why they decorated a tomb is unknown. They may represent the rule of death over all creatures.

In the tombs were notices giving the names of the dead and their family history. The wealthy owners came from Sidon and settled, living in Marisa between 300 and 100 BC. They mixed with the local people so that the children born there had local names, some of them Idumean (Edomite) and, as time passed, more and more of them Greek.

Marisa illustrates very well the mixed culture of many Palestinian places just before the birth of Christ. Towns and cities of the Near East have always had a medley of races and beliefs. Alexander's adventure brought new and very influential ingredients to the mix.

JEWISH COINS

Archaeologists are glad to find coins in their excavations because a coin can often give an exact date and so help in working out the age and history of a building.

In the ruins at Qumran, for example, the excavators found two small hoards of copper coins which the Jews issued during their revolt against Rome. The coins have dates on them, many in year 2 and a few in year 3 of the revolt, that is AD 67 and 68 (see *Dead Sea Treasure Trove*).

As none were found dated later than year 3, and out of seventy-two coins, four only bore that date, the rest being from year 2, the archaeologists deduced that AD 68 was the year when the Romans captured the place.

In contrast, in the fortress of Masada, where the rebels made their last stand against Rome, some of their coins were found with dates in year 4 and year 5, AD 69 and 70. These coins agree with historical reports that the Romans did not capture the fortress until AD 73, after they had taken Jerusalem, where the

coins were minted.

Coins offer other information as well. From the time when the first pieces were struck, perhaps about 600 BC, in Lydia in western Turkey, they were a good means of communication. In the days before there were newspapers and broadcasting by radio or television, it was not easy for governments and kings to make their policies known. A coin with the name of a king impressed on it, or the symbol of a city, carried the authority of the king or the city.

A new king could announce himself by issuing a large number of new coins with his name on them, or a message about his rule. Greek and Roman coins repeatedly provide examples of coins used to spread propaganda.

After the conquests of Alexander the Great, coins began to be common. For the 300 years before that, they were made of silver or gold only, so most people did not need to use them. When copper or bronze coins were minted, with lower values and in much larger numbers, people of

The silver denarius was a day's wage for the working man at the time of Christ.

A gold coin bears the name and image of Augustus, during whose reign as emperor of Rome, Jesus Christ was born. The census Augustus ordered was intended to bring in more tax.

The coin of Ptolemy V, ruler of Egypt, dates from the second century BC.

The Jews minted their own coins during the Jewish revolt against Rome in the first century AD.

The bronze coins date from Hasmonean times.

Coins discovered on a dig can often give an exact date. The bronze pot and silver coins are from the last centuries BC and the first century AD.

all classes used them freely. The rulers of small and relatively poor states could strike copper coins and so proclaim their existence, even if they could not afford to mint in silver.

This was what the Jewish high priests did when the Greek kings of Syria allowed them to rule Judea, following the Maccabean War. The first to do so was John Hyrcanus (135–104 BC). His small copper coins bear the words 'John the High Priest and the Council of the Jews'. They are written in the Old Hebrew script. Both the words and the writing assert the Jewish nature of the state, and the title marks its religious basis, the

priest sharing the rule with the Council (which later became the Sanhedrin — the Council before which Jesus himself stood trial).

Successive rulers issued similar small coins, using them to publicize themselves. Alexander Jannaeus (103–76 BC) saw their value for this purpose. He made himself king, then had coins struck with his name and title in Hebrew on one side, and in Greek on the other.

Placing Greek on the coins displayed their origin to neighbouring countries. It is also a sign of the deep penetration of Greek in Jewish society.

When Herod gained control, Hebrew inscriptions

were omitted. They only reappeared on the coins of the Jewish rebels in AD 66–70 and in AD 132–35.

The large numbers of small, poorly made copper coins issued by the high priests, and then by Herod, his sons, and the Roman governors implies that they were of little value. They illustrate how very poor was the widow who put the only two she had into the Temple collecting-box. Seeing her gift, Jesus was moved to say, 'I tell you that this poor widow put more in than all the others. For the others offered their gifts from what they had to spare of their riches; but she, poor as she is, gave all she had to live on.'

PETRA, THE HIDDEN CITY

Burning incense was a common act of worship in ancient temples and shrines. The strong, pleasant fragrance was thought to rise up to the deity being worshipped. Smoking incense also masked the sharp smell of animals roasted and burnt as sacrifices. Incense was also burnt to sweeten the air in the presence of Assyrian and Persian kings, and other people may have used it for that purpose too.

Enormous amounts of incense were needed to supply the demands of the Greek and Roman world. The basic ingredient was frankincense, the sap of a tree which grows in southern Arabia. Caravans of merchants with strings of camels and donkeys plodded from south to north through the desert, transporting consignments of incense to Gaza and Damascus for export all around the Mediterranean. They took back, in exchange, fine metalwork, pottery and glassware from the factories of Egypt, Syria and Greece. In southern Arabia the states of Sheba, Ma'in and Qataban grew rich from this trade.

As the caravans travelled, they stopped where there was water and shelter. Some of these resting-places grew into major towns. The most famous of them is Petra. This city was built in a valley between cliffs of red and pink sandstone, where the high desert plateau breaks down to the great rift valley south of the Dead Sea.

In the centuries from 300 BC to AD 150 one of the main incense roads came past or through Petra, turning west to the coastal city of Gaza. The

citizens sold provisions and lodgings to the travellers, and the kings taxed them. So the city grew rich.

The people of Petra were an Arab tribe which had settled and begun to live in the fashionable way, under Greek influence. The tribe was called the Nabataeans. Without the work of archaeologists in Petra and other towns, little would be known about these people.

They were great borrowers. Their towns and temples and tombs have designs and decorations taken from Egypt and Phoenicia, from Greece and Rome. Their language was an Arabic one, but they borrowed the Aramaic alphabet for writing it. From the Nabataeans, that alphabet passed to the Arabs, the shapes of the letters having changed through the centuries.

After the Romans conquered Petra in AD 106, the city lost its power. People lived there for centuries, but earthquakes and neglect led to the ruin of its buildings, until no houses were left standing, and it was forgotten. Modern explorers first reached and identified Petra in 1812. Some excavations have been made by American, British and Jordanian archaeologists, but there is much yet to be learnt about the city.

In its heyday, during the first half of the first century AD, the Nabataean kingdom controlled much of Transjordan, the southernmost part of Palestine (the Negev). Under its most powerful king, Aretas IV (about 9 BC to AD 40) the kingdom even ruled Damascus for a while. (The apostle

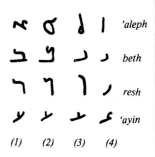

Letters in forms used in Hebrew handwriting of Herod's time (1), Nabataean inscriptions (2), Nabataean handwriting (3), and Arabic (4).

Petra, 'the rose-red city, half as old as time', is built in a valley between cliffs of red and pink sandstone. The magnificent façade of the Treasury (opposite) instantly catches the eye. It is in fact a rock-cut tomb.

On top of a great rock, high above the city, is a Semitic 'high place', designed according to age-old custom for worship involving animal sacrifice. The Old Testament frequently mentions such high places, warning God's people against idolatrous forms of worship.

Once a resting-place for desert caravans, Petra was settled by Nabataean Arabs who adopted a fashionable Greek lifestyle. The city flourished in New Testament times, but lost its power after the Roman conquest in AD 106. Here is a series of tombs, cut in the cliffs.

Paul escaped 'the governor under King Aretas' in Damascus by being let down from the city wall in a basket.)

At this time, recent studies indicate, a grand street was laid through the centre of Petra, and splendid buildings set on terraces beside it. The road led to a square temple, built to the ancient plan of porch, holy room, and shrine that Solomon had followed.

Spreading over the valley from either side of the main street were the houses and workshops of the city. Some were built with finely-cut stones, the plaster on the walls inside decorated with mouldings and paintings.

In one product the Nabataeans

excelled. That was their pottery making. Nabataean potters learnt how to make pottery as thin as porcelain, but made by hand on a potter's wheel, not in a mould. Their dishes are especially fine, painted in brown with floral designs.

Such thin ware breaks easily, so complete examples are very rare. But so many broken pieces are found on Nabataean sites that it is clear this pottery was in quite common use, not made by a single craftsman for wealthy patrons.

The city of Petra was protected by a wall with towers, and by the rocks and cliffs around it. In the soft stone of those rocks, the people of Petra cut the monuments which make their city famous. They wanted to bury their dead so that they would not be forgotten, and they found the sandstone very suitable for carving.

Their masons hacked into the rock, making a doorway to lead to a large room. Some burials might be made in that room, or other chambers might be cut leading from it for the burials. Some of the rooms were apparently

designed so that relatives could visit the tombs to hold celebrations in honour of the dead.

The rock face outside the tomb was prepared for carving, too. In most cases it was cut smooth, carved to look like a stone-built doorway and, high above, like a roof.

The wealthiest citizens, the royal family and their associates, had even more magnificent tombs. For them, the rock was sculptured to take the form of a Roman temple.

Visitors to Petra see the finest one first. As they make their way through the narrow gorge 2 km/1¼ miles long leading to the city they see nothing but the rocky walls. Suddenly, facing them at the end of the crevice is a marvellous pink carving.

Above a pillared entrance are columns carved in the stone with delicate figures in relief between them. On top, on the pediment 30 metres/100 feet above the ground, is a great stone vase. It is solid, but local people shot at it for years, hoping to break it open and find gold inside.

The tomb is still called Pharaoh's Treasury, El-Khazne. Whose tomb this was, no one knows; one leading scholar argues it was made for Aretas IV.

Petra's spectacular rock-cut tombs and the tumbled stones of the once-great city are evidence of the luxury and skill the Nabataeans enjoyed at the time when King Herod was erecting his splendid buildings (see *Herod, the Great Builder*).

In addition to the temple built at the end of the main street, there were other sacred places in Petra, and one is of particular interest. Hundreds of feet above the city, on top of a great rock, is the High Place. This is not a temple in a Greek or Roman style, it is a Semitic 'high place' fashioned after an age-old custom.

A processional road cut through the rock, with carefully hewn steps, led up to the top of the hill. There the worshipper came to the sacred area. Two stone pillars marked it, not built from blocks of stone, but created by cutting the rock away until they stood alone. They are each about 6 metres/20 feet high, and they stand several metres/yards apart — so a lot of rock was removed. These pillars echo the pillars found in Canaanite temples (see *Conquered Cities of Canaan*).

Beyond the pillars the summit of the rock is cut away. A level area about 14 × 6 metres/46 × 20 feet was made, with a bench cut in the rock on three sides. At the fourth side, facing east, is a rock-cut altar, approached by a flight of three steps. To the left of the altar other steps rise to a circular basin cut in the rock. A drain running from it suggests it was the place where animals were slaughtered. Although the altar is big enough for a person to lie on, there is no evidence that the Nabataeans sacrificed human beings.

For long centuries the Nabataeans and their city lay forgotten. Their recovery is another achievement of archaeology, and a contribution to the cultural background of the New Testament.

DEAD SEA TREASURE TROVE

It was a winter afternoon in 1946–47. Three shepherds were watching their sheep and goats near the edge of the Dead Sea. The animals scrambled about the stony hillside finding tufts of grass to nibble. The herdsmen's eyes were alert, watching their flock and the landscape around them.

One spotted a hole in the cliff face, and threw a stone inside to see how big the hole was. The stone fell and made a strange noise. They wanted to explore, but the sun was setting and it would soon be dark, so they left.

It was two or three days before the youngest of them, Muhammed edh-Dhib, came back. He scrambled up to a bigger hole, just above the first one, and fell into a cave. He looked about.

Was there treasure waiting for him? His cousin was always hoping for a cave full of jars of gold, like Ali Baba's.

Around him in the cave were pottery jars, some standing by the walls, some lying on the floor, broken by rocks which had fallen from the roof. Most of the jars were empty. There was no gold. Only two had anything in them, a roll of leather and two bundles wrapped in cloth.

Muhammed had found his treasure, though he did not know it.

He scrambled out of the cave and took his find to show the others. They did not know what to make of it. When they opened the bundles, two more leather rolls appeared. There was writing on the leather, but none of them could read it.

The rolls were left in a bag in their tent for several weeks. Eventually, the shepherds took the rolls and two jars to a shopkeeper friend in Bethlehem. At first no one was interested in them. Then a Syrian Orthodox Christian clothes-merchant saw them in Bethlehem and agreed to try to sell them. The shepherds did not trust him, and so called in a local cobbler, Kando, as their agent.

The Syrian Christian took a sample of the rolls to the head of his church in Jerusalem. He thought they might be quite old and decided to buy them. After a few weeks the sale was made. The three rolls, with another the shepherds had taken from the cave on a return visit, were bought for about £24 (at that time just under $100). Three other rolls, also brought out during the second visit to the cave, were sold to an antiquities dealer for £7 ($28), and they were bought for the Hebrew University later in 1947.

The first group of rolls was carried from Palestine to America and sold to the State of Israel in 1954 for $250,000. All are now together in The Shrine of the Book, attached to the Israel Museum in Jerusalem.

A year or so after the first discovery, the rolls sold to the Syrian were taken to the American Schools of Oriental Research in Jerusalem where a young American, John Trever, interrupted his study of the plants of Palestine to photograph them. He saw at once that these rolls were ancient Hebrew books, and soon identified one as the biblical book of Isaiah.

The style of the Hebrew handwriting puzzled him. Checking

Some of the Qumran scrolls were stored in the caves in pottery jars. The community's library was saved from destruction at the hands of the advancing Roman army.

with pictures of other early Hebrew books, he came to the conclusion that this writing was older than any other Hebrew manuscript, except for a tiny scrap in Cambridge. That seemed to be an impossible conclusion.

Trever wrote immediately to the leading American biblical scholar, W.F. Albright. A reply came as quickly as the bad political situation in Jerusalem allowed. This was 'the greatest manuscript discovery of modern times'! The news was made public on 11 April 1948.

What was this discovery? Why was it so important?

The four rolls Trever photographed are written in Hebrew. One of them is a copy of the biblical book of Isaiah, a roll of leather 7.34 metres/24 feet long and 26 cm/10 ins high, made of seventeen sheets sewn end to end, covered with fifty-four columns of

Hebrew writing.

Rolls, or scrolls, are normally used in synagogues for the Hebrew Bible, but when they wear out they are buried or hidden and left to decay naturally, so that men do not destroy God's Word. As a result, no very old scrolls have survived. The oldest copies of the Hebrew Bible are some made for private study about 1,000 years ago, as books with pages.

Trever concluded, and Albright agreed (as do all scholars now), that this scroll of Isaiah was written 1,000 years before those oldest copies.

When scribes copied books by hand they sometimes made mistakes. (Anyone who tries to copy two or three pages from a book will find how easy it is to mis-copy.) Jewish scribes took great care when they copied their holy books, but still mistakes crept in. The Isaiah scroll, and many more found later, allows us to jump back 1,000 years and see how far the Hebrew text had changed in that time. The scroll also takes us much closer to the time when the book of Isaiah was written, although there is still a gap of several hundred years.

What is the result, when we compare the Isaiah scroll with the oldest copies previously known?

Scholars were surprised to find that there was very little difference. The Jewish copyists had worked with great care. Over the 1,000 years one or two words had been wrongly written here and there, and some small changes made. The scroll proves beyond doubt that the Hebrew Bible on which all modern translations are based has hardly changed at all since the time of Jesus.

In the years following the first discovery, archaeologists explored the cave where the scrolls were found, and many others. They found pieces of more scrolls, all badly damaged because they had not been hidden in jars. The shepherds and their friends had not lost interest. They searched the cliffs even more thoroughly, and found

The Isaiah scroll from the caves at Qumran is 1,000 years older than any other copies of the Hebrew Bible. The fact that there is so little difference in the text is a tribute to the great care taken by the copyists. It gives fresh ground for confidence in the reliable transmission of God's word down the centuries.

more caves where scrolls had been hidden.

One which they came to in 1952, called Cave 4, had an enormous quantity of fragments in it. The shepherds took some, then the archaeologists caught up with them. Altogether, about 40,000 pieces came from Cave 4, representing about 400 scrolls.

These discoveries made the shepherds' tribe wealthy, for after the first scrolls were proved to be so old, they found they could charge a high price for any more they found. The price was set at £1 per square inch (at that time $2.80) and, from limited resources, the Jordanian government which then ruled the area, made available much of the money that was needed.

Other governments and private institutions also supplied funds, so that all but a few fragments have been kept together in Jerusalem. There, a small team of experts has worked for years piecing together the fragments and trying to identify them. This is a long, slow task. The nature of the research, and the small number of people able to do it, are the main reasons for the fact that many of the documents are still unpublished — not, as some claim, a deliberate plot to prevent sensational information harmful to the Christian

church from reaching the public!

On the contrary, if the Isaiah scroll is anything to go by, those who take a high view of the authority of the Bible have nothing to fear, and much to gain, from this research. It is a staggering fact that in the course of 1,000 years of copying by hand no errors have crept into the text which in any way affect the Bible's teaching.

A stone, casually tossed into a hole in the cliff-face triggered the remarkable manuscript discoveries at Qumran, on the edge of the Dead Sea. They brought undreamed-of wealth to the shepherds' tribe — and opened up a whole new world to scholars.

A LIBRARY LOST AND FOUND

All that remains of the Essene community at Qumran is a ruined stone building that was their headquarters — apart from the library stored in the nearby caves.

Sharp-eyed shepherds and eager archaeologists found eleven caves beside the Dead Sea which were hiding-places for ancient Hebrew books. Who hid the books, and why?

These are questions archaeology tries to answer by studying all the evidence available. In this case there are two main lines of evidence: first, the contents of the books; second, the pots found with them and the ruins of a building close to the caves.

The books are almost all religious. Over 100 of them are copies of parts of the Old Testament. They include at least seventeen copies of Isaiah, beside the one from the first cave, and more than two dozen copies of Deuteronomy. Those seem to have been the favourite books. Joshua, in two copies, and Ezra, in only one, were less popular.

Every book of the Old Testament had a place in the collection except for the book of Esther. The owners may have rejected that because of its lack of religious teaching. There are no religious books in the library that do not depend on the Old Testament. So we can see that the people who owned these books were a group of deeply religious Jews.

Among the other scrolls there are some which are their own writings. These people studied their Bible earnestly to find out what it meant for their own situation. They wrote some of their conclusions as commentaries on the biblical text. They identified themselves as the true Israel, persecuted by faithless Jews and ruled by foreign powers. Where a prophet mentioned the Chaldeans of Babylonia as enemies of God's people, the commentator said that meant the Kittim, a name used for the Romans. The prophets had not spoken about their own times, their ' words were about the age in which the commentators lived.

As well as commentaries there are books of rules. They are rules for a community of religious people, like monks or nuns, living under a very strictly organized system. This strictness is the sort that characterizes any group of people who claim they alone are God's people. Anyone who wanted to join the society had to go through a two-year probation period. Once accepted, all property was held in common and everyone had to obey the leaders.

A very long scroll, now known as the 'Temple Scroll', hidden by an antiquities dealer after it was first found and only recovered in 1967, lists all the regulations for worship in the Temple, describes its arrangements, and gives instructions for keeping the people holy.

These people looked forward to a time when they would triumph. In one book they described a war between themselves, the 'Sons of Light', and the 'Sons of Darkness'. With God on their side they would win, the proper way of worship would be set up, and God would send two Messiahs, a king and a priest, to lead the people.

From the commentaries and the rule books we can pick up clues about the origin of their authors. They respected a man called the Teacher of Righteousness. Much of their distinctive thought seems to stem from him. As far as can be learnt from the scrolls, he lived in the middle of the second century BC. He held unusual views about the dates of the main Jewish festivals, and so the priests in Jerusalem stopped him celebrating the holy days because they were not at the same time as their own.

One man, called the Wicked Priest, who ruled in Jerusalem like a tyrant, persecuted the Teacher. The commentators call him wicked, the liar, and describe how he met an agonizing death at the hands of his enemies, a punishment from God. The Teacher led his disciples to a refuge in 'the wilderness'.

The ruins afford the second line of evidence. The archaeologists who

The plan shows the complex of buildings occupied by the monastic community at Qumran. It began life about 150 BC and flourished during the first century AD until its destruction by the Romans in AD 68, during the Jewish uprising.

1 Main entrance
2 Entrance of aqueduct
3 Cisterns
4 Tower
5 Writing-room
6 Kitchen
7 Assembly-hall and refectory
8 Potter's workshop

0 ⊢ 10 metres
0 ⊢ 10 yards

explored the caves after the first discovery soon turned their attention to a ruin just above the sea-shore. They excavated there from 1951 to 1956.

The building they uncovered was unique. It was not a palace, a fort, or a house: it was a centre for all sorts of activities. Potters made and baked dishes, bowls, cups, and jars. Farm produce was stored in silos and prepared in a kitchen. Weavers probably made wool from sheep and goats into clothing, and there was a dyeing plant to colour it, and a laundry to wash it.

In one room were pieces of plastered brickwork fallen from an upper floor. When these were pieced together they formed three benches. Since two ink-wells lay among these pieces, we can be fairly sure the upper room was a writing-place. Unfortunately, no scrolls or other written documents remained there.

The region where the building stands is very dry. There is no spring of fresh water close to it. In order to obtain water for their work, the people made a canal to draw rainwater from the hills behind. They stored the water in large cisterns, enough, it is calculated, to supply the needs of 200 residents. But where did they live? A hall over 27 metres/70 feet long seems to have been a dining-room. In one corner lay over 100 pottery vessels, perhaps ready for a meal.

A thousand or more other pieces of tableware were piled on the floor of a small room at one side of the hall. They had been covered with rubble when an earthquake damaged the building, and left, discarded, when repairs were made.

The large hall indicates that everyone ate together. It is possible they slept in dormitories upstairs. It is also possible they lived in the numerous caves in the cliffs all around. Pottery found in the caves is identical with pottery found in the ruins. Further, the jars found with the first group of leather rolls, large and uncommon in shape, have their counterparts in the building.

There is no good reason to doubt that the people who hid the book were the people who lived in the unusual building. The rules about their way of life in the scrolls agree in general with descriptions we have from other writers of a Jewish religious sect called the Essenes.

The Essenes flourished during the first century BC and the first century AD. Those are the dates when the building was in use. Its life began, perhaps, as early as 150 BC and ended in AD 68. In that year Roman troops, marching through Palestine to crush the Jewish Revolt, advanced to Jericho and the Dead Sea.

Coins found in the ruins include Jewish ones of the year 68, but none later. Fire and mining destroyed the building, then Roman soldiers turned part of it into a look-out post. Their coins, minted between AD 65 and 73, lay in the ruins of their rooms.

The advance of the Roman forces is the obvious moment for the hiding of the scrolls. Their owners did not live to rescue them. Some were lost in landslides or through dampness. But many survived, to become 'the greatest manuscript discovery of modern times'.

JESUS AND THE DEAD SEA SCROLLS

'Christianity is a sort of successful Essenism' declared the radical French scholar Ernest Renan in 1893.

After the Scrolls brought so much fresh knowledge of Essene beliefs to light, one of Renan's successors in Paris, A. Dupont-Sommer, took up his approach. Writing one of the first surveys of the discovery, he said:

'Everything in the Jewish New Covenant (as found in the Scrolls) heralds and prepares the way for the Christian New Covenant. The Master from Galilee, as the New Testament writings present him to us, appears as an astonishing reincarnation of the Master of Justice (the Teacher of Righteousness) in many respects . . . Like him, he was condemned and put to death. Like him, he ascended to heaven, near to God . . . Like him, he will be the supreme judge at the end of time. Like him, he founded a church whose members eagerly awaited his glorious return . . .' He then claimed that wherever there is a resemblance between the Scrolls and Christianity, the Christians had borrowed from the Essenes.

Here was a wonderful supply of ammunition for critics of Christianity, for sceptics and for humanists. No longer did Jesus stand as an isolated figure, he was a product of his times. Still, time had demonstrated one major difference. One man's teaching had failed to bring his followers through the war with Rome, the other's lit a flame which persists to the present day.

What is the truth about the Dead Sea Scrolls and Jesus?

● In the first place, there is no sign that Jesus had direct contact with the men of Qumran. John the Baptist may have done, but he did not follow their teaching when he preached.

● Both the New Testament and the Dead Sea Scrolls have their roots in the Old Testament. A lot of the ideas and the language they share come from the Old Testament.

● The similarities between

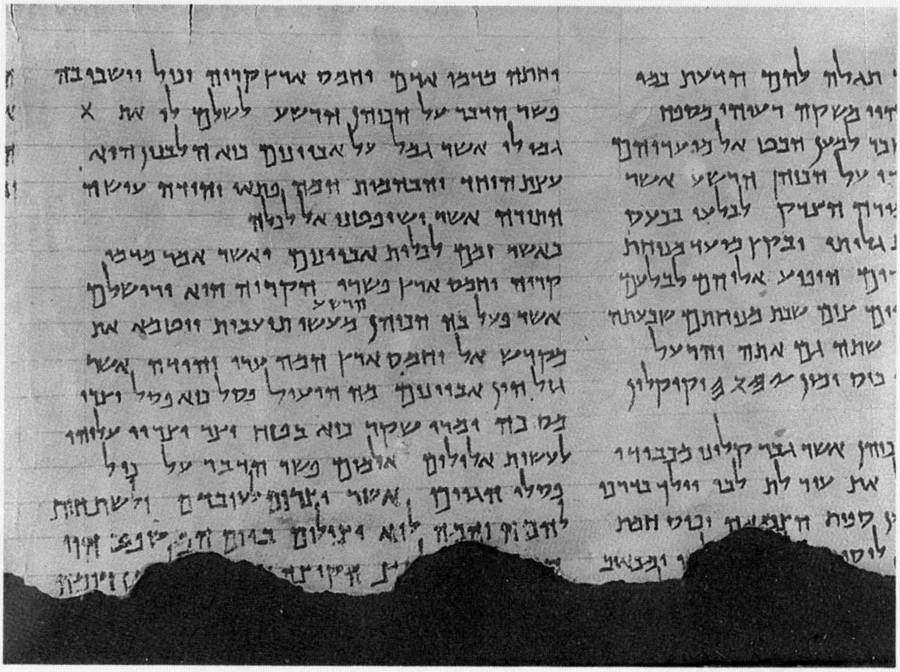

At the bottom of this column of the commentary on Habakkuk a French professor filled the gap with the words, 'he persecuted the Teacher of Righteousness', and made them the basis for a comparison of the Teacher with Jesus.

the Teacher of Righteousness and Jesus are not as close as the French scholar tried to prove. He based his sensational assertions on one scroll, a commentary on the book of Habakkuk. The scroll is quite well-preserved, except at the bottom, where the last lines in each column of writing are damaged. It was by filling in one gap with the words 'he persecuted the Teacher of Righteousness' that Dupont-Sommer manufactured the basis for his claim that the Teacher 'was judged, condemned, and put to death'.

No one now upholds him; most authorities accept that the dreadful fate of the Wicked Priest is described here, for that is what the nearby passages describe. If the Teacher of Rightousness was expected to reappear in the future, which is not certain, he was not to be a judge seated beside God.

● The differences between the Teacher of Righteous-ness and Jesus are huge.

The Teacher taught a meticulous observance of the Jewish ritual laws, and hoped for a time when his followers could offer sacrifices in the Temple again.

Jesus and his followers gave the Temple a diminishing part in their faith, and did not feel obliged to keep the ritual laws. This difference meant that the Teacher led his disciples into an exclusive community (although not all Essenes left the towns); Jesus told his to mix with people.

The Teacher was seeking to please God by obeying the words of the Old Testament. He was waiting for God to send the Messiah, the specially chosen leader. He does not seem to have claimed to be the Messiah.

The Christian church stands on the conviction that Jesus came as the Messiah, and that men can please God only by putting their faith in him. As Messiah, Jesus behaved in a way the Teacher of Righteousness did not, in a way that might have shocked him more than it shocked the Pharisees. The concept of one man's death making atonement for all mankind, not for Israel only, would have been hardest for the Teacher to accept.

● The Scrolls include rules that seem similar to Christian customs.

New members should be baptized, having repented of their sins. Although this sounds like John the Baptist's baptism and the Christian sacrament, it is not the same. For the Essenes could repeat it, apparently each year, to purify themselves, not to find pardon.

Members ate a meal together and some have likened this to the Last Supper and the Holy Communion. There may be a common background, but the meals at Qumran looked forward to a banquet with the Messiah. They had no sense of remembering the Messiah, or even the Teacher of Righteousness, in the way Jesus' words require: 'Do this in memory of me.'

● Lastly, the commentaries the owners of the Scrolls wrote on the Old Testament depended on the way of interpretation the Teacher taught them. They applied the prophecies to their own situation and still looked for their fulfilment, often using some phrases arbitrarily.

In the New Testament, the prophecies apply mostly to the situation that has come into being with the arrival of the Messiah. There are similarities of treatment, but the Scrolls lack the unifying element of interpretation and the certainty that Jesus brought.

The Dead Sea Scrolls are especially important because no other books written by religious Jews in Palestine during the period immediately before the fall of Jerusalem survive in reliable Hebrew texts. From the Scrolls there is a new view of one area in Judaism at the time of the Gospels. This discovery has brought much fresh air into New Testament studies and, as more of the fragments are published, the background to the Gospels will grow more intelligible. We have to remember that the Scrolls present only one part of Jewish thought at that time. Early Christianity arose in the context of the whole.

HEROD, THE GREAT BUILDER

It was to be bigger and better than any temple that had ever stood in Jerusalem. No expense would be spared. This was the king's present to his Jewish subjects, a new temple for the God of Israel. But there was a temple there already, the one the Jews had built when the Persian king Cyrus allowed them to go back from their exile in Babylon. There was no question of building the new one in another place, the site was sacred. Nor could builders interrupt the temple services; in fact, ordinary workmen could not go in to the inner parts of the Temple.

How did Herod solve the problem? He had a thousand priests trained as stone-masons and carpenters. Everything was made ready, so that the work could be done as quickly as possible.

The central building followed the same plan as Solomon's Temple: a porch, a central hall, and a shrine. It was about 50 metres/164 feet long, and the porch was the same in width and height. Inside, the main part was only 10 metres/33 feet wide, but a range of rooms surrounded it. All this part, built of white stone blocks, was finished in about eighteen months (20–18 BC). Crowning the roof were golden spikes to prevent birds perching or nesting on it.

Although the Temple building was quickly finished, Herod planned that it should stand in the middle of a great courtyard with colonnades or cloisters running round the sides. Here Herod could build as he liked, not limited by any existing structure.

He made the courtyard area nearly twice as big as it was before, and to do that he had to build up an artificial terrace because the hill sloped steeply away at the southern end. At the southeast corner the rock surface is 47 metres/150 feet below the level of the courtyard, whereas the difference is about 30 metres/100 feet at the southwest corner.

Herod's Temple enclosure is now the Haram esh-Sherif in which the Dome of the Rock stands today. Part of the massive stone-work of the platform at the western side is the famous 'Wailing Wall'. Stone blocks in the wall average 1.2 metres/4 feet in height, and from 1–7 metres/4–23 feet in length. Most of the building was complete by 9 BC, but work went on at certain points until AD 64. In John's Gospel the Jewish authorities declare: 'It has taken forty-six years to build this Temple!' How could Jesus possibly say he would build it again in three days? (But the temple Jesus was speaking about was his own body.)

In AD 66 the Jewish people rebelled against the authority of Rome. Herod's Temple became a fortress and the Romans attacked it. In August of the year 70, all of Jerusalem was in Roman hands except the Temple, where a group of Zealots held out. In the face of their refusal to surrender, Roman soldiers set fire to the woodwork of the buildings, and one threw a flaming torch into the Temple itself. A few of its precious furnishings were rescued, to be paraded in the victory procession of the Roman commander, Titus, whose father had

just become the Emperor Vespasian.

When the Roman soldiers had finished, the Temple was in ruins. All that remained of Herod's work was the great level platform on which it had stood, as Jesus had forecast. 'You see these great buildings?' he said to his disciples. 'Not a single stone here will be left in its place; every one of them will be thrown down.'

From 1968 onwards the Israeli scholar Benjamin Mazar made extensive excavations outside the southern end of the courtyard, up against the wall. He cleared away a great heap of heavy stone blocks fallen from the Temple walls to reach the original street level. The paved street led along the wall with steps for the changing level of the hill. In the centre at the south end were uncovered the remains of a great stairway up to the gates that led into the Temple court.

Among the masonry fallen from the walls were stone slabs carved with geometric patterns and flowers. They had been part of the ceiling of the gateway or of the colonnade. These few fragments, and the quality of the masonry, point to the magnificence of the original Temple.

Jerusalem's Temple was only one, the most costly, among many grand buildings Herod had erected. At Hebron, to the south of Jerusalem, Herod put a great wall around the caves where Abraham and his family were said to be buried, and another wall around an ancient tree Abraham was reputed to have planted at Mamre nearby. The wall around the tomb still stands, showing what the outside appearance of the Temple walls would have been like.

These buildings were to please the Jews, to help them to accept Herod's

rule. He himself was not Jewish in origin. His father, Antipater, belonged to a family from the south, a family of Idumaeans, the Edomites of the Old Testament. The Jewish king, John Hyrcanus (134–104 BC), had conquered these people and allowed them to live only if they converted to Judaism.

When he was not in Judea, Herod did not pay much regard to Jewish customs. No more than 56 km/35 miles north of Jerusalem he built another temple. He had rebuilt the ancient city of Samaria, calling it Sebaste in honour of the Emperor Augustus (Sebaste is Greek for Augustus-burg). Crowning the town was Herod's temple, dedicated to Rome and Augustus. Excavations have uncovered parts of the temple.

He built other cities in Palestine (Caesarea and Antipatris were the most important) and added public buildings to others further away. At Tyre and Sidon he built theatres, at Damascus a theatre and gymnasium. He paved the main street of Antioch and gave funds to Greek cities, including Athens.

In Athens the people set up a statue for him. The stone base was discovered there, with an inscription, 'To Herod, the friend of Rome'. Another inscription calls him 'friend of Caesar', and yet another 'benefactor'. In response to an argument amongst his disciples as to who should be greatest, Jesus said, 'The kings of the pagans have power over their people and the rulers are called "Friends of the People". But this is not the way it is with you.'

The remains in Jerusalem and the wall at Hebron illustrate the scale of Herod's work, and the recent discoveries at the south end of the Temple area show how it was decorated. Herod's other public

The city of Caesarea, on the coast, with its high-level aqueduct was built by Herod the Great.

buildings followed the most fashionable designs of the day, we may be sure.

Herod spent freely on palaces and fortresses for himself and his family. In Jerusalem he built a palace, but nothing of it remains. Part of the citadel there dates to his reign, especially 'David's Tower' (called 'Phasael's Tower' in ancient times, after Herod's brother).

Away from the capital, Herod fortified the hill-top of Machaerus, east of the Dead Sea, to guard his frontier with the Nabataeans of Petra. (It was at Machaerus that Salome danced for Herod's son Antipas, pleasing him so much that his rash promise of reward led to the execution of John the Baptist.)

Little is known about that site, but another has been excavated in the hills south of Jerusalem. For a long time it was called 'Frank's Mountain', until Edward Robinson and later travellers identified it as Herodium, a fortress, and Herod's burial place. The circular walls sit on top of a prominent hill, with four round towers to protect them. Within the walls were a garden, a large dining-room, and a suite of baths. Private rooms would have been at a higher level.

At the foot of the hill stood another palace, its walls plastered and painted in various colours to imitate masonry. Several rooms had black and white mosaic floors and stone pillars with carved capitals to support the roof. Other buildings include store-rooms with jars still standing in them and a pool in a garden.

Herodium had a counterpart near Jericho. Jewish rulers had a winter palace there about 100 BC, so that they could escape the cold of Jerusalem (the temperature there can fall below 10°C/50°F in December, January and

February, Jericho staying 10 degrees warmer). Herod made a new palace on the site of the old one, and, towards the end of his reign, built a much bigger one with an elaborate bath-house of six rooms, a great reception hall and a dining-room.

Excavations in 1950–51 and 1973–74 revealed ruins of these rooms and traces of their mosaic floors and painted walls. They make it clear Herod wanted nothing but the best for himself! This was true even at Herod's most extraordinary and impregnable castle, on the rock of Masada overlooking the Dead Sea (see *Masada–The Last Stronghold*).

Excavations in Herod's forts and palaces give substance to the descriptions left by the Jewish historian Josephus, who wrote about their splendour later in the first century AD, having seen some of them himself. His accounts of buildings that cannot be excavated, such as Herod's palace in Jerusalem and Herod's Temple, both completely destroyed, are no doubt equally reliable.

Herod's most extraordinary and impregnable fortress stood high on the rock at Masada, overlooking the Dead Sea. It was luxuriously planned and furnished, and included a fine bath-house.

Herod spent freely on palaces and fortresses for himself and his family. The fortress of Herodium was his burial-place.

A NEW TOMB IN A GARDEN

'At the place where Jesus was crucified, there was a garden, and in the garden a new tomb in which no one had ever been laid.'

'Joseph took the body, wrapped it in a clean linen cloth, and placed it in his own new tomb that he had cut out of the rock. He rolled a big stone in front of the entrance to the tomb . . .'

The burial of Jesus, recorded in the New Testament Gospels, is one of the few events in the story which archaeology helps us to understand better.

His resurrection, the basis for the existence of the Christian church, is a matter for faith. No excavation or archaeological research could ever prove or disprove that Jesus rose from the dead. If someone were to find Joseph's tomb, and to find it empty, he could still say nothing about its occupant.

What archaeology can do is to show what Jewish tombs were like in the first century AD and set the gospel accounts beside that information.

Jerusalem stands on the ridge of limestone hills that form a spine through Palestine. There is very little soil on the hills, so burials were frequently made in caves or tombs cut in the rock. As a result, the area around a long-lived city like Jerusalem is honeycombed with graves of all ages.

Cutting an underground tomb was expensive, so usually the tombs accommodated the remains of several people. Often the dead would all be members of one family, but in some places it was possible to buy a share in a tomb.

Scores of tombs made between about 50 BC and AD 135 have been discovered around Jerusalem, most by accident, some by archaeological excavation. The majority have the same basic design, and it is this that relates to the tomb of Jesus.

The stone-masons began by cutting a level area in the rock so that there would be a wall at one side in which they could hollow out the tomb. In the level area the wealthy might afford a water supply and a garden for the benefit of mourners and visitors. Entry to the tomb chamber was normally through a doorway so low that one would have to stoop or crawl through. The entrance was kept small in order to make it easy to close. This was essential, otherwise dogs, jackals, and hyenas might enter.

To close the tomb, the mourners

The body of Jesus was laid to rest in a rock-cut tomb and the entrance sealed with a great stone to keep out predators. Examples of this kind of tomb, from the time of Christ, can still be seen in Jerusalem and elsewhere.

rolled a large boulder, roughly shaped, to fit into the entrance like a plug. A very few magnificent tombs in Jerusalem have round wheel-like stones which roll across the doorway. In other places this style was followed more often; an example can be seen in Nazareth.

Having cut the doorway, the masons would chisel downwards and upwards to make a chamber large enough for a man to stand in. On each side of this space, except where the doorway was, they would cut away the rock from the ceiling to about waist height to leave a shelf or bench up to 1 metre/3 feet wide. From the bench they would drive two or three horizontal shafts into the rock wall, up to 2 metres/6 feet long and 1 metre/3 feet high. How carefully the walls were cut and finished would depend on the client's wealth.

The tomb was now ready for the first burial. If convenient, this took place on the day of the death. Jewish sources indicate that the arms and legs were bound with strips of linen and a cloth was wrapped around the head, binding the jaws. A shirt, or perhaps a long linen band, covered the body. Perfumes were sprinkled on the cloth. Once the body had been prepared, the mourners would carry it into the tomb and place it on the rock-cut shelf or bench, blocking the doorway as they left.

After some time, when the flesh had decayed, relatives would re-enter the tomb, collect the bones together and place them in a box, an ossuary. They would then push the ossuary into one of the shafts in the tomb wall. Sometimes they wrote the name of the dead person with charcoal or ink on the box or its lid, or scratched it into the stone surface.

There were variations: the body might be placed immediately in a shaft and left there permanently, the opening blocked with stones. Or the ossuaries might be piled on the benches or the floor.

A tomb used in this way seems to be what the Gospel writers describe. A stone blocked the doorway, too heavy for the women to move. Visitors to the opened tomb stooped down to look inside. They saw the grave-clothes heaped together with the cloth from the head at one side. According to Mark (16:5) and John (20:12), an angelic being or beings sat inside the tomb, presumably on the rock bench, where the body had been.

In this way archaeology helps us to envisage the tomb. Can it identify the tomb? Not without original inscriptions.

Through the centuries builders have altered the landscape around Jerusalem so that it is impossible to locate even the hill of Calvary, the site of Christ's crucifixion, with assurance.

Since the fourth century, Christians have identified the tomb of Jesus with one now enshrined in the Church of the Holy Sepulchre. No one can be sure this is correct, but it is part of a complex of first-century burial places of the sort we have described.

Visitors to the Holy Sepulchre who go beyond the Shrine of the Tomb to the 'Tomb of Joseph of Arimathea' will find themselves among the rock-cut shafts of a first-century tomb. The tradition may be wrong, but it does have that in its favour. The alternative site, the 'Garden Tomb', does not conform to first-century fashion at all. Indeed, it is more like tombs from the days of the kings of Israel and Judah found near Jerusalem. Christians will agree that knowing the actual site of the tomb of Jesus is less important than knowing that he rose from it.

Inside the tomb the rock was cut away to form a shelf on which the body, wrapped in perfumed grave-clothes, was placed. Later the bones would be placed inside a box — an ossuary.

The decorated limestone ossuary (top), which was found in Jerusalem, dates from about the time of Christ.

MASADA — THE LAST STRONGHOLD

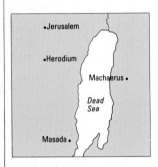

Safe, he must be safe! All his life Herod lived in fear. He knew that no one really liked him. If someone could take his crown and his life, the people would make the assassin a hero. So Herod killed anyone he suspected might be a rival — even two of his own sons and the baby boys of Bethlehem, any one of whom might be the infant king for whom the Wise Men sought. Indeed, one ancient author reports, the Emperor Augustus himself once said: 'I would rather be Herod's pig than Herod's son.' Only the knowledge that Herod had Rome's protection stopped the Jews from revolting against him. His fear made him build fortress-castles: Machaerus and Herodium, the citadel in Jerusalem, and others besides — above all, Masada.

This isolated rock, rising in the wilderness west of the Dead Sea, was a natural fortress. Herod used it to keep his family safe when he went to Rome to win the support of the man who was to become Caesar Augustus, and Masada resisted a siege then. On his return he fortified it strongly, and continued to add to it during his reign so that it should be as secure as possible, and comfortable too.

After Herod died, in March of 4 BC, Masada had a garrison. Then the Jewish rebels captured it in AD 66 and made their last stand there. Roman military camps were set up at the foot of the hill and, eventually, the Romans captured the fort by heaping earth and stones to make a great ramp up one side of the hill. As they breached the walls, the defenders killed their families and themselves, rather than fall into the hands of the Romans. All this Josephus tells us in his *History of the Jewish War*, completed in AD 79.

The rock of Masada was one of the sites Edward Robinson identified in 1834. Various later explorers visited and wrote about it, but only since the outstanding discoveries of the Israeli archaeologists directed by Yigael Yadin in 1963–65 has the place begun to be well understood.

A good water supply is vital for anyone wanting to live on a hill-top in the desert. Masada was well provided with rock-cut reservoirs, and with channels and aqueducts to bring water to them. Even so, men and donkeys would have had to carry water from the lower cisterns to those on the top. Masada's ability to resist attack depended to a considerable degree on its water system.

A side-view of Masada clearly shows the great ramp the Roman forces had to build in order to reach the massive gates and storm the fortress walls. There was no surrender. The invading soldiers were greeted by an eerie silence.

All around the flat top of the hill, right at the edge, ran a double wall with towers at intervals, and four gateways where paths climbed down to the foot of the hill. Inside the walls were barracks, store buildings and living quarters for the staff of the castle. There were also two palaces.

One was on the top of the hill near the western side. This was for official occasions. A hall paved with a fine mosaic opened on to a small throne-room, and not far away was a small suite of hot and cold baths.

But for relaxation Herod created a second palace, a pleasure palace, at the north end of the hill. On the end of the hill itself were living-rooms with black and white mosaic floors and painted walls. Looking out from the end of the hill was a semi-circular pillared porch where the king and his friends could

A view from the air gives some idea of the impregnability of Herod's fortress at Masada. He built his palace on the terraces in the foreground. Here the Jewish resistance made their last long stand against the might of Rome, and by a final mass-suicide cheated the enemy of the full savour of victory.

look out across the barren hills.

Lower than the surface of the hill at this north end, 20 metres/65 feet below the living quarters, was a terrace on which a round building stood. Only the foundations and pieces of carved stones and pillars remained, not enough for the archaeologists to discover what the building was for. Beside it are ruins of other rooms, including a painted hall.

About 15 metres/50 feet lower still, down the end of the hill, was another terrace. On a square platform were porches with painted walls and gilded pillars, apparently a place for meeting and talking. Yet another small bath-house stood on this terrace, for the comfort and refreshment of Herod and his favoured guests. Broken wine jars in various buildings were labelled 'for Herod, king of Judah'. Here is further

The plan shows Herod's palaces and store-rooms, taken over by the Jewish zealots in their last stand.

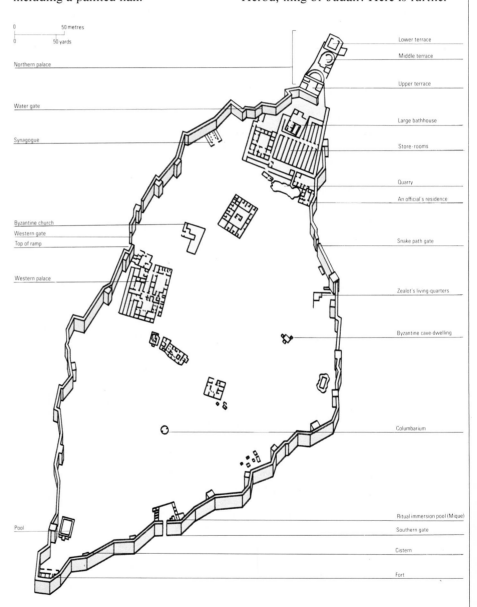

evidence of Herod's love of luxury.

Masada's last phase as a fortress was when the Jewish zealots held out against the Romans. It is from those years (AD 66 – 73) that the most startling discoveries came. The rebels remodelled some of the buildings. They built a small synagogue for their worship, as they did at Herodium, and they made two ritual baths in other parts of the hill, built according to the rules preserved in later Jewish tradition.

Herod's palace at the north end gave a good supply of timber from its floors and roofs. The other buildings and the rooms in the wall round the hill were turned into living quarters and workshops. Most of them had been burnt. In the rubbish were broken pots and pans and glassware, tools and weapons, piles of dates and remains of other foods. Hidden in some of the rooms were small hoards of the silver shekels issued by the rebels.

The hot, dry atmosphere of the Dead Sea coast allowed unusual things to survive. In the synagogue and nearby, the excavators came upon fragments of leather scrolls. Some bear biblical texts, parts of Genesis, Psalms, Ezekiel and other books. There are also pieces of Ecclesiasticus and books known among the Dead Sea Scrolls.

In the bath-house on the lowest of the northern terraces were the skeletons of a man and a woman and a child. Beside them were fragments of a woollen prayer shawl, the woman's sandals, and her braided hair. Broken pottery had served as scrap paper; several hundred pieces were found. Dozens bore one or two Hebrew letters. The excavator thought they had been tickets in a sort of food rationing system.

Other potsherds carried names, or were labels for the tithe or for sacred use. Twelve had written on each one a single name, one apparently the name of the commander of the rebels. Yadin believed these to be the actual lots which, according to Josephus, the last defenders drew to decide who should kill the others and then himself. Archaeology casts one of its most vivid rays of light on history at Masada.

Among the objects which remained from the Jewish Zealot occupation of Masada were these kohl spoons, mirror lid, sandals and a comb.

NO ENTRY — EXCEPT FOR JEWS
The Story of a Stone

There was a riot when Jews thought that the apostle Paul had taken one of his Greek friends into the Temple court. This was strictly forbidden. Notices, written in Greek for foreigners to understand, forbade entrance to all but Jews, on pain of death. In 1871 one of these notices, engraved on limestone, was found in Jerusalem. Part of another came to light in 1936.

The Roman garrison in Jerusalem was used to dealing with riots. For the Jews, religion and nationalism went hand in hand — and that meant trouble. The soldiers had a clear duty to keep order, to control the people, and to try to make sure justice was done.

On one particular day in AD 59, a riot broke out inside the Temple itself. As soon as he heard the news, the Roman commander took some of his men and marched quickly to the scene. Before he arrived, the crowd had pushed its way out of the Temple into the streets and the heavy metal-bound doors had swung shut.

The ringleaders were attacking one man, obviously wanting to kill him. When they saw the soldiers and the tribune coming, they stopped, and simply held on to their victim until the Romans arrived. The mob quietened as the man was chained. They all began shouting again when the officer asked what it was all about. The full account is recorded in the New Testament book of Acts (chapter 21).

The victim was Paul, apostle and preacher. The riot had been started by Jews who had met him earlier in Asia Minor, and wanted him silenced. Now, in Jerusalem, they had seen him going round with a Greek friend. Surely Paul must have taken him into the Temple court? At last they had a good reason to make trouble.

From the beginning of Israel's existence as a nation, the Israelites had known they were God's people. No one could worship God properly except by becoming a Jew and obeying the Law of Moses. No one but a Jew could go into the sacred area of the Temple.

King Herod rebuilt the Temple in Jerusalem between 19 and 9 BC. He made it much larger than it was before (see *Herod, the Great Builder*). There was a great open courtyard, with colonnades along the sides, which anyone of any race or religion could enter. It was here that the teachers walked and taught their disciples, and all sorts of business was carried out.

In the middle of the courtyard stood a low wall or fence of stone about 1.5 metres/5 feet high. This enclosed the Temple building, and none but Jews might pass through. To make the position quite clear, notices were placed along the wall. Josephus, the Jewish historian of the first century AD, says they were written in Greek and Latin.

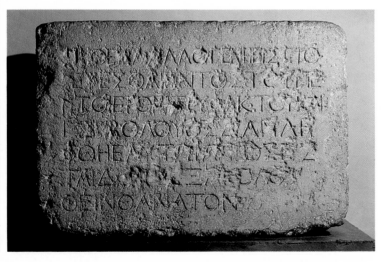

Just over 100 years ago, in 1871, an example of one of these notices, written in Greek, was discovered in Jerusalem. It is engraved on a block of limestone 57 cm/22½ ins long and 85 cm/33½ ins high. Part of another copy came to light in 1936, and shows that originally the letters, each about 3.8 cm/1½ ins high, were painted red so that they would show clearly on the creamy-white stone.

The inscription reads: 'No foreigner may pass the barrier and enclosure surrounding the temple. Anyone who is caught doing so will be himself to blame for his resulting death.' No one could doubt its meaning. And anyone who disobeyed would almost certainly be lynched.

The force of the warning was widely recognized. Josephus reports that the Roman general Titus, later to become emperor, admitted that it even applied to Roman citizens. Rome's authority was supreme and only the Roman governor could order an execution. Yet the Romans respected the Jewish religion and left the control of the Temple area in the hands of the priests. So a blatant offence against religious laws, such as a non-Jew entering the restricted area, could be punished straight away.

But in Paul's case the officer could

The reconstruction shows the western and southern walls of Herod's great Temple, built to win the favour of the Jewish people, who hated him.

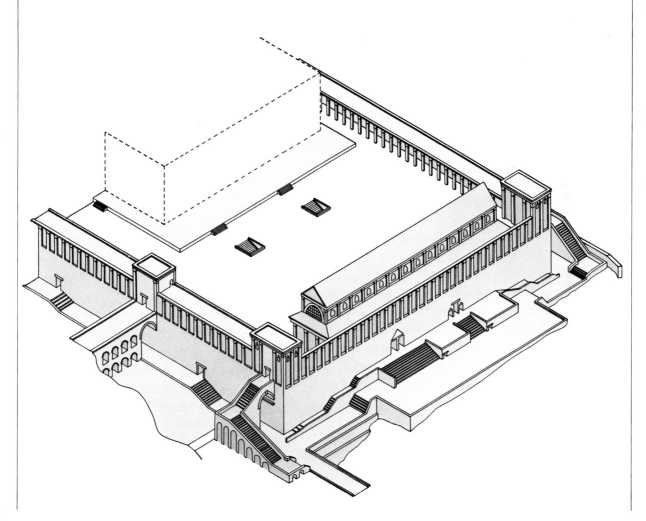

not get a clear case, and so he took him into custody, and, eventually, he was taken for trial in Rome.

This complete copy of the warning is now in a museum in Istanbul, Turkey. (Jerusalem was a part of the Turkish Empire at the time when the stone was found.) For Paul, too, a museum would have been the right place for it. For him, the warning had lost its force.

Paul seems to have had the inscription in mind when he wrote to Christians in Ephesus and other cities of Asia Minor. He told them that the distinction between Jews and others no longer exists. Jesus Christ has taken it away. 'He has broken down the dividing wall.' As a result, anyone can approach God through him. All who

do so are like stones being built into a single temple for God.

The stone in Istanbul, and the fragment in a museum in Jerusalem, appear to have been carved in King Herod's reign. They must have stood in the Temple throughout the time of the gospel story. They are among the most interesting of the few things which we can still see and be sure Jesus and his disciples also saw. And they still have a message for us today: not as a wall of partition, separating Jew from non-Jew, but as witnesses of a new message.

Jesus has broken down the dividing wall. People of different nations and races and backgrounds can be 'made one' through Jesus Christ alone.

SECRET SIGNS — A CHRISTIAN CONNECTION?

Scholars are always keen to make new discoveries, and sometimes they are tempted to exaggerate the importance of what they find. The quest for traces of first-century Christians has led to several claims that appear plausible, yet are surrounded by doubt. Three are well known.

Christian burials?

A tomb of the New Testament period, opened in 1945 in Jerusalem, contained fourteen ossuaries, stone boxes in which the bones of the dead were placed (see *A New Tomb in a Garden*). Five had writing on them. Three bore the names of the dead in Aramaic.

The other two, the discoverer affirmed, were different. On one were words he read as 'Jesus, woe!' and on the other he read 'Jesus, alas!' The second one also had a large cross scrawled on each side in charcoal. These, he claimed, were 'the earliest records of Christianity'.

This was a big claim to make. It attracted a lot of attention and now features in many books. Since their publication in 1947, other scholars have examined the writings. Their verdicts destroy the case for a Christian connection.

Instead of 'Jesus, woe!' should be read 'Jesus son of Judas', and the word 'alas' — it has an odd form not explained properly — is another name, an uncommon one, giving 'Jesus, son of Aloth'.

As for the cross marks, they may be no more than marks to single out one ossuary for some temporary reason in the tomb. Other ossuaries have cross marks which served to match the lids with the boxes.

There is one burial which does have a better claim to a Christian connection. An ossuary found in a tomb in the Kidron Valley, immediately to the east of Jerusalem, is inscribed in Greek 'Alexander son of Simon' and in Hebrew 'Alexander of Cyrene'.

When the writing was read, the echo of Mark's Gospel was obvious. 'Simon of Cyrene, father of Alexander and Rufus' was the man found to carry Jesus' cross.

The names were common in the first century AD, but with the home-town Cyrene (now in Cyrenaica, part of Libya) there is a strong possibility that this was the burial of that Simon's son. Nothing distinguished it in any way from other Jewish tombs, and we cannot assume Alexander became a Christian.

A Christian Code?

Scattered across the Roman Empire, from Dura Europos on the Euphrates, at the eastern fringe, to Manchester in Britain, near the northern frontier, archaeologists have found examples of an ingenious Latin word-square. It reads the same in every direction, horizontally and vertically.

```
S A T O R
A R E P O
T E N E T
O P E R A
R O T A S
```

This can be translated 'The sower Arepo holds with care the wheels.'
This is hardly a vital statement. It is not even very intelligible! Puzzling over the square, someone has observed that the letters can be rearranged in a cross to spell the opening letters of the Lord's Prayer in Latin. The two extra As and Os can be put at the ends of the arms as the first and last letters of the Greek alphabet, *alpha* and *omega*. In the book of the Revelation these letters symbolize Christ's eternal existence.

```
          A
          P
          A
          T
          E
          R
APATERNOSTERO
          O
          S
          T
          E
          R
          O
```

If this is right, the square is apparently a sort of secret sign. Only Christians would be likely to understand it at once. The two oldest examples come from the town of Pompeii, destroyed by the eruption of Mount Vesuvius in AD 79.

Not everyone accepts the PATERNOSTER explanation. However, no other solution to the square offered yet is as satisfactory.

Doubt will always hang over the Christian interpretation. Yet the number of examples, their wide distribution, and the care taken in writing some of them, together suggest that the square may have had more significance than a game with words, that it was a sign of some sort.

A Christian shrine?

A house in Herculaneum, a small town near Pompeii and destroyed at the same time, has a strange mark on one wall. In a small room there is a cross-shaped mark in the plaster. Something was once fixed there, then taken away.

Was it a crucifix? That is what some believe. In that case, a wooden cupboard standing below it might be for the bread and wine of the Communion. On the other hand, there may be nothing Christian here at all.

When it was found, the cupboard held lamps and gaming dice. The mark above could be simply the imprint of a bracket supporting a piece of wall furniture. The fact that there is no other mark exactly like it does not mean a crucifix made it!

Each of these three cases has aroused discussion and resulted in differences of opinion. There is obviously no certainty about any of them, without clear information in writing. The best that can be allowed, even for the word-square, is that a Christian origin is just possible.

WHAT KIND OF EVIDENCE?
The Early Christians

For some events archaeology gives no evidence. The beginning of Christianity is one of them. The earliest archaeological evidence of Christianity is from the second century AD. Nothing belonging to the first century has been dug up which is clearly Christian. This is true in Palestine, in Rome, and elsewhere; there is no trace of Christianity.

Does this mean that the history books are wrong, that the church only came to life after AD 100? There are some who would like that to be true, for then they could dismiss the New Testament as unhistorical, and so not worth believing. But the fact that no traces of first-century Christians are identifiable does not mean there were no first-century Christians. It is simply a reminder that archaeologists cannot discover everything about the past.

The nature of the most important discoveries about Christianity from the second century explains the situation. These discoveries were made in Egypt. They consist of tattered pages and scraps of Christian books. In almost every other part of the Roman Empire damp would quickly rot papers buried in the earth. Without these fragments there would be no sign of second-century Christians in Egypt, either.

Obviously, there were Christians living in Egypt and the other Mediterranean countries. Why cannot archaeologists detect them?

The explanation is simple. In terms of their physical environment, Christians were no different from their neighbours. They lived in the same kinds of houses. They used the same utensils. They did not take up totally different customs which changed the plans of their houses or the shapes of their pots and pans — and those are the things archaeology can discover.

Without written indication, Joseph and Mary's house would be just like any other, the houses of Christians in Rome like the houses of Jews or Romans. Changes in behaviour towards other people, in morals, in language, fall beyond the scope of archaeology.

There are two areas of human activity which do reveal something about religious beliefs. They are forms of worship and types of burial. Even here, no Christian examples, churches or tombs, have come to light which date much before AD 200. The most that can be said is that some Christian churches and cemeteries known from the third century probably had their origins in the late second century.

The memorial uncovered beneath the high altar at St Peter's basilica in Rome may be one, a memorial which Christians later treated as the tomb of St Peter. But the oldest undoubted Christian church so far found was built shortly after AD 230, not in Jerusalem or in Rome, but far away to the east at Dura Europos on the mid-Euphrates.

So we are driven back to the manuscripts from Egypt for the earliest relics of Christianity. They are pieces of papyrus books written in Greek. There are thousands of pieces of papyrus from Roman Egypt in the world's museums. Most of them were thrown on to rubbish dumps where they were never intended to be seen again. Happily for us, some of those rubbish dumps dried out and so the papyri survived. They cover every aspect of life, from preparations for the emperor's visit to schoolboy letters.

Scholars were delighted to find among them copies of famous Greek books made long before any previously available. Among these are parts of the Old Testament in Greek, two or three of them copied as long ago as the first century BC. For the New Testament there are over 80 papyrus manuscripts, ranging from complete Gospels to tiny fragments of a single page.

Out of all these papyri, four are Christian products of the second century. Two were probably copied at the end of the century. One contained the Gospels of Matthew and Luke, the other the Gospel of Matthew.

The third is a scrap from the top of a page of John's Gospel. It turned up in a box of odds and ends of papyrus bought by the Rylands Library at Manchester in 1920. Only in 1934 did an expert identify it. He recognized that its style of handwriting belonged to the period AD 125 to 150, making it the oldest copy of a New Testament book ever found.

Although it is so small, it proves the existence of Christianity in Egypt early in the second century. It also testifies against theories put forward in the nineteenth century, and still aired from time to time by those ignorant of the facts, that John's Gospel was not composed until after AD 160.

In the year in which that piece of John's Gospel was identified, the British Museum bought three other scraps of papyrus. Their handwriting dates them about AD 140 to 160. These are parts of a book of sayings and miracles of Jesus, drawn mainly from the Gospels.

Again, these fragments show the spread of Christianity in Egypt. They also indicate that the Gospels were well enough known for someone to imitate them. The papyrus is unlikely to be the author's original copy, so the date of the original book is to be placed slightly earlier.

That is all archaeology can offer. But there is no doubt at all that this new religion did exist in the first century AD. In addition to the New Testament and other early Christian books, some Roman writers mention the Christians. The historian Tacitus reports that the Emperor Nero made

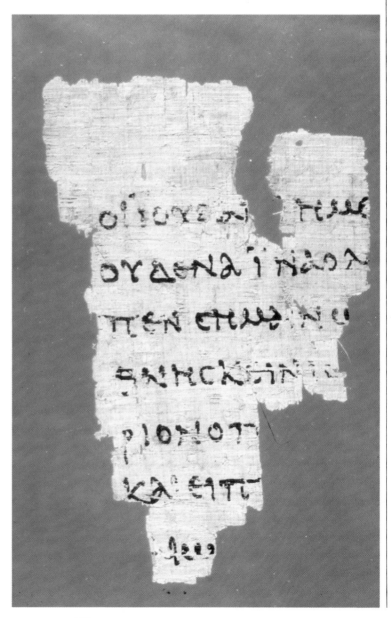

The earliest surviving copy of a New Testament book is this papyrus fragment from a copy of John's Gospel. It is written in Greek and dates from about AD 125-150. Evidently Christianity was alive and growing in Egypt (where the fragment was found) early in the century after Christ.

In the nature of things, archaeology can offer little evidence of the lives of those ordinary Christians who made known the good news of forgiveness and new life in Christ in the first centuries of the Christian church. The fact that they did exist and were active — beginning, as the book of Acts says, 'in Jerusalem, in all Judea and Samaria,' — is evident from the way the flame of faith spread wider and wider in the years that followed, even 'to the ends of the earth'.

them take the blame for the fire of Rome in AD 64.

Without question there were Christians in the first century AD. Few of them are known by name. Thousands died and all physical trace of them has vanished. The real evidence for their existence lies in the faith to which they testified, a faith passed on to others — a living flame which spread and grew. Their legacy, like that of so many other ordinary men and women down the centuries, is the world-wide church of God, a church of all races and nations, alive and growing still today.

For Further Reading

A great many books describe archaeological discoveries in the Near East; among the most useful are:

W. F. ALBRIGHT, *The Archaeology of Palestine,* fourth edition, Penguin Books, 1960

R. N. FRYE, *The Heritage of Persia,* London, 1962

R. GHIRSHMAN, *Iran,* Penguin Books

J. M. COOK, *Greeks and Persians,* 1983

O. R. GURNEY, *The Hittites,* Penguin Books, 1969

A. LOGAN-SMITH (editor), *An Introduction to Ancient Egypt,* British Museum, 1979

J. RUFFLE, *The Egyptians,* Oxford, 1977

K. M. KENYON, *Archaeology in the Holy Land,* fourth edition, London, 1979

J. OATES, *Babylon,* Thames and Hudson, 1979

H. W. F. SAGGS, *The Greatness That Was Babylon,* Sidgewick and Jackson, 1962

M. AVI-YONAH and E. STERN (editors), *Encyclopaedia of Archaeological Excavations in the Holy Land,* four volumes, Oxford University Press, 1976-79

History books that make use of archaeology are:

SIR ALAN GARDINER, *Egypt of the Pharaohs,* Oxford, 1961

W. W. HALLO and W.K. SIMPSON, *The Ancient Near East, A History,* Harcourt Brace, 1971

G. ROUX, *Ancient Iraq,* Penguin Books, 1966

The first three volumes of the *Cambridge Ancient History,* third edition, editors I.E.S. EDWARDS, C.J. GADD, N.G.L. HAMMOND, E. SOLLBERGER, which analyse in detail the mass of information now to hand, Cambridge, 1973-83

Translations of ancient texts are given in J. B. PRITCHARD (editor), *Ancient Near Eastern Texts,* third edition, Princeton, 1968, abridged as *The Ancient Near East,* volume 1, 1958, volume 2, 1975, and in D. WINTON THOMAS (editor), *Documents from Old Testament Times,* Torchbooks, 1958, Harper and Row, 1965.

Many books survey archaeological discoveries related to the Bible. Two classics, now out of date in many respects, are:

G. E. WRIGHT, *Biblical Archaeology,* second edition, Duckworth, 1962, and SIR FREDERICK KENYON, *The Bible and Archaeology,* London, 1940. DAME KATHLEEN KENYON offered a supplement to her father's book, drawing especially on her own work in Palestine, *The Bible and Recent Archaeology,* London, 1978.

E. YAMAUCHI, *The Stones and the Scriptures,* Inter-Varsity Press, 1978, shows how archaeological discoveries can affect biblical interpretation

K. A. KITCHEN, *The Bible in Its World: The Bible and Archaeology Today,* Paternoster Press, 1977, demonstrates the positive contributions they can make when the Bible is read as objectively as any other ancient document, in contrast to the excessively sceptical opinions offered in:

MAGNUS MAGNUSSON, *B.C. The Archaeology of the Bible Lands,* London, 1977

Also combatting positions Magnusson reflects is A. R. MILLARD, *The Bible B.C. What Can Archaeology Prove?,* Inter-Varsity Press, 1977

For the New Testament period see:

J. FINEGAN, *The Archaeology of the New Testament,* Princeton, 1969, Croom Helm, 1981

M. AVI-YONAH (editor), *The Herodian Period, World History of the Jewish People,* Volume 7, London, 1975

E. YAMAUCHI, *The World of the First Christians,* Lion Publishing, 1981; in USA, *Harper's World of the New Testament,* Harper and Row, 1981

Entries in standard reference books, such as *Encyclopedia Judaica, The Illustrated Bible Dictionary, The Interpreter's Dictionary of the Bible, The New Bible Dictionary Revised,* give information on specific persons, places and discoveries.

Index

Acknowledgements

Design
Peter Wrigley

Illustrations
Mark Astle: 69, 95, 120; Dick Barnard: 40, 48, 51, 56, 93, 98, 107, 114, 131, 137, 153, 165, 178, 181; Simon Bull: 179; Pauline O'Boyle: 102, 121, 141; Vic Mitchell: 133, 135, 144, 175; Angela Pluess: 79; David Reddick: 105; Stanley Willcocks: 17;

Maps
Roy Lawrence and Lesley Passey

Photographs
J. C. Allen: 50, 134
Bodleian Library Oxford: 149, MS Pell Aram bag recto (left), MS Pell Aram IV Int. (right)
British Museum: 27 (top), 52 (left), 104 (right), 116 (both), 130, 155 (below right), 161
Cairo Museum: 100 (right)
Werner Forman Archive: 65, 103
Sonia Halliday Photographs: Sonia Halliday: 16, 60, 63, 66, 75 (below), 78, 127 (both), 146 (right), 152 (below left), 155 (below left), 156, 170–171, 172, 175; Barrie Searle; 151; Jamie Simson; endpapers, 20, 35, 36, 41; Jane Taylor; 15, 24 (top right), 38–39, 94 (below), 96, 97, 158 (below), 176
Robert Harding Picture Library: 52 (right), 143; Rainbird 69 (top and below left), 71, 72, 73 (both); John Ross; 37, 105
Georgina Hermann; 29, 144 (both)

Robert Hunt: 173
Illustrated London News Picture Library: 19 (above), 24 (below left), 68
Israel Museum: 104 (left), 112 (right), 113 (above), 162, 167
Jericho Exploration Fund: 24 (top left)
Kenneth Kitchen: 13, 100 (left)
A. H. Layard, Nineveh and its remains, 1849: 21
Lepsius Denmaker III, 40: 58
Lion Publishing: David Alexander; 22, 89 (right), 107, 129, 164, 174, 180, 186–7; by courtesy of the Trustees of the British Museum, 5, 19 (below left and right), 26, 30 (below), 42, 44, 45 (both), 46 (both), 67, 74, 75 (top), 88 (below left), 89, 90 (above), 91 (right), 108, 109, 110 (both), 111, 113 (below), 118, 119, 120, 121, 122, 124, 125, 126, 133, 140, 141, 142 (both), 145, 146 (left), 152 (below right), 155 (top three)
Macquitty International Collection: 148
Mansell Collection: 30 (above)
Alan Millard: 27 (above), 31, 32, 34 (both), 49, 85 (left), 86 (both), 88 (below left), 94 (above), 115 (right), 150, 151, 157, 158 (above)
Musée de Louvre: 81, 85 (right), 117
Picturepoint London: 55, 57, 61
D. Quatrough, University of Liverpool: 25, 112 (left)
John Ruffle: 77, 106
John Rylands Library: 185
Staatliche Museen zu Berlin: 136
H. Williamson: 115 (left)
ZEFA: 12, 117